Fingleton on Cricket

FINGLETON
ON CRICKET

—

Jack Fingleton

FOREWORD
BY IAN PEEBLES

COLLINS
LONDON & SYDNEY
1972

William Collins Sons & Co Ltd
London · Glasgow · Sydney · Auckland
Toronto · Johannesburg

First published 1972
© Jack H. Fingleton 1972
ISBN 0 00 211180 2
Made and Printed in Great Britain by
Alden & Mowbray Ltd
The Alden Press, Oxford

To my Cobber and Friend,
Laurence John

Acknowledgements

Permission to use copyright photographs is acknowledged as follows: Central Press Photos, 5, 7, 9, 10, 11, 12, 15, 16, 18, 25, 26, 27, 30, 31, 32, 33, 34, 35; The Press Association, 14, 19, 20, 23, 24; *The Rhodesia Herald*, 36, 39; *The Advertiser*, Adelaide, 29; *The Courier Mail*, Brisbane, 1; *The Sydney Morning Herald*, 6; Sport and General, 17; *The Natal Mercury*, 37; West Australian Newspapers, 38; *The Melbourne Herald*, 8. The author is also grateful to the following for permission to use material originally published by them: The *Sunday Times*, chapters 6, 19, 20, 21, 24, 26, 27, and 28; William Heinemann Limited, chapters 2, 7, 8, 9, 10, 11, and 15 (from *Masters of Cricket*, 1958); Cassell and Company Limited, chapters 3 and 14 (from *Cricket Crisis*, 1946), *The Australian Cricketer*, chapter 4; *World Sports*, chapter 5; *The Canberra Times*, chapter 25.

Contents

Foreword   *page* ix

Introduction   xiii

PART ONE: – MATCHES TO REMEMBER   I

  1. The Greatest Test of All   3
  2. You Never Know in Cricket   36
  3. A Yorkshire Gesture – 1938   43
  4. Out of the Old Trafford Pit   54

PART TWO: – GREAT BATSMEN OF THE PAST   61

  5. Donald Bradman   63
  6. Wally Hammond   74
  7. Victor Trumper   77
  8. Jack Hobbs   85
  9. Bill Ponsford   95
 10. Charlie Macartney   102
 11. Warren Bardsley   112
 12. Stan McCabe   123
 13. Denis Compton   136

PART THREE: – SIX BOWLERS   141

 14. Bill O'Reilly   143
 15. Syd Barnes   157
 16. Clarrie Grimmett   166
 17. The Fast Men: Larwood, Lindwall, Miller   175

PART FOUR: – CRAFT, CHARACTER AND
CONTROVERSY   185

 18. The Brilliance of Left-Handers   187
 19. Test Openers are Gloomy Fellows   200
 20. When Cricket Turned to Near-Murder   205
 21. The Big Boot Hoot   211
 22. A Classic Example   215
 23. Pepper and Salt   225

Contents

24. The No-Balling of Ian Meckiff   236
25. Barbadians Love the Tumult   240
26. 'Tiger' Pataudi   243
27. No Play at Lord's   247
28. Cricket Farewells   250
29. On Politics in Sport   253

Foreword

Some years ago, Fingo and I, the joint representatives of the *Sunday Times* sat, gloomy and barren of ideas, in the press box at Lord's. The rain poured down and what little juice the Test Match had produced in two days' play had been wrung from it by our daily colleagues. After a number of blank weekends, we had already drawn heavily on the history of the game and there was no convenient row or controversy to hand.

In the midst of our agonies a letter arrived for me from a Scots friend enclosing a cutting describing a match between Ross-shire and Elgin. This fixture had a special interest for me as Ross-shire had been Walter Robins' adopted county when on holiday, and Elgin was at one time our local club for whom I had played on occasions. The point of this particular contest was that Ross-shire had been all out for nought. Having read it I passed the cutting over. 'Fingo,' I said, 'You can have this Test Match all to yourself. I'm going to write about Ross-shire.' On the morrow Fingo's article started: 'Ian Peebles has told me that I can have this dreary day all to myself as he is going to write about Scotland. Thus, while he sits smiling happily I sit biting my pen.'

This passing incident is not, to me, just a pleasant triviality. It is one of many warm memories of a very happy association. It was a joy to work with Fingo as an old friend with his humour, warmth and splendid company. It was a privilege and a revelation to work with a great and truly professional journalist. The incident I have quoted epitomizes his generous and positive spirit of cooperation.

Amongst sports, cricket is extremely well served by writers and commentators of competence in their craft and great love and knowledge of their subject. It is no belittlement of this devoted band to claim for Fingo a unique place in their midst. His chosen career as a political journalist was a very good training for his natural powers of intelligent observation and analysis. Armed with these he was ideally equipped to take full journalistic advantage of a distinguished and extremely varied cricket career. The result, so happily seen over the years, is the complete cricket writer and commentator.

First the cricketer. Amongst many distinctions Fingo could fairly claim to have had the most exacting introduction to Test Match cricket of any man. As a very young man, after one respectable appearance against South Africa in the 1931/2 visit, he was heaved straight in to face the fury of Douglas Jardine's battery of fast bowlers in 1932/3. He batted so well at no. 3. in the first match that when Ponsford was injured he went in first in the second to make 83 out of a total of 288. True, he got a most honourable pair in the Third Test, but he had acquitted himself with such resolution against the thunderous bodyline attack that Lol Larwood was moved to say of him that he was the most courageous batsman he had ever bowled to. His disappearance from the confused and bitter scene of the bodyline series would seem to have been premature, but it is nice to record that between him and his chief opponent, Lol Larwood, there has, from that moment, been a warm and lasting friendship.

Fingo was a cricketer of the best Australian school, which is to say well-tutored, fit, and a dedicated man of the team. I first saw him bat at Oxford in 1938. Having expected something on the solid lines of his erstwhile captain, Woodfull, I was immediately and pleasantly surprised. True, the backlift was restricted by MacLaren or Dexter standards, but the stroke was in every case crisp and, when necessary, forceful. Also there was such a grand, full range of shots directed to every point of the compass, starting from a very neat delicate slice which I should call a late and he a back-cut. It was in watching this innings, which ran to a century against an adequate University bowling side, that I was strengthened in a theory I had long pondered. It is that where, in general, English batsman tend to make a clear distinction between the defensive and the scoring stroke, the Australian played every stroke with, at least, the intention of getting a run from some quarter. Thus a batsman as reputedly staid as Bill Woodfull, whilst ostensibly playing a defensive stroke, would constantly be pushing and deflecting with just sufficient force to make the fieldsmen move and, with the superb Australian running, this usually meant a constant flow of singles and a harassed field. Ponsford and Fingleton brought this industrious quality to a fine art.

In after years Fingo and I took the field at various levels of club cricket. He loved to bat and play his strokes and, perhaps as a consequence, he always offered the opposition the ultimate courtesy. However lowly the standards to which they played he took them seriously so that where, on occasions, condescension and levity had become tedious, he would provide a greatly appreciated measure of real entertainment.

His record for Australia is remarkably good. Despite his 'honourable pair' in 1933 and some disappointment in the English series of 1938, he averaged 42 having made three successive centuries against a good South African side in 1935/36. This, coupled with his superb fielding, marks him clearly as being in the higher bracket of Test Match cricketers.

Although a very fast man in the field, with a sure hand and powerful return, his great joy was to field very close at forward short leg to a batsman bombarded by O'Reilly's beautiful and fiery variations of spin and pace. The friends made a deadly combination for this was a key position. With O'Reilly's quality of bounce any mistake in judging or picking the 'wrong-un' almost certainly resulted in the ball popping up in the area of the short legs. So wide was Fingo's range and so swift and prehensile his grasp that, to the apprehensive striker, he must have appeared in the (very uncharacteristic) light of a voracious and sprightly spider in the midst of a comprehensive and efficient web.

I promised to write this Foreword 'warts and all'. In honesty I find myself after twenty years of friendship and association hard put to gather any suitable material in this direction. If, for the sake of keeping my promise, I was to say that he had a good Australian pugnacity it would hardly meet the point. For what in fact he has is the staunchness of a man who feels deeply about all the things that matter to him, his country, his religion, his family and his friends. Being, as Lol Larwood noted, a courageous man, he is not inclined to sit silently by should any person or thing near to him be disparaged within his hearing. This admirable courage and clarity is to be seen and appreciated in all his writings. In fact the reader will find in the pages of this book clearer testimony to these qualities of the man than my few words can convey.

The scope is very wide and affords ample space for the author's firm touch on every aspect of the game of cricket. This touch is as happy and sure in the lighter moments of personality or incident, as it is on the delicate matter of cricket and politics, a realm in which the professional training of the political journalist keeps emotions and prejudices in their proper perspective.

The general scheme of the book is very much to my taste, for cricket is a game which lends itself to categorization. For me it is a great pleasure in this case, to be able to dip into any of the very interesting sections but with an understandable bias toward the great bowlers. The bowlers the author has chosen to describe are of inexhaustible interest and he has a close practical knowledge of the majority, and makes a penetrating study of all. My only complaint is that he did not give further rein to his considerable imagination and let us have a reconstruction of Spofforth and, say, Lohmann, and an estimate of their quality to modern standards. Also I would have liked to see something about Gregory and McDonald, the most picturesque and spectacular pair of all time (not forgetting Barnes and Foster). However, there is never space for everything and perhaps Fingo will sometime oblige us with an encore.

I would like to end where I started with a footnote which is quite irrelevant except that I think it would please the author. When Fingo and I parted at the end of that rainy but happy season, I went to Scotland. There I met the captain of Ross-shire, an erudite man with a twinkle in his eye. After some talk he said 'When you wrote about the match you did us a great injustice'. Cricket writers have been known to drop clangers and I eyed him warily. 'What did I do?' I asked. 'You omitted to mention that we were one man short,' said he.

Should he chance on this book I feel he will be amply compensated.

IAN PEEBLES

Introduction

To those who have never played it and thus don't understand it, cricket seems an odd game, indeed a boring one. To those who play it and, therefore, love it, cricket can be a fascinating game, full of character, humour, tactical moves, technique, a beauty difficult to define, and a game which produces infinite goodfellowship. It is at its best when played with challenge and it takes two sides to issue and accept a challenge. Those who know the game immediately recognize the poseurs, those who pretend to aim for victory but run for cover in the guise of slow overs and wasted time. Also easily recognizable are the 'bluffers', those who roar and jump in appeal, hoping to put it over the umpire.

Arthur Mailey, who had a lovely whimsical humour in his cricket cartoons, always depicted the umpire as a humble little fellow, wearing a white coat and hat much too big for him and weighed down by bowlers' sweaters. Television, and radio (I suspect some Test umpires have a tick-tack system worked out with some commentators to 'put them in the picture'), have made the modern Test umpire a pretty important fellow. His name is constantly repeated and, mean fellow that I am, I sometimes suspect that one or two of them project an image for the camera. I know one in particular who now signals a boundary with a flourish that would do credit to a conductor at the Albert Hall!

I only comment upon this in passing but it was unfortunate to see such open conflict and disagreement between players and umpires in the Test series between Australia and England in Australia in 1970–71. Some of it suggested wrangling more in keeping with the soccer field – or, rather, one should say, wrangling and argument that *did* occur on the soccer field. The booking of players for 'back-chat' in soccer has had a salutary effect upon behaviour in that game and, arising out of the series in Australia, one presumes that 'booking' of players could come in cricket. It will be unfortunate if it does and in hoping that it doesn't, one could also express the hope that umpires will make themselves as unobtrusive as possible, as a good umpire should. A few of them have held an exalted opinion of their importance in the game.

Enough of that. I have to explain the reason for this book. No sport could possibly have provided a more thrilling game than the Tied Test, the only one of its kind, between the West Indies and Australia in Brisbane in 1960. It remains the highlight of my playing and watching career and as my book *The Greatest Test of All* is out of print, that Test was one reason why I thought of collating various pieces of my cricket writing over the years.

Much of my writing has been done under the pressure of newspaper deadlines. Journalists have precious little time, under such circumstances, to prune and polish and so I have permitted myself the liberty of some additions to various articles in this book. In the chapter on Bradman, for instance, which was published in *World Sports* (London), I have added and told for the first time the story of how our 1938 team in England threatened to strike if the Australian Board of Control would not give permission for Mrs Bradman to join Don in England before the tour finished. Don was not present at our team meeting, at which I suppose I played a part. We won our point!

I am indebted to the London *Sunday Times*, in particular, for permission to use some of the innumerable articles I have written for them over the years. I began writing for the *Sunday Times* in 1951 and I think an Australian can be proud of such lengthy service for such an outstanding newspaper. I certainly am. My long association with Ian Peebles on that newspaper was one of infinite pleasure and joy to me and I am honoured and most happy that he has written the Foreword to this book. Peebles and I knew at close quarters what Test cricket was all about. He once got Don Bradman's wicket in a Test in England for 14 and as that was the 1930 series when the Great Man hit Test scores of 254, 334 and 232, Peebles's feat rightly made national headlines. One could never have a more delightful working companion than Ian Peebles. On my arrival in London, we would discuss many matters over his festive office board (he is a wine merchant and would produce some magnificent bottles of well-chosen and happy grapes) and this atmosphere of mellow bliss and contentment with each other's company would carry on through the summer. Peebles is in a rare class as a cricket raconteur, extremely droll and possessing the facility not always known to raconteurs of being able to tell a story against himself. I like exceedingly his tale – much abridged here – of how the then Governor of West Australia, a cricket fanatic who not only didn't like being beaten but indeed never was to this time, induced Peebles and Hassett to play for his GH side. The two worthies failed to 'register' in either runs or wickets. At all events, the Governor's side suffered its first and only loss. Obviously moving faster in a car than they did on the field, Peebles and Hassett were 'booked' by the police for speeding after the match. They pleaded they were anxious to escape the scene of vice-regal felony!

After my own playing days, I never made a practice of getting close to cricketers. It is not a good policy when one has to write about them. Some younger pressmen, I am afraid, are too prone to wear a path to the dressing-rooms, where they are avidly received, it seems, and could be fed, human nature being what it is, inspired information. Bill Woodfull would never allow the press in the Australian dressing-room and I think this was correct. I tell in this book of how I got the blame for 'leaking' the sensational story of the bodyline Test in Adelaide in 1933 when Woodfull, after being badly hit by Larwood, told Sir Pelham Warner and Mr R. C. N. Palairet, the English manager and assistant manager who had come into our room to sympathize with Woodfull: 'There are two sides out there. One is playing cricket and the other is not.'

Warner and Palairet left our room quickly and in acute embarrassment. Later, in a book, Sir Pelham wrote: 'Unfortunately, there was a professional journalist in the Australian team and next day the story was blazoned all over the newspapers.'

Years afterwards, Sir Pelham accepted my word that I had not given the 'leak', although I don't think he had any justification for believing that such a story should not have been made public. I carried the blame for the story for a long time. Claude Corbett, who wrote for the Sydney *Sun*, as I did in those days, early told me who gave him the scoop. He said he got a telephone call from an Australian player and arranged to rendezvous with him, in the player's car, on North Terrace, Adelaide. There, Claude got the whole story.

It doesn't matter a fig to me now who was the informant. Possibly, as Woodfull told me long afterwards, it cost me the 1934 tour of England. I toured South Africa in 1935–36 and England in 1938 and have gone every tour since to England. I got most satisfaction out of the 1953 tour when I took my wife, Philippa, and our four young children to England (Jacquelyn came along later in the innings).

As I say, I have not made a practice of getting close to the players. All I would appreciate from them is the occasional humorous story. But I was a little staggered once when a modern demanded to know how I could interpret happenings on the field from the press-box (this modern showed no lack of alacrity himself in interpreting field actions when he later did a short stint in the press-box). I reminded him that I had once trod the field myself and a journalist is taught to observe and interpret. Evidently, on his basis, had I been fielding on the fence and not been just outside it, I could have justified my opinions. But the point is piffling. I think I interpreted too correctly for his liking.

Probably, I could have included in this book more material that I have written on modern players and I am none too sure now that I wouldn't agree with those who think the ripple-soled shoe, under some circumstances, is somewhat suspect. I have worn the shoe and it is most comfortable, but I have seen a lot of slips on the field since John Benaud had his tilt with authority. On lush grass and when the field is wet, I think a fully-sprigged boot is more reliable. A Test cricketer should carry shoes and boots for all occasions.

Old cricketers often perpetuate dreams, ignoring a probing of reality, yet cricket is a nostalgic game and perhaps that is the reason why I have favoured other times and other players, although I have been pleased to discuss champions like Richards, Sobers and Graeme Pollock, all moderns, at considerable length. Sobers hit a classical 254 in Melbourne in 1972. It will remain an unforgettable innings. Two matches later, playing for the World Eleven against Australia, Pollock played a century innings of tremendous character on a dubious Adelaide pitch.

These two innings were of the highest possible order. I don't think I live too much in the past, yet, if South Africa can produce two like Richards and Pollock and the West Indies one like Sobers – and I hasten to add that Rohan Kanhai, also of the West Indies, is one of the really *great* batsmen of the modern age – what ails England and Australia now when it comes to producing batsmen of the classical order?

Some will advance Boycott, of England, and Walters, of Australia, to refute my general argument. Boycott is the very epitome of a professional cricketer. He immerses himself in himself . . . which is one reason why too big a number of his fellows have been run out when batting with him. . . . And he has perfected an impregnable defence, so watertight that when the loose ball comes along Boycott will sometimes succumb to it in his flurry to unlimber. Many Test batsmen have the capacity to bat better than they do. They realize this, unfortunately, mostly in retirement. The urge or the inspiration to attempt is the big disability. When Boycott infrequently cuts loose, he can play as attractively as anybody but runs will always be Boycott's horizon. That is his character.

I don't think even Yorkshiremen will claim that Boycott is of the same school of genius to which Denis Compton belonged. Recently, I was tinkering with a difficult television set, trying to get a splendid programme called, I think, *The Summer Game*. It was infuriating that I could get the sound but not the picture. Suddenly the picture broke out and showed us Compton dancing yards down the pitch to drive. I could not have wished for a more perfect snippet to set in motion my vivid memories of Compton at the crease and he completed my enjoyment by dashing off, as he so often did, for a horribly short run and just getting it amid a general upsurge of arms, legs, bat and appeals. This was vintage Compton. I think it fair to observe that English batsmen don't get down the pitch like that these days; nor, Peter May apart, have England produced another since like Hammond or Compton.

Why not? The English field is wide open for an exciting batsman to invade and dominate it. Just the very sight of Jack Hobbs coming to the middle warmed his countrymen, they were so proud of him. Some years ago, I wrote in the *Sunday Times* a prediction that the policy of employing players from other countries to bolster the strength of county teams would react to the detriment of English cricket. It would deny chances to many young Englishmen, as it would sap the strength, the playing ardour and the novelty of internationals from other countries. I think some of this has come to pass. Many complain of being 'stale', but I think most harm has befallen the young Englishmen in their denial of chances. Some English county sides seem to have almost as much country as county flavour these days.

As I write this (I had a celebratory drink only yesterday with Harold Larwood to mark the birth of his tenth grandchild – all Australians – and my third), the 1972 team to tour England is only three days off selection. Newspaper columns are replete with critics, some of whom are not abashed at never having seen an English pitch, telling us who should be chosen. Ian Craig says Inverarity must go but Craig has not seen Inverarity on English pitches as I have. Craig, himself, had a horrible tour when he went in 1953, yet I think this was mainly due to a technical fault that should have been corrected immediately. Craig gripped his bat wrongly so that when he thought he was playing straight down the pitch, his bat's face was turned to the leg-side, where he was often caught.

English county bowlers are great probers of technique and keen swoppers of information. I early perceived in England in 1968 that to every ball Inverarity took a big back-swing towards the middle stump. This made him a most proficient leg-side player but the English didn't bowl at him there. They kept the ball outside his off stump and Inverarity always had trouble there. He couldn't orient his swing. There is in this book one of the best and most graphic cricket pictures I have seen. It was taken by Barry O'Brien, the gifted photographer of the Adelaide *Advertiser*, and it shows Tony Greig, of Sussex, sitting on top of Inverarity at point on the Adelaide Oval.

Greig's feet are almost on the pitch. He is 6 ft. 7 in., and when he leaned over he was almost breathing into Inverarity's face. Once in each of Inverarity's innings at Adelaide, Greig was motioned back by the umpires but his tactics completely unsettled Inverarity, who made 11 and nil. Greig was playing the 'old soldier's' trick of bluff and intimidation and it came off, yet it would not have been possible but for the defect in Inverarity's technique. If this picture is further studied, it shows Inverarity's front foot pointing down the pitch, thus turning his left shoulder, thus swinging his bat across the line of flight. His front foot should have been side on, thus keeping his shoulders side on, not full face.

One other point is that Greig was so close he could fairly be said to have impeded Inverarity. I don't think any fieldsman should be allowed to stand within the follow through of a stroke by a batsman. I asked Hilton Ackerman how he would react if his fellow South African stood close to him like this. Ackerman grinned 'I'd whack him in the shins for a start,' he said.

Inverarity in England in 1968 had eleven successive innings under 20. He was sent to Scotland, to get away from cricket, and returned to make a sound 56 in the final Test. He could correct his fault, although it is now late in the day for him. Walters has tons of natural ability but he, too, baulks at times in technique. Many of my young countrymen have much ability but lack concentration and application. Perhaps they have won Test honours too easily. One of the reasons I included Warren Bardsley in this book is because he was an object lesson in application, hard work at the nets, and attention to small details. It is of interest that the former Englishman, Barry Knight, now in Sydney runs Australia's biggest coaching school.

Coleridge once asked Charles Lamb: 'Pray, Mr. Lamb, did you every hear me preach?' 'Damme,' said Lamb, 'I have never heard you do anything else.'

So to an end to my preaching. I end on a note of thanks to many. Apart from the London *Sunday Times* and *Times*, I have covered many tours for the *Argus Group* of South African newspapers, the Singapore *Straits Times*, the *Hindu*, Madras, and the *South China Morning Post*, Hong Kong. Oddly, perhaps, although I prefer to be a free agent, I don't write on cricket for my native Australian newspapers. Sometimes, understandably, I wish I did. I have enjoyed warm friendships with English journalists. Many long hours in the press-box have been enlivened by good-natured banter with them – Swanton, Wellings, Manning, Wilson, Woodcock, Wooldridge, Chapman, White, Bray, Bannister, Taylor, 'Tiger' Smith, Easterbrook, Bowes, Preston, Kilburn, Williams – and others whose innings sadly have been declared closed. Our Australian contingent – Goodman, O'Reilly, Butler, Tresidder, Benaud, Simpson, Beames, Mathers – usually managed to keep our end up. Then, too, are the many BBC characters with whom I worked in England – Brian Johnston, Arlott, Alston, Robert Hudson, Anthony Craxton – and in this regard I must also mention Freddie Brown and Norman Yardley, with both of whom it was always a pleasure to broadcast.

Neville Cardus must have a niche on his own. As a youth, I had the temerity to write to him from Sydney. He answered me and, ever since, we have been warm friends. I always enjoy his wonderful company and no day at Lord's has been too busy but that I couldn't spare an hour to sit and yarn with Neville.

I am indebted to my publishers over the years – Collins, Cassell, and Heinemann – for the books from which I have taken some of these chapters. Sydney Goldsack was my first splendid friend with Collins. Then came Ian Chapman, who has been both a friend and my publisher. I am also indebted to Mark Bonham Carter, who has helped me over many publishing stiles. I would also like to express my deep sense of gratitude to Ian Wooldridge for his generous and capable professional help and advice in the assembling of this book at a distance of 12,000 miles. I would also like to thank Irving Rosenwater for his help with the illustrations.

Cricket has been exceedingly kind to me and I acknowledge the debt. I end by mentioning my deep gratitude to Pat Murphy, Ken Compston and John Lovesey, successive Sports Editors of the London *Sunday Times*, and Denis Hamilton, Editor in Chief of the *Times* newspapers. It is extremely pleasant to have warm friendship in working associations.

Sydney, March, 1972 JACK FINGLETON

Part One

MATCHES TO REMEMBER

There comes a time in many matches when a decision can make it live or die. It is up to the skipper or, in some cases, to both skippers. I am sure the Tied Brisbane Test between Australia and the West Indians is the greatest game of cricket that has been played any-where, yet it could so easily have died on the final day. That it didn't – and due credit must be paid here because most were in-clined to over-tribute the West Indians at the end of the brilliant, unforgettable series – was mainly because Richie Benaud took up the challenge. I wrote a book on this series and called it *The Greatest Test of All*. I recall this section from it with relish because I loved every minute of that epic game. Some in the press-box lost their heads in those final tumultuous minutes – indeed, some, deciding that the game would end in a tame draw, had even flown out of Brisbane! – but I kept jotting down the details as they happened and my note-book gave me everything I wanted at the end of the hectic day. So I wrote it. Not many saw that final day's play. Those who did will never forget it.

Hundreds of thousands of Australians saw that miraculous finish on television or heard it on the radio. I have chosen the New South Wales–Victoria match, and its sequel, as an instance of the ups-and-downs in cricket – and a score of over a thousand in an innings made the game remarkable. The Yorkshire games choose themselves, even though they are separated by a long span of years. I hope young Australians yet to play for their country in England will read of these games and appreciate just how different from other games is one against Yorkshire at Bramall Lane. It has colour, it has edge. The 'Yorkies' play cricket hard, as Australians once used to do, and Ray Illingworth gave a good instance of this as he led England in Australia in 1970–71. This last game at Bramall Lane convinced me that Freddie Trueman would have made a capital Test captain. He far out-manœuvred Bill Lawry. Bowlers rarely get the nod as an international captain, although there is no valid reason for this. One of the best 'thinkers' in the game is Bill O'Reilly and he showed clean captaincy heels to his fellows when he led New South Wales to victory after the Second World War. Not even Bradman excelled him as an after-dinner speaker, a requisite for a touring skipper.

'Out of the Old Trafford Pit' recalls a most interesting Test of 1961, a game that *should* have gone England's way. Even the Australians thought England had it in the bag. That it slipped out was due to several factors – a bold, captaincy move by Richie Benaud which he had previously discussed with an Australian hard-head, Ray Lindwall; and, undoubtedly, some hysterical batting by one or two Englishmen in a time of crisis. Who can say what would have been the run of Tests between England and Australia in the next series or two had England won that day at Manchester? For a surety, I think Peter May would not have foreshortened his Test career.

1. The Greatest Test of All

FOREWORD

I titled this book *The Greatest Test of All*. I might equally have called it 'Cricket Reborn' because that greatest of all Tests between Australia and the West Indies in Brisbane from 9–14 December 1960 breathed new and lusty life into the ailing spectre of a once great game.

From something which seemed inexorably headed for the text books of the antiquarians, international cricket emerged from this breathless, spine-tingling Test as a game that can be played as a game – for the enjoyment of the players themselves and the enormous delight of those who pay at the gate.

What was the principal cause of this stupendous transformation?

To me the answer is clear. The principal cause was the simple, the unsophisticated, the generous, the essentially carefree and *good* cricketing behaviour which Frank Worrell and his happy band gave to Australia from the moment their tour began.

Good behaviour evokes good behaviour. It is difficult among the carefree to be a prophet of gloom; indecent among the generous to behave meanly; impossible, if you are an Australian international, to play timidly when courage and challenge form the hallmark of your opponents' game.

So did Richie Benaud and his men rise to the West Indian challenge, and in doing so they sloughed off the degeneracy into which Test cricket between England and Australia has, in recent times, descended. So did they match good cricketing behaviour with behaviour that was no less good.

Just thirteen hours after that Brisbane Test had ended in a tie, the first tie in Test history, I saw the Woolloongabba cricket ground far beneath the starboard wing of our climbing plane. Brisbane, from the air, is a pretty city with the river winding a picturesque path down to the bay. In the early morning sunlight of this day after, the cricket ground was not yet awake. Its red-roofed pavilion looked drab; the ground, of course, was deserted and the tawny pitch stood out clearly, as did the vacant scoring-board. A few bare moments and the ground was lost to view, a ground on which cricket history such as to defy belief had been made only a few short hours before.

We were not a sparkling lot that morning. Few had had much sleep. Some had not even bothered to turn in at all, our start from the various hotels being a dawn one, and those last few hours of play, with their teeming, unbelievable happenings, had been discussed over and over. There was still, this morning, a light in the eyes of all who had played in the game and those who had seen it. Not many saw it that final day – only 4,160 – and a few who should have been there, working on it, ducked off early in the day, thinking the game would be drawn. One, indeed, who had flown away early, next day wrote a most graphic account of the tie he hadn't seen, but the names of those who flew off early are professional secrets.

Yet hundreds of thousands of Australians listened to that tumultuous last hour and tens of thousands watched it in Brisbane on television. Streams of cars out of the cities that afternoon had their radios on and when the fight got hardest, many pulled into the kerbside the better to listen and many others crowded around their cars. The national broadcasting stations re-played the film of the last ten minutes of play many times that week. They have done so, often, since.

The afternoon after the game I was back in my Canberra office, 800 miles from Brisbane, but work was impossible. Fellow members of the Parliamentary Press Gallery crowded in and plied me with questions. They told me how everybody had hung on their radios the afternoon before. One said some sixty members of his club had deserted the bar for the radio. For many Australians not to have a beer in their hands at six o'clock was almost as historic as the Tie itself!

Yet neither radio nor television could give the atmosphere of that demented finish. It had to be seen to be believed and, of a truth, those few hundreds who witnessed it could barely believe that what was happening under their very eyes was actually happening. It all seemed impossible; so much did drama pile upon drama to an excruciating climax. W. J. O'Reilly wrote that a gifted entrepreneur with a rare flash of genius could not have conceived this finish. He considered it the greatest happening that all sport had yielded. So did everybody who saw it and, as the years go by, it will give to cricket a breed of bores – I will be one – who will boast, 'I saw the Brisbane Tie.'

My first editor was a charming and sagacious man, A. R. B. Palmer. He impressed upon me that a journalist was not present on any occasion to participate. He was there as a recorder, to note, to form his impressions and to be certain of his facts. It was intensely difficult over that final hour not to be completely immersed in the happenings; not to be transported into the delirium of ineffable excitement ineffably prolonged. But I jotted and jotted and jotted. Here, then, while my notebook re-lives the match, is the story of the Brisbane Tie as I saw it.

AN IMMORTAL INNINGS BY SOBERS

I saw Frank Worrell's men play in Melbourne and Sydney and thought them a typical West Indian side – in the heights one hour, in the depths the next. Kanhai had played a spectacular innings for 252 against Victoria and Ramadhin had got two good crops of wickets. Worrell still looked a prince among batsmen but what they gained in Melbourne, they lost in Sydney. Particularly, also, as Sobers, who did not play in Melbourne, failed in Sydney in both innings, the first time to a monstrous lbw decision. He had one ball from Benaud in the second innings and it took his middle stump.

Sobers left the Sydney field looking a most disappointed young man. Those of us who had not seen him make runs began to doubt the lavish praise given him by English critics and recalled that England had no ogre of spin like Benaud to test him.

Nor did Kanhai look impressive against Benaud in Sydney. He played him cautiously from the crease, always a point in the spinner's favour because it allows him to dictate terms. On a humid day, Davidson's swing had nonplussed the West Indians in the first innings against New South Wales. Worrell, alone, seemed possessed of the technique to counter Benaud and Davidson but, now thirty-six years old, he strained a leg muscle in Sydney and stood down the next game against Queensland. This side, one thought, relied very much upon Worrell.

On the eve of this Test in Brisbane, the sixteenth between the two countries, I thought of the West Indians in terms of Marechal Bosquet's famous remark about the Charge of the Light Brigade: '*C'est magnifique, mais ce n'est pas la guerre.*' On their best days, the West Indians played magnificent cricket but one had the nagging notion that it wasn't the way to win Test matches – or so most Australians thought.

There was not a cloud in the sky when the Test opened. Worrell won the toss and accepted its favour. Those inured to a customary hour of cautious skirmishing at the beginning of a series got their first surprise when Hunte brilliantly drove Davidson's third ball of

the match to the boundary. He slammed the very next square to leg
for another four and in three minutes we had seen as much aggressive
action as we had seen in many sessions of the last Test played in
Brisbane – England v. Australia – that aptly earned itself the title of
the Battle of the Snooze.

Cammie Smith – no relation to the brilliant Collie who had lost
his life in a road accident in England, an accident which also could
have cost Sobers his life – had opened so brilliantly in Sydney that
some people began to compare him with Trumper. He swung with
the 'tide' againt Davidson and hit him from the bowling crease – one
thrilling pull going high over the square-leg fence – in three overs.
Davidson had quick revenge in Brisbane. He angled the ball across
the pitch, Smith followed it with a swishing bat, but not his feet, and
Grout took the catch behind.

Hunte kept up the pressure. Right-handed, a most graceful
stander at the crease, he has a surfeit of strokes but, seemingly, not
the capacity to lard them with discretion. Again Davidson delivered
from the extreme edge of the crease as he bowled left-hand fast over
the stumps. Davidson pitched well up, feeding Hunte's eagerness to
drive. Hunte took the bait but again the batsman took no cognizance
of the angled delivery; again the ball touched the bat's edge, not its
middle; and Benaud took a handsome, difficult, face-high catch at
third slip.

Now came Sobers, tall, graceful, quick in his walk, bare-headed.
With the aplomb of youth and the skill of a veteran, he beautifully
forced Davidson square off his toes for four the first ball. As if the
careless strokes of Hunte and Smith had no significance for him,
Kanhai made a full-blooded drive at another angled ball from
Davidson without getting his front foot to the ball and Grout had yet
another catch. Davidson had all three wickets and, at noon, after
only an hour's play, the score was 36 for three. There was not an
unproductive minute in the hour.

Worrell came now with his languid, graceful walk, exuding
avuncular urbanity and easy charm. Champions wear their flannels
well and none more so than the athletic Worrell. He came with
heavy responsibility. Not only had three wickets gone but Sobers had
also shown an inclination to rashness outside the off stump. The
innings stood badly in need of intelligent solidity, some law and
order, and Sobers could have had no better partner than his skipper,
one with icy coolness to temper youthful impetuosity; one, too, to
bring a judicious calm into the calling of runs.

Meckiff had presented no difficulties. Labouring with his changed style, a change ordained by higher authority in Australia on the evidence of films which clearly showed a crook in his elbow at delivery, he didn't look at all happy. With his arm now high at delivery, the ball came sedately off the pitch and behaved itself coming and going. Benaud came on at 87 for three and was given immediate respect. Sobers's first scoring stroke went behind square-leg. It could have yielded two but Sobers wanted only one. Aha, we all said, Sobers is in no hurry to tilt with Benaud!

Sobers immediately showed the futility of such thinking. He very carefully watched Benaud's second over and then in the third lambasted him. He had three boundaries in four balls – a scorching drive left mid-off standing; the next screamed back past Benaud and the third was a thrilling back-cut. So quickly, then, did Sobers dispel the belief from Sydney that he had a chink against spin; that Benaud would over-awe him.

The third boundary gave Sobers 50 in 57 minutes, with eight fours. The 50 partnership came in 41 minutes and of them Worrell, the watchful, had made only nine. The game now had swung to the West Indians, Sobers in particular. He again vigorously square-cut Benaud, this time for three, and Worrell eloquently drove him for four. At lunch, after 120 minutes, the West Indians were 130 for three. It had been a morning of absolute delight.

Benaud bowled again after lunch and Worrell pulled him for four. Nor did Davidson command respect, 10 coming from his first over, and when Sobers precisely placed Benaud through the covers for 4, Sobers had hit twelve boundaries in 79 runs. This last boundary took him past 3,000 in Test cricket. There was now no stopping him. He slammed Benaud straight again to the fence and the 100 partnership was up in 90 minutes. Worrell had made only 38 of them, but he was the rock on which Sobers built.

Completely at ease, Worrell played some admirable cover and off-drives and placed neatly to leg, but it was Sobers who had everyone, and particularly the Australian bowlers, gasping. Mackay had earned a reputation in Pakistan and India as an inexpensive medium-paced bowler and in this match he was expected to rest Davidson and Meckiff while keeping the game tight. He bowled three overs and Benaud sacked him. One shot by Sobers showed complete scorn for Mackay's bowling. The ball was pitched well up on the leg stump. Sobers drew back and with a full sweep of the bat across the line of flight of the ball, hit it unmercifully square to leg for four.

Benaud had taken the brunt of the onslaught. He had his field deep, but still Sobers found the gaps and he once pelted the Australian skipper so hard straight back that Benaud, wisely, made no attempt to stop the ball. In such a manner, a few months earlier, he had fractured a finger when on a short tour of South Africa.

A century by Sobers was as inevitable as the hour. It came after only 125 minutes and it had 15 fours. The ground rose to him in its ovation. Benaud walked up and warmly shook his hand. It was his tenth Test century.

And so the new ball at 200 came at the fantastic time of 25 minutes past two. Again, we thought back to that other Test here when Bailey was in the middle for 7½ hours for 68 and the daily totals of run-getting were 142, 148, 122 and 106, setting a record as an all-time low for slow scoring in Tests.

The new ball did not curb the batsmen. Davidson must have wondered what hit him when, resting after his first spell of opening bowling, he had the new ball in hand again. Neither he nor his skipper, seemingly, had much hope of the new ball achieving anything. The umbrella field, so called, with fieldsmen grouped around the batsman like Australian males around a nine gallon keg of beer at a party, was not summoned, was not considered.

Davidson had his field strung out as if bowling medium-paced with an old ball and Sobers made the placement of McDonald at deep mid-off memorable by surely the swiftest daisy-cutter seen on this ground. McDonald was in its direct path. Far out and all as he was, he barely got his fingers down in time and then, obviously, wished he hadn't. The ball seared through them to the fence and for some minutes the unhappy McDonald stuck his stinging fingers under his armpits for relief. It was for all the world like getting a 'sixer' with the strap on a cold, winter's morning at school.

Davidson and Meckiff had no effect upon Sobers until, at 132, he fell to the worst ball of the day. It was from Meckiff, a full toss and wide of the leg-stump. Sobers parried half-heartedly at it, the ball hit the back of the bat and spooned up, a 'lolly' catch to Kline at mid-on. Sobers didn't conceal his shock and disgust with himself.

Sobers slowly turned and walked in, clapped every yard of the way by everybody. Uncapped, his bat on high to acknowledge the applause, Sobers passed from view below us in the press-box. He had batted 174 minutes; he had hit 21 boundaries; he had played an immortal innings.

With four more runs added, Worrell fell to Davidson, who moved one away and Grout took the catch. So, in a trice, the game had swung again. Two who had the Australians seemingly where they wanted them for the rest of the day, were both back in the dressing-room within five minutes. Worrell had batted 159 minutes for 65, with 8 fours. One, a delectable late-cut off Davidson, was not excelled even by Sobers. Worrell was the perfect foil for Sobers, guiding and inspiring him by his cool presence.

Joseph Solomon, a thin wisp of a man who plays with his sleeves buttoned to his wrists, batted on with the apt wisdom of his name. His footwork is not expansive but it is correct. There was much in his innings of 65 in 141 minutes to admire but the partnership of 174 in 152 minutes by Sobers and Worrell had left us limp and comparatively unappreciative of anything less than Homeric. This batting day belonged in large doses to Sobers and what was left was Worrell's.

Lashley once picked up a ball swinging away to leg from Meckiff and, being left-handed, lifted it with rare timing over the fine-leg fence – there to be caught by a bespectacled spectator. Alexander hung on defensively for 21 in 105 minutes and at stumps, with the West Indians one run behind the clock, the total was 359 for seven. Never had I seen an Australian attack so torn to tatters in a single day's Test cricket.

I was invited to meet Sobers at the day's end. We talked of various things and he still hadn't forgiven himself for getting out as he did against Meckiff. No, he assured me, he hadn't worried when dismissed for small scores in the preceding state games. 'The Tests,' he said, 'are all that matter.' I did not agree with him in that but said nothing. He had looked a most disappointed young man trudging back after Benaud had bowled him in Sydney. Moreover, a batsman on tour in a new country is always avid to get a good look at the pitches and opposing bowlers. I put his remarks down to understandable over-excitement.

'Never,' he told me, in his deep, gurgling voice, 'have I set out so keenly to fathom a bowler as I did Benaud today. That is why I was so annoyed when I got out. I meant to "farm" Meckiff safely away for a single. I knew that Benaud would be on again soon.'

I saw a weary Davidson with his legs up on a rail and I complimented him on his grand bowling. Though I am not one for dressing-rooms (I considered this an unusual occasion and I wanted to study Sobers), I must say the press are more warmly received by modern players than in my own playing time. On this same ground, for instance, the autocratic Jack Hutcheon, President of the Queensland Cricket Association, wielded the big stick over everybody. Jack, who once ordered a woman out of the Members' Stand because, he told her, she wasn't suitably dressed, died before the mini-skirts.

There was, in the old days, a barbed wire fence between the players room, a shabby little weather-board room that would have made a better sweat-box, and the adjacent grandstand. Nowadays, a magnificently comfortable press-box is perched on top of the new dressing-rooms and a new spirit pervades Woolloongabba.

The good relations between modern players and the press is due in the main to Richie Benaud, who is a professional journalist. In my day, both players and officials scowled whenever a pressman passed by and, from some, there would be the infantile whispered warning of 'look out, press!' Conceivably, we have swung too far, the other way. Some of the press have a path worn to the dressing-room door so that their opinions often bear the suspicion of being coloured. One interprets their pats on the back accordingly. Their favourites – or their informants – inevitably 'justify their places'.

Benaud was exuberant about the day's play. To him, the entertainment of it was uppermost. 'I have never seen a better innings than the one by Sobers,' he said. 'The amazing thing was how he so consistently hit good length balls to the fence. I would think I had put down a good length ball that would take some playing and then, whizz, off to the fence it would go. And how he found the gaps!'

Worrell had this to say of Sobers: 'I have seen him play some great innings but this is a Test match and we were in an awkward position. All things considered, I think this is the best innings I have seen him play.'

I sat that evening, after my work was finished, looking out into the gloaming of the ground, casting my mind back over the years. I didn't see Bradman make his great score at Leeds – a century before lunch, another before tea and yet another before stumps. I saw Bradman once decimate a Victorian attack in Sydney and, before and since, I don't think I have seen the like of that. Sobers's innings, however, was in a Test and this carries a gloss of responsibility and occasion that no other game has. Moreover, as Worrell stressed, the West Indians were in trouble when Sobers came to bat.

Stan McCabe came instantly to my mind. His 187 not out in Sydney in 1932 was made against the ferocious bodyline bowling of Larwood and Voce. McCabe's 189 not out in Johannesburg in 1935 was made on a 'bumping pitch and in a blinding light'; and there was also the incredible 232 McCabe hit against England at Trent Bridge in 1938. I had seen all these innings, playing in all these games. I remembered, too, the peerless double century Wally Hammond had hit against us at Lord's in 1938; and the unforgettable double century Dudley Nourse had made in that same Johannesburg game in 1935. Len Hutton had a small masterpiece in Sydney; Colin Cowdrey had a similar innings in Melbourne in 1959 and Denis Compton had several of the greatest Test innings against the fury of Lindwall and Miller in England in 1948.

It is not easy to decide which innings is the greatest one has seen. In the circumstances, one would give the accolade to McCabe's in Sydney in 1932, yet I considered myself fortunate to have seen this one by Sobers. To be assessed, also, is the fact that it came to Australian Test cricket after long years of dour, intense games between England and Australia in which a batsman who tried to give 'colour' to the game would have been considered a national liability, so much had victory come to count. Yet this victory cult had defeated itself. This innings by Sobers showed us just what we had been missing in Test cricket.

The Australian attack against which Sobers had scored his runs was that which had subjugated England in Australia two years before. It had not been demonstrated then that it was insufficient yet Sobers showed this day that it had some gaping holes. Davidson, in thrust, in steadiness, was high above all the other bowlers. Benaud was his reliable self, but the others fell away. Benaud seemed to lack confidence in using Kline against the two champion West Indians. Mackay was well below Test class as, also, was Meckiff. This attack, therefore, was not comparable to that which McCabe bedraggled in Sydney in 1932. One, therefore, listed this innings by Sobers below that by McCabe but in all other ways it measured up – in grace, range of strokes, command of the attack and of the situation. No ball this day quietened Sobers. Tall, lissom, upright in his stance, a full flow of his bat, he demonstrated the true attribute of the genius – the ability to know instantly whether the ball was made for a drive, a cut, a glance or a forcing stroke. Defence hardly seemed to feature at all. No bowler can deliver on a length when batting genius is at work and it was so this day.

HALL – ALEXANDER – DAVIDSON

There should not have been many more runs left in the West Indian tail on Saturday morning. Alexander had shown the evening before that he could keep one end fast but he had shown no disposition to stroke-making, although in an earlier match in Perth he had indulged in some big hitting. Ramadhin was his partner this morning and even if Alexander held the Australians out, it was thought that the Australian spinners would quickly finish off the innings.

There were still 41 runs to go to the new ball. Benaud undoubtedly reasoned that he would not need it and that was the reason he opened with Davidson. A man who had done so much hard 'grafting' on the first day was richly entitled to trap the 'rabbits'.

The match began according to expectations. Davidson soon had Ramadhin out. The end was now in sight. The aim was to keep Alexander down one end and concentrate upon Hall, then Valentine, at the other.

Hall had other ideas. His batting is always good for humour. He carves big strokes at the ball and when he often misses, he meticulously goes through the motions of the stroke again. Worrell, this morning at the nets, had had a look at Hall's batting grip and suggested that he should change the position of his left hand. Hall did so and now, in the middle, was batting with his revised grip.

Hall began with a square-cut off Benaud that would have delighted Worrell. Then he magnificently pulled Davidson for four. He reached double figures and then began to play 'polished' strokes. Six times against Davidson he made big arcs and missed six times. Hall played his strokes all over again and the crowd howled with laughter. Each minute looked as if it would be Hall's last and the Australian slips rubbed and warmed their hands in anticipation. But Hall crashed Davidson past mid-off for four and square-cut him imperiously for four, bringing up the 400. Benaud took the new ball immediately. He had had his fill of Hall. Davidson and the new ball would put an end to this batting nonsense.

But Davidson didn't do so in the first over and Meckiff took the red ball at the other end. Surely, no other Australian fast bowler with the new ball has been so roughly handled; and by the tail-end! The first two balls Alexander drove furiously back past Meckiff for four apiece. Then Hall got up to the striking end and he also hit Meckiff for two crashing fours. One almost went for six, to the left of mid-off —a most remarkable stroke. That over cost Meckiff 19 runs.

Benaud, who is also a proficient journalist, wrote later that at the end of that over he reflected that in one whole pre-lunch session of the preceding Test here between England and Australia, only 19 runs had been scored altogether. And he wrote, too, of a remark he heard from a barracker over the fence, 'Hey, Benaud, which one of these blokes is Sobers?' Good Australian wit!

Alexander ran to his 50 in 173 minutes and still the onslaught on Meckiff continued. Hall swung him fine for four and then tore down the pitch for an exceedingly cheeky single to gain his 50 in 69 minutes with eight fours. Every minute was chockful of action.

Benaud's throw-in hit Hall and the big fellow was travelling with such momentum that he ran ten yards beyond the stumps before he sprawled flat on his face. He rose, covered in dust, cleaned himself down, grinned hugely and waved to the crowd with his bat. Meckiff's three overs with the new ball had cost 39.

Kline was given the ball and Hall, going for more glory with a huge hit, was stumped immediately by Grout. Left now only with Valentine, Alexander also decided to 'dip' and, skying Kline, was well taken by Davidson. The West Indians were out for 453 in 445 minutes – ahead of the clock. Some 250 had come from boundaries.

Back in the pavilion, I heard later, a grinning Wesley Hall explained to his skipper that he had 'thrown' his innings away. 'Why, man', he said, 'Wes Hall could have got a century easily. Yes, sir. Then I suddenly say to myself, 'Wes, man, you're not in this side as a batsman only. You've got to do some fast bowling.' So I tell myself to be sensible and be satisfied, man, and get out – and so I get out.'

Alexander's innings was a most useful one. The score was 283 when he came in, 453 when he was last man out. The last 50 between Alexander and Hall had taken only 35 minutes. Davidson was, undisputedly, the Australian bowling hero. His fast ball had plenty of pace, but he judiciously mixed his speed and concealed it adroitly. His stock ball comes in to a right-handed batsman, particularly when the ball is new, but he has the capacity to send it the other way also. His length and direction are always good. So often Davidson looks at his last gasp, dragging one leg wearily after the other, yet a good hour or two after first gaining this impression, one is surprised to note that he is still bowling at his top. Benaud knows how to handle him. Davidson looks hard at Benaud as much as to say, 'I can't possibly do another over, Richie,' and Benaud says, 'Just one more over, Al.,' and Davidson seems barely to possess the energy to hand his cap to the umpire. He is an unusual cricketer; also a great one. I doubt that I have seen a better left-handed bowler with the new ball.

Opening batsmen are always delighted to see the opposing fast bowler make some runs at the end of an innings. It takes a lot of steam out of his bowling. Yet Hall, this day, seemed to have an extra boiler. He got up pace enough to hit McDonald a hearty smack on the ribs with the fifth ball of his first over. McDonald looked very groggy and sick of being hit by Hall. McDonald had played in an early game in Perth against the West Indies and had there taken a physical battering from Hall. He said to Hall after that match, 'I don't mind being hit about the body, Wes, but there is one place

I don't want to be hit and that is here.' McDonald dramatically put a finger to the middle of his head. Hall, completely unabashed, replied, 'Man, when Wes Hall is bowling, that's just up to the batsman.' After lunch, in Brisbane, McDonald got another body-cruncher from Hall in the ribs.

After all the brilliant batting that had gone before, the crowd of 16,000 became restive on this Saturday when the Australians scored slowly. I did not think the Australians entirely to blame. McDonald, like most openers, is not a dasher and Simpson, originally a brilliant stroke-maker at four or five, concentrates very much upon defence as an opener.

This day he got his runs much slower than McDonald, who took most of the charging Hall. It took the Australians 65 minutes to make 40, McDonald 28 of them.

I noticed, however, that Worrell showed an inclination to keep the game tight and I searched for reasons for this. I really believed Worrell had come to the strange conclusion, which was perfectly feasible, that his team had scored its runs too fast for a five-day Test. He had won the toss; his side had scored 453 (its previous best score in a Test in Australia had been 362 in Sydney in the 1950–51 tour), but the Australians had come to bat before lunch on only the second day. This meant that the Australians had got the pitch at its batting best. All life had gone out of it and four hours were left for play on this Saturday. Three more days after this one remained for play and a captain winning the toss and batting, naturally aims to have his opponents bat last on a wearing pitch. By scoring so fast, and especially if the Australians hit back powerfully, the West Indians could find themselves batting last.

Worrell, in his formative years, learnt more things in Manchester than at the University where he graduated in arts. He had played much cricket in the cauldron of the Lancashire League and these tight tactics savoured of it. Hall bowled eleven overs straight (he takes from six to seven minutes to bowl an over) and Sobers and Worrell, changing ends and relieving Hall, each bowled eleven overs of medium-paced bowling to a strong leg-side field. I thought these tactics admirable. I could understand them; but I felt that those who barracked the Australians didn't.

After a neat, plucky innings of 57 in 111 minutes, McDonald was caught at the third attempt by Hunte off Sobers, close in at leg. Harvey came and for over an hour was ill at ease. It was the most unconvincing innings I have seen from this champion. Simpson, over-cautious and no doubt worrying about whether he would stay in this Australian team, had an odd way of countering Hall's bumpers. He left his stumps open and swayed his body away. This looked dangerous for his stumps, if not to his limbs, yet it was noticeable that when Hall put one down on the stumps, Simpson was always in position to counter it. He batted 140 minutes before he hit his first four.

Harvey, who had several close lbw calls, fell eventually in drawing away to cut Valentine. Harvey cut him all right, but into his stumps. It was one of those occasions when a batsman, knowing it is not his day, was not sorry to get out. Harvey seemed out of form although a fortnight before, against the same bowling in Sydney, I had never seen him bat better.

O'Neill began unpromisingly, as he usually does, and hereabouts the Australian batting was markedly inferior to that of the West Indians. No doubt, Hall was the reason for this. No Australian appreciated his bouncer. Against Hall in Sydney, O'Neill twice hooked bouncers off his nose for four. This was the counter to Hall but on this occasion no Australian seemed to possess it. Hall flattened O'Neill after he had scored one. He didn't pick up the pace of the ball and it hit him in the groin. That could well have cost O'Neill much confidence.

Simpson had more than his share of good fortune. Like McDonald, he played a weak stroke to the on but it fell safely amid three fieldsmen. There was a very confident appeal for a catch behind when he was 76 and at 88, Smith should have caught him at short-leg off Worrell. And, like McDonald, there was the odd snick that missed the stumps.

Simpson, who seems as if he will play his Test cricket for 'keeps', denying his better parts, tried rashly to sweep Ramadhin five minutes before stumps and was bowled for 92. It took 260 minutes to make, and included seven fours. He batted nicely from 50 on, but was the butt of much barracking. Some of Simpson's critics claim that he plays too much for himself. The time to criticize him for that is when he makes his Test place assured. Unlike some of his contemporaries, he has had no easy path in Test cricket.

Two years ago on this Woolloongabba ground, O'Neill provided the only batting life that that Test knew but this was not his day. He lacked confidence and his 28 took 89 minutes. Although 3–196 looked a fair reply on paper by the Australians, they finished way behind the West Indians in public favour. Some of the batsmen grumbled at how tightly Worrell played. Of the 59 overs bowled, 45 were by the pace men and only 14 by Ramadhin and Valentine, Ramadhin at one stage not playing a slip.

Yet, by playing more attacking cricket by bowling his spinners, Worrell would have taken the risk of allowing Australia to build up a lead by sometime on Monday. If that lead had been considerably increased on Tuesday, the West Indians would undoubtedly have faced trouble on the last day of the match.

The morning apart, it was not a brilliant day's cricket. It was a day more for the student and the connoisseur than the average spectator. It was interesting, for example, to one who had known reactions in other days to bouncers, to see the tell-tale manœuvres of some Australians against Hall. Plainly, they didn't like them.

O'NEILL'S LUCK AND SKILL

Hall soon had the new ball on Monday morning. All life had gone from the pitch and Hall, after his week-end's rest, had surprisingly little also. O'Neill early got a hit from Hall on the upper left arm that carried on up into his face and he received another from the same bowler when he ducked to a ball that didn't rise high. This time he was hit on the left shoulder.

It was an oddly hesitant O'Neill we saw before lunch. He had begun this Australian season with a run of small scores which he broke against the West Indies in Sydney, hitting 156 not out for New South Wales. He was, too, a jerky, scrambling, nervous starter of an innings, threatening constantly to run somebody out with his hasty, ill-considered calls.

Favell was much more impressive. He had moved above Mackay on the Saturday, being chosen as nightwatchman, and it was absorbing to notice his batting change in stance. This, for a batsman in his thirties, is remarkable. Whereas before Favell had had a most pronounced crouch at the crease, his bat mark well away from his feet, which took his body outside his stumps, he now stood upright like a Grenadier Guard on duty outside the Palace. This new stance seemed to give him confidence against Hall, in particular, and he lofted the fast bowler repeatedly with audacious shots to the on-side. Of the first 50 of the day, Favell had 28.

Hall bowled five overs for 37 runs and then Worrell replaced him. Worrell, left-handed medium paced, bowls with his head as well as his arm. He moves the ball slightly off the pitch and he probes at a batsman's weakness. He should have had O'Neill immediately, the batsman not getting over a cut, but Sobers put the chance down at second slip. O'Neill was 47. He got a hard-won 50 in 148 minutes, including six fours, and then Alexander dropped him behind off Valentine at 54. O'Neill drew well away to cut.

No batsman could have had more luck than O'Neill between 47 and 54. At 52, O'Neill doubled up as he swung at Sobers. The ball hit him in the stomach and went on to the stumps – without knocking off the bails! This was stupendous good fortune. Alexander got his chance into both gloves.

It was Favell, not O'Neill, who celebrated this good fortune. Favell is always looking for runs – I put him down as Australia's unluckiest cricketer never to have got a tour of England – and he decided that as Valentine had no outfield he would exploit the wide, open spaces. Twice, from successive balls, he hit Valentine thrillingly over mid-off for six. We were still exulting in the splendour of it when Favell pushed one to the on-side, called O'Neill for a single, which O'Neill refused, and Favell scrambled back.

Favell thought he had made his ground in time. The umpire didn't and Favell left with misgivings. This happened right on lunch and a photograph developed during lunch showed that Favell was in error and the umpire right.

This was unfortunate for Favell and the crowd, but the West Indians had something owing them after O'Neill's three escapes.

Mackay, bending, flexing, chewing gum unceasingly, was now on view and one reflected what a remarkable sight he presents at the crease. His stance is unusual. He holds his bat out and away from his body in an old-fashioned manner. He swivels from the hips and, after going through innumerable, preparatory motions of flex, bend and chew, presents the full blade to the bowler. He performs with a minimum back-swing and follow-through and a minimum of footwork. He pushes, rather than swings, at the ball and it is amazing what power he gets when he tries. His wrists must be very powerful.

Most of O'Neill's runs came from pushes and glides. He seemed, momentarily, at least, to have lost those glorious drives of two years ago and it wasn't until he was 58 that he played his first full-blooded off-drive. Then, more like his old self, he hit Ramadhin for three fours in one over. At 4–306 at lunch, O'Neill 80, Australia was well placed, only 147 runs behind.

Mackay also had some luck. He once almost holed out on the on-side and then, at 34, was dropped by Alexander off Worrell. Fortunately, this made no difference (or did it at the finish?) as, after another single, Mackay played all over a ball from Sobers, now bowling spin, and was bowled. One reflected that thrice this summer

Martin, now the Australian twelfth man and a spinner similar to Sobers, had got Mackay's wicket.

O'Neill improved when joined by Davidson. He rushed through the eighties with four fours to reach 97 and then got his century in 235 minutes. Whereas he had hit only six fours in his first 50, O'Neill hit nine in his second. This was his first Test century in Australia and his fourth in all – two against India, one against Pakistan. His first 50 had the taste of corked wine; his second bubbled like champagne, if one overlooks his extreme good fortune in the fifties.

O'Neill was now in full spate and his score from 70 to 120 had eleven fours in it. Davidson, too, batted beautifully. Indeed, Davidson looked the best of the Australians, his defence sound, his movements against Hall full of confidence, his strokes excellent and varied. He could hold his place in this side for batting alone. At tea, the Australians were 346 for five, O'Neill 151, Davidson 21, and the two hours had seen 120 added. It was grand stuff to watch.

The new ball held no terrors for Davidson. He stepped inside one bouncer from Hall and thrashed it to the leg boundary. Hall seemed busted but, in what appeared likely to be his last over with the new ball, he got one to rise which Davidson snicked and Alexander held it.

This was a valuable wicket for the West Indians. It fell at 469, with the Australians ahead. Hall now went on to big deeds. He had Benaud lbw, then Grout. Meckiff fell while trying to give the strike to O'Neill, and O'Neill, with the last man Kline in, tried to hit Hall straight for six and was caught by Valentine off the resultant skier. In 36 minutes, Australia's last five wickets had fallen for 36 runs. The West Indians had broken back spectacularly into the game. The last half of the side could manage only a lead of 52 for the Australians.

When clouds are about, the Brisbane light fades early. So it was this day and as Hunte and Smith came out it was apparent that a light appeal would be upheld. It was, and the game finished 35 minutes early.

Chances had been lost and taken. The West Indians would have been in a commanding position had those chances been taken from O'Neill around the fifties. No side can afford to give a talented young man like O'Neill more than one innings. He reached 181, batting 401 minutes, and he hit 22 fours. His last hundred runs was replete with red meat.

Worrell's men gained in the finish with those quick five wickets. Hall took 4–18 in his last three overs to finish with 4–140. He had been 0–122! The Test was still wide open. The pitch had stood up well. I noticed no abnormal turn from the spinners.

DAVIDSON AGAIN THE STAR

Hunte and Smith began in characteristic West Indian fashion next day, each a four for his first scoring stroke. There had been an exceptionally heavy storm overnight. Once upon a time, before the pitch was covered, this game would have finished quickly because a heavy storm followed by a steamy sun would have left this pitch an unplayable glue-pot. In the deluge of 1946, the stumps had floated away.

But the pitch was still its somnolent, peaceful self for this fourth day. The West Indians had to push the score along. There was a lee-way of 52 and the clock had to be considered as well as the Australian attack.

Smith was destined to have a poor Test. He clipped Davidson well on the off-side but not along the ground and straight to O'Neill, the only fieldsman on the off-side in front of the stumps. A yard either way and Smith would have had a boundary. O'Neill dived and took a grand catch, inches from the turf. In such a manner does a batsman's luck run!

Kanhai wasted no time. He banged two full tosses from Davidson for four, one through the covers, the other backward of point. Thirty runs came in 30 minutes. Hunte was relishing Davidson. He hooked a short one so ferociously that few could follow it in flight and the next ball he drove straight to the fence. He took three for a well-placed on-side force, making 11 from Davidson's over. The score was 41 in only 35 minutes.

Meckiff, who had an injured ankle, bowled only three overs and Benaud relieved him. Hunte on-drove his first ball for four and then Benaud almost got through him with a top-spinner. Hunte jabbed down hurriedly, just in time. The 50 partnership came in 48 minutes and the leeway was wiped off when Kanhai brilliantly back-cut Benaud for four.

Mackay took over from Davidson and should have had Kanhai in his third over, Benaud dropping a sharp slips chance with Kanhai on twenty-eight. After an hour, the West Indians were 75 for one, a good, strategic position for a victory thrust. Hunte and Kanhai were fulfilling Worrell's instructions to perfection.

At this stage, however, the Australians got the scoring under control. Benaud sent down three successive maiden overs. Hunte

anchored so long on 39 that he seemed to lose patience and chased a
ball very wide of the off-stump. He snicked it and was safely taken by
Simpson's very reliable hands at first slip off Mackay.

Sobers came and Kanhai greeted him with a succinct pull for four
off Benaud. Sobers began with a superb on-drive for four off Mackay,
turned one for two, back-cut another in the same over for four and
the 100 came in 98 minutes.

Davidson came back for Mackay and in his second over got the
perfect yorker under Sobers's bat. Undoubtedly, Davidson bowled
for this. Sobers has a big back flourish with his bat and obviously
Davidson had worked it out that an early yorker would trouble the
West Indian champion. It is one thing to know what to do; another
to do it. I recalled that Lindwall always tried for such an early ball
against Tom Graveney, of England.

Davidson was so elated at his success that he jumped and shouted
and, in his joy, went whooping down to the other end of the pitch to
join his happy fellows. Sobers took an interested look at Davidson as
he walked out. He probably thought such an outburst a little out of
place and made a mental note of it for the future.

Kanhai drove Benaud through the covers for four to reach 50 in 97
minutes (7 fours), but in the last over before lunch, Worrell was
dropped off Davidson. Worrell hadn't scored. The snick was going to
Simpson at first slip, but an exuberant Grout dived, didn't get to it,
and obscured Simpson's vision.

The West Indians were 119 for three at lunch, Kanhai 51. In
effect, they were 67 for three and the Australians were well on top.
Much depended upon the Kanhai–Worrell partnership. Benaud had
not got a wicket in this session but he had bowled well and one
sensed that the worry he gave all the batsmen at one end had something to do with their downfall at the other. Kanhai has one strange
mannerism. He begins to bat without a sweater but once he gets a
start, no matter how hot the day, he calls for a sweater. He says he
gets cold across the shoulders.

Kanhai didn't stay long enough after lunch to get warm. He
chased another wide one from Davidson and Grout took yet another
catch. The Queenslander was having a fine Test in front of his own
folk.

Benaud, who had bowled 14 overs straight for only 38 runs, gave
way to Kline and Mackay came for Davidson. Worrell and Solomon
were now together and the game bogged down. Kline bowled
around the stumps, possibly hoping to pitch into Davidson's marks,
but after four overs from Kline, Benaud had himself back again.

Worrell cracked one good four through the covers but there was now little sparkle in the batting. One sensed that the West Indians realized they were facing defeat.

Simpson bowled and the 50 partnership came in 77 minutes, Solomon scoring only 13 of them. Worrell drove Simpson for four and swung him high for another one. He got his 50 in 110 minutes and the West Indians their 200 in 240 minutes. They were only 152 ahead, six wickets in hand and eight hours left for play. More than ever, one got the impression they were prepared to settle for a draw and with only slight hopes of that.

Even the draw vision faded after tea when Davidson, with the new ball, got one to come back off the pitch to Worrell. It hit the inside edge of Worrell's bat and deflected many feet to Grout's left but the Queenslander, a superb catching wicket-keeper, still managed to get there. Worrell had scored 65 in 151 minutes. His six innings on this tour had been 65 not out, 68 not out, 82, 51, 65 and 65 – the latter two in this Test. The sight of Worrell batting never palls. He is a consummate artist, paralleling Alan Kippax in the late cut.

Lashley soon had his stumps uprooted by Davidson and that great Australian player, after his five wickets in the first innings, now had five of the six that had fallen in this. The first hour after tea produced only 12 runs from 12 overs, three singles only to Solomon.

Alexander and Solomon continued to sit on the splice. A draw was now obviously their intention. Solomon poised almost monumentally for 222 minutes before Simpson again got him, this time lbw. Alexander's innings must have tried his own patience. After 67 minutes, he was bowled by Benaud for 5. It was, oddly, the first wicket of the game to the Australian skipper. It came in his 48th over and at a cost of 153 runs. He emulated Davidson in jumping for joy and doing a victory run down the pitch.

At stumps, the game looked all over. The West Indians were 259 for nine, only 207 ahead. The pitch was still behaving itself. The Australians had reason to think that tea-time on the morrow would find victory theirs. This day's play had been only fair to mediocre in quality. Davidson was the undisputed star. He now had ten wickets in the match.

WORKING UP TO THE CLIMAX

This final day brought an early setback to the Australians. Hall and Valentine stayed together for 40 minutes, a reflection upon the Australian spinning attack as Valentine is a batsman of ordinary

425,015

parts. This last wicket added 31, a useful contribution, 25 of them in this morning, and it had a double value. One was in the runs scored; the other in the diminished time left to Australia. Australia needed 233 to win in 312 minutes – about the rate of 45 runs an hour.

This, for the Australians, was a comfortable target. The pitch was still excellent, with no life for the fast men. They would have to earn every whit of lift they got but those most in the minds of the Australian batsmen were 'Ramadhin and Valentine, those two spinning pals of mine', as the Victory Calypso ran at Lord's on that unforgettable day in the early fifties when the two spun England out and their madly-excited countrymen weaved in happy crocodiles over the sacrosanct cricket turf.

Not that the Australian spinners, and Benaud in particular, had covered themselves in glory or suggested any spinning picnic for Ramadhin and Valentine. Kline, with a chill, was off-field. McDonald, with ribs sore after his battering from Hall in the first innings, was also absent. Meckiff, the third Victorian in the side, was on-field but not in a bowling sense. He had an ankle injury. Martin was fielding and Burge had been called into the fielding gap.

Davidson finished off the innings, hitting Hall's stumps with a yorker. This was fitting, giving Davidson eleven wickets for the match. He thus equalled C. V. Grimmett and H. Ironmonger, slow leg-break bowler and medium left-hand medium-paced spinner respectively, as the only Australians who had taken such a number of wickets in a Test against the West Indians.

Davidson's figures deserved a special bowling tablet to themselves. They were:

	Overs	Maidens	Runs	Wickets
First Innings	30	2	135	5
Second Innings	24.6	4	87	6
Match Total	54.6	6	222	11

The big left-hander had done enough work for two bowlers and, to be added to this stage, was his splendid innings of 44. He was entitled to take a cut lunch and a cold bottle of beer and retire to the shade of one of the colourful poinsettia trees that fringe this ground and there spend the remainder of the day contemplating his triumph at ease, cooling his bare and aching toes in the breeze.

Benaud once warned Hall to run off the pitch. Benaud wanted no more wear on it for the opposing spinners than was inevitable, although his own bowling figures were historic for him in their frugality. They were:

	Overs	Maidens	Runs	Wickets
First Innings	24	3	93	0
Second Innings	31	6	69	1
Match Total	55	9	162	1

McDonald, his ribs padded, opened with Simpson and we had not long to wait for a sensation. In Hall's second over, Simpson buckled at the knees and offered one-handed a limp stroke to a short ball in line with his body. It propped up a 'sitter' catch to Gibbs, substitute fieldsman for Smith, at short-leg.

Not only was this a bad start. It demonstrated concern against Hall's pace which, surely, on this final day, was at its least dangerous. Harvey had an immediate force to leg for four but in Hall's next over, the usually reliable little left-hander propped at a ball outside the off-stump and snicked it fast to the slips. Sobers dived forward, tumbled head over heels and came up triumphant with the ball. Up went the umpire's finger. This was a glorious catch but in its making Sobers dislocated the little finger of his right hand. He was given aid on the spot by wicket-keeper Alexander (a veterinary surgeon) but there was a cut, also, and Sobers left for dressing-room attention.

This made Australia two wickets down for seven. Hall gave O'Neill a bouncer first ball and the Australian sat unceremoniously on the pitch in avoiding it. Worrell, using the new ball at the other end, was economical. Next over Hall fired in fury at McDonald, who defended stoutly. It was a maiden over and from five overs Hall had 2–6. O'Neill took 24 minutes to make his first score and at lunch, 2–28 after 70 minutes, Australia were well behind the clock. McDonald had made 14 in that time and O'Neill eight in 44 minutes.

Hassett had appointed himself Chairman of the Clock in the press-box. His rate of runs needed per hour ran steadily higher: from 45 to 55.

O'Neill brought the first batting brilliance into the innings after lunch when he forced Hall for three; leg-glanced him for four and then, in Hall's next over, brilliantly late-cut him twice for four. The West Indian supporters among us began to grumble over Worrell's field-placing to Hall. 'Why the dickens,' they asked, 'doesn't Worrell keep a third man on the fence? He's letting O'Neill have it all his own way.'

But Worrell had intentionally left that gap. O'Neill, obviously with the gap uppermost in his mind, cut again but this time the ball wasn't made for it. O'Neill wasn't over the top of it and the snick went to Alexander, who snaffled it. Hall, thus, had 3–32 from 8.7 overs and the big West Indian threw his hands to his head in agony next ball as he almost bowled Favell.

Australia went further downhill next over when Worrell got one past McDonald's bat to bowl him. McDonald had hung on for 91 minutes for 16 but it was a grim and doubtful suspension for the most part. Hall had him most uncomfortable but nobody looked more incapable against Hall than Mackay, who three times failed to gauge the West Indian's pace.

Worrell again demonstrated superb captaincy when he moved an extra man across to the leg-side for Favell to Hall's bowling, attacking him on his strength. Favell didn't seem to notice the field change but what followed was clever cricket, well construed and perfectly consummated. Hall gave Favell a loose one outside the off-stump for 'burley' and to take his attention away from his leg-trap. Favell made the most of it and crashed it past point for four but two balls later, when Hall put the ball perfectly on the right spot, Favell picked it off his toes – straight into the safe hands of Joe Solomon, the extra man on the leg-side! As he departed, Favell probably felt like kicking himself on his way, so blindly had he fallen in the trap.

The game now belonged entirely to the West Indians. Hall, the big heart, had 37 for four from 10.3 overs. The last three Australian wickets had crashed for only eight runs. The Australian position was so desperate that Hassett had abandoned his time calculations. Hall, legs and arms flaying everywhere and sometimes in his wild enthusiasm running twenty yards to field to his own bowling, looked the very epitome of a West Indian typhoon – but even these blow themselves out in time. It was now twenty minutes past two. Australia were 57 for five. Taking twenty minutes off for tea, this left Australia 176 to make in 200 minutes.

Dripping with perspiration, Hall came off at last after 12 overs straight for 38 for four. He had done his job, a memorable fast bowling one in Test cricket. He had blasted a hole right through the centre of the Australian batting. He had made victory certain. The two spinners, Ramadhin and Valentine, could surely now drop the guillotine.

But, strangely, it was Sobers who took over Hall's end and to bowl medium-pace. One doubted Worrell's captaincy here. Sobers had earned himself bowling respect from the Australians but mostly as a slow spinner. He is amazingly versatile – fast, medium and slow spinners – and some of the Australians were none too certain in reading his bosie. Indeed, a few feared him more as a spinner than Ramadhin and Valentine and with two left-handers now batting, Mackay and Davidson, one thought Worrell would have had Sobers bowl spinners to the batsmen's legs off the marks of Davidson and Hall. Then, too, one recalled how Sobers had got Mackay in the first innings.*

For a while little happened. The batsmen concentrated upon defence, Davidson looking particularly safe, his bat and pad always moving close together. Ramadhin took over from Sobers and should have had Mackay with his first ball. A catch went to Gibbs at slip but it was dropped. Australia's sixth wicket should have fallen at 80; it fell instead at 92 when Ramadhin slipped one past Mackay and hit his stumps. In an hour, Davidson and Mackay had put on 35.

Benaud had an early fright. Ramadhin shaved his stumps with his second ball. Davidson then hit two successive twos from Valentine, and Benaud opened his score with a crashing off-drive to the pickets off the same bowler. This brought up the 100 in 175 minutes. Benaud was tentative in his approach, his forward play suggesting a wobbling probe, but they were together at tea, Davidson 16, Benaud 6. Australia needed 123 in the 120 minutes left for play. It still looked very much like a West Indian victory.

Obviously, there were keen councils of war in the dressing-room over the tea-cups. The Australians had two powerful hitters in possession with Davidson and Benaud. I had seen Benaud, in particular, play three sensational hard-hitting innings – one at Bradford in 1953, one at Lord's the same year and another at Scarborough, also in 1953. In addition, he had hit a momentous Test century in the West Indies – one of the hardest-hit of all time. Benaud, however, for all his ability, rarely does himself batting justice and seems lacking in confidence at the start of an innings. He has an odd grip with his left hand – in emulating Bradman's grip with that hand he has gone even further around the handle so that all his knuckles face the bowler. Davidson, in his time, has played many a merry innings, his best a hard-hit 67 in the Lord's Test of 1953.

There would come a time after tea when the Australians would begin their victory onslaught. They had to turn from passivity to pugnacity. It was apparent how it would start. The two Australians would try to rattle the West Indian bowlers and fieldsmen by taking

---

* I asked Worrell afterwards if there was any reason why he had not asked Sobers to bowl early spinners against Mackay. 'I'm afraid,' he confessed, 'the penny hadn't dropped by then' – in other words, he had not come to realize how much Mackay disliked this type of spin.

short runs. If successful in that, they would then try some hard hitting along the ground to gain confidence and then they would begin to put the ball in the air to find the gaps.

Worrell probably had recurring visions of what happened to the West Indians in Melbourne in 1951 when Ring and Johnston put on a hilarious 38 runs for the last wicket and snatched victory away from the West Indians. The manner of the victory, from the West Indian viewpoint, was as unforgettable as it was tragic. The Australians ran for everything and the West Indians became wildly excited. There were over-throws, there were missed run outs and of a sudden some extra skippers seemed to emerge so that the West Indians were in a tangle. Worrell had to make sure nothing like that happened again. He had to keep a tight rein on his men.

Soon after tea, off Valentine, Davidson got his first four. It had taken him 84 minutes. Benaud also off-drove Valentine for four. Worrell quickly switched back to Hall but Benaud had now gained in confidence and was batting extremely well. At ten past four, the Australians were 128, needing another 105 in 100 minutes.

Umpire Egar, in his first Test, held Hall up and directed him to tuck his flying shirt into his trousers – an odd thing to do as Egar, himself, like most Australian umpires, is a swinger and a bender. He swings low and bends in behind the bowler to stumps' height as the ball is delivered. If the end of a shirt, one thought, unsights a batsman, what would much swinging and bending do (Egar in later years gave up this practice)?

Hall tried hard but he was obviously busted. Worrell gave him only three overs and wisely took him off. There would be a new ball at 200. If need be, Worrell would keep Hall for that final fling. Davidson, one of the best of all hookers, showed Hall had little, if anything, left when he stood inside a bouncer and pelted it with gusto for four. This shot made the partnership 53 in 55 minutes.

Minute by minute, this partnership was looking more dangerous. It had begun after tea as expected in a flurry of short singles, and a suggestion of hysteria began to appear in the West Indian fielding. They began to peg wildly at the stumps; fieldsmen got in one another's way. 'Steady now, steady now,' admonished Worrell.

Worrell came on himself at twenty to five, Australia 148 for six, Davidson 31, Benaud 21. Benaud hit him immediately for four past mid-off and the Australians now had almost gained on the clock, 80 being needed in 75 minutes. Ramadhin was on at the other end and one sensed that Benaud had an eagle eye cocked for a straight hit to the outfield to the first ball well up. Worrell had an eye on it, also, and had a man back fairly deep but, unknown to Worrell, Ramadhin shifted the man and brought him up much closer.

That took much of the danger out of Benaud's intentions and, sure enough, he lifted Ramadhin over the man's head to the fence, the ball hitting the pickets first bounce. Worrell's thoughts were easily imagined. He sent the man back immediately but Benaud had gained more than four from that stroke. A big hit that soars safely gives a batsman tremendous confidence.

Worrell was extremely tight in his bowling but Ramadhin was the one the Australians had set their sights on. Davidson majestically square-cut the first ball of Ramadhin's next over for four; 67 runs were now needed in 65 minutes. The Australians were running for the slightest tap and with an hour to go 60 were needed – a run a minute. They were on terms with the clock for the first time of the innings.

Now came a drink to give everybody a chance to settle down. It was badly needed. Only a pitiful crowd of 4,160 was there to see this spine-tingling stuff but they made noise enough for a crowd thrice their size. The air was laden with drama and atmosphere.

Still Worrell persevered with Ramadhin, and Davidson made a huge hit against the spinner that was almost a six forward of square-leg. This gave Davidson his half-century in 141 minutes, with four fours. Big hearts, big temperaments, skilled strokes were needed in this crisis and the two Australians were full of all requirements.

Worrell had bowled three overs for nine and Sobers came on at last to bowl spinners with 54 runs to get – but from the top end. The other end, one thought, was the one for spin, into the rough, and there were now not many runs to play with for an experiment with Sobers's slow stuff. Benaud swung him square to leg for four and 49 were wanted in 48 minutes.

Still Ramadhin continued at the far end and Davidson straight-hit him for four – how perfectly were the Australians picking the right ball to hit for four! – and now 45 were wanted in 46 minutes. Davidson swung Ramadhin for four to go to 60, Benaud 41, and this entrancing century partnership had come in 95 minutes. Davidson now stole a single, the fieldsmen knocking over the stumps, and the single was turned into two. Ramadhin came off after bowling 15 overs straight for 1–49 but, it transpired, only to change ends.

Worrell was showing tremendous faith in Ramadhin but probably he had by now realized that the new ball with Hall was the only gamble left to him and it didn't matter much how quickly the 200 and the new ball came up. Perhaps, even, Worrell was thinking the quicker the new ball came the better, as Hall consumed time with his long run.

Ramadhin experimented with a round-armer and the shock to Benaud was such that it almost got under his bat. Benaud jammed down on it in haste – and the pair stole a single. Their running between the wickets was as thrilling and as dangerous as it was masterly. Australia now needed 36 in 31 minutes.

Sobers came on for Ramadhin and gave Benaud a full toss which he hit with tremendous power. Worrell, ten yards away at mid-wicket, brilliantly fielded it one-handed – a certain four saved. But the West Indians just couldn't plug the stolen singles. Still they came and Ramadhin went on at the bottom end with the score 198. With the new ball thus imminent, one sensed that the Australians would let fly with everything at Ramadhin this over to cut down the margin needed against the new ball. Two more singles came, Davidson cut Ramadhin for two and then most beautifully drove him for four. Worrell signalled to the umpires for the new ball. Umpire Egar held it up to the batsmen and to the scorers, and Hall took it at 5.30 p.m., with 30 minutes left for play, and Australia needing 27 to win with four wickets in hand.

Hall with the new ball was the last card in the West Indian pack – their sole, remaining gamble.

THE UNBELIEVABLE FINISH

Divine Providence, with Dr Grace possibly the chairman of the advisory committee, surely must have ordained and controlled the tumultuous final minutes of this Test. No earthly mind could have conceived such a plot. It was beyond the bounds of human credibility.

Everybody now knew that Hall alone could win this match for the West Indians but it was a desperate, almost hopeless chance. Benaud viciously cut his first ball for a single. Davidson flashed at the next and missed. One wondered, at this moment, what were the thoughts in the dressing-room of Grout, next man in. Or, for that matter, the thoughts of the remaining batsmen. Then came a no-ball from which the batsmen ran a single. Then Benaud skied one to the leg-side that fell only inches away from the grabbing Hunte. That yielded another single so that 24 were wanted in 25 minutes.

Hall's long, slow trudge back to his mark, 34 paces away, gave everybody a chance to breathe and think yet it intensified the drama on this sunny, Brisbane late-afternoon. Hall this time came down with a bouncer and Davidson, without a thought of the physical risk involved, stepped inside it and poorlessly hooked it high to leg for four. Just 20 runs to go. Next ball Davidson blocked and the Australians scampered off for a ridiculously short run. Hall charged in after the ball but couldn't gather it for the run out. He stood there despondent, arms on hips. Worrell moved in and patted him comfortingly on the stomach and, as I learnt afterwards, said to Hall, 'No more bouncers, Wes, no more bouncers.' He knew how well both these Australians could hook.

There was a mix-up of Keystone-comedy pandemonium in the same over. Benaud pushed one to point and started for the run. Davidson screamed 'No' and then, strangely, began to run to Benaud's end where Benaud, after Davidson's call, had immobilized himself. Davidson suddenly realized that they would both be at the same end. So Davidson stopped, wheeled about and began his long, desperate return. The throw, obviously, should have been back to Hall, who was standing guard over the stumps but Valentine, in the muddle, threw to Benaud's end where Alexander had to sprawl to take the wide throw and then, for the life of him, he couldn't get the ball back to Hall in time. Davidson scrambled home, a lucky escape. The West Indians all looked infinitely depressed at this misfortune. The ground rocked with excitement.

Hall takes a very long time to bowl an over. There were loud calls from the outer to him to 'Get a move on – get a move on, Wes.' The umpires now stopped play while boys were removed from the top of some pickets. Sobers took the new ball at the other end at 21 minutes to six – Australia needing 19 to win.

A leg-bye came from the first ball and Benaud got a single from the next. Davidson shaped for a drive which turned into a cut, got a single, and 16 were wanted in 19 minutes. It was as good as in the bag for Australia, surely, and especially when Benaud played a scorching on-drive from Sobers to the fence that left Ramadhin bereft at deepish mid-on. Now came a no-ball and eleven were needed to win. Benaud took a sharp single that gave him his 50 in 124 minutes, with six fours, an innings of incalculable character, and at a quarter to six, Australia needed ten, only ten, in fifteen minutes with four wickets standing.

Hall took up his burden again. Benaud pushed at one, dangerously, and missed. A rearing bouncer (Hall ignoring Worrell's instructions!) came next and almost took Benaud's nose with it. Then, Benaud just managed to keep out a lovely, late-swinging yorker, and they ran a quick single to Worrell, at mid-wicket. Hall was doing his utmost but it seemed hopeless. When that over ended, at ten to six, Australia needed only nine runs to win. And with four wickets in hand.

Davidson had come to bat at 2.19 p.m.; Benaud at 3.21 p.m. Each single minute for them had been laden with responsibility and endeavour that had to be larded with cool heads and consummate judgment: each minute since tea had been doubly impregnated.

Two quick singles were taken from Sobers but now, breeding all the time in the taking of these thrilling yet highly-dangerous singles, disaster broke at last for the Australians. Benaud pushed one wide of square-leg and shot off for a very, very short run. Davidson responded immediately to the risky call but the little Solomon, picking up and throwing with the one action, hit the stumps over from the acute angle and Davidson was out, well out. His innings was a master-piece. He had batted 194 minutes for his highest score in Test cricket, 80, and he had hit ten fours.

The West Indians chivalrously clapped the gallant Australian all the way to the pavilion. Few greater Test innings, considering the accumulating tension and responsibility, have been played anywhere and Davidson's 80 followed upon his outstanding success with the ball and his runs in the first innings. He had taken 11 wickets and made 126 runs!

Now – and already we had had more than enough to make this day memorable – purple drama mounted upon purple drama. Grout passed Davidson at the halfway mark to the middle. No minutes would be lost so far as Grout was concerned. Australia now needed seven runs in six minutes, three wickets to fall. If necessary, there would be one more over after this one by Sobers, which had four balls left.

Grout took strike and scurried for a quick single from the seventh ball. This, surely, was an error in tactics as it left Grout at the other end to face Hall's last over. That was if Benaud did not get a single from the last ball of Sober's over. Six to win, nine balls to go with Sobers to bowl the last ball of his over.

This ball was to provide an intense battle of wits. Quite obviously, Benaud wanted a single to get down and take Hall away from Grout. Quite obviously, the West Indians intended that Benaud would re-main where he was and Grout would remain the sacrificial victim for Hall. Sobers put everything he had into that final ball. He put it down on a length with every particle of strength he had in his left arm. Benaud tried desperately but he couldn't get it away. Six converging West Indians were almost in Benaud's pocket as he played the ball. There would be no stolen single here! Grout must face Hall at all costs.

And so Wesley Hall, of magnificent physical stature, of unlimited courage, came to bowl the last over of the match to Grout with the clock at four minutes to six and Australia, three wickets in hand, wanting only six to win.

I will never forget the memory of Hall as he walked back, ever so slowly, to begin this death-or-glory over. He wears a jangling cross on a chain around his neck and I could see him fingering the cross as he walked back towards the press-box. I could imagine him praying: 'Please, Lord, I'll do my best – You know I always do – but what I ask, Lord, is a miracle. Yet not one but two or three. Please, Lord!'

The shadows lengthen quickly across the Brisbane ground at this time of day. The sun was cutting slanting swathes across the field. Hall stood in one of them, poised on his mark, taking huge gulps of air into his lungs for the final fling. He got balance and then he was away, arms and legs flying, surely a petrifying sight to Grout as he stood waiting. It was a ball of length and pace and got up to hit Grout in the groin. Under ordinary circumstances, Grout would have gone to earth on the hit but as he was in the process of doubling-up in pain he saw Benaud charging down at him. Benaud, most wisely, didn't call. To do so would have alerted the West Indians – and so, with the ball in the very block-hole and under the noses of some three fieldsmen, Benaud stole what was barely one-third of a run.

Five runs to win, seven balls to go!

Hall trudged back extremely slowly, bitter, no doubt, that Grout had been spirited away from him – but Hall's invocation was in mind on high and now came the first miracle. Contrary to Worrell's orders, Hall let fly another bouncer. It drew Benaud's bat in temptation with it as it rose, there was a touch of bat or glove, and there was Alexander, screaming his appeal in concert with his fellows, tossing the ball on high. Benaud was out. Hall had given that ball everything he had. If Benaud had hooked it for four, Hall would have had to face his accuser, Worrell, in the dressing-room later. But now Benaud was sadly walking back after an unforgettable innings over 136 minutes, six fours.

Five to win, six balls to go, two minutes to six but the clock now of no account because an over started must be finished.

Meckiff, walking in slowly as if to make sure that his limbs all came with him, would have been tingling in heart, head and stomach. He middled the first ball and there was no run. Now came a flash of absolute genius from Grout. Hall's next ball went wide down the leg-side to wicket-keeper Alexander and Grout began to run and call as he saw the ball going through to Alexander.

Now ensued another muckle of cricket-pickle reminiscent of the village green. Like a startled hare, Meckiff, not expecting such a call, nevertheless responded and took off helter-skelter for the other end. Hall had followed down the pitch and Alexander, burdened by his gloves, threw to Hall. Hall gathered, wheeled, threw at his end, missed (Meckiff would have been out otherwise), and some West Indian hurled his body at the ball to envelop it and save overthrows. Australia had gained another golden run in 'perhaps the strangest manner seen on a cricket field. A run to the wicket-keeper! The inspired Grout had comfortably made good his ground.

Four to win, four balls to go!

The whole ground, madly delirious over the past hour and more, went completely berserk next ball. Grout aimed for the boundary to win the match but mis-timed his stroke and the ball spooned up high to the leg-side, about mid-wicket. At least four West Indians could have taken the catch. Kanhai – his teeth clenching in cold determination, his eyes never leaving the soaring ball – positioned himself perfectly underneath the ball. This would be one catch he would never miss. But alas, as Kanhai waited and waited, the frenzied, emotional Hall charged in, jumped high over Kanhai's hands – and muffed the catch!

Horror of horrors! The crowd yelled in disbelief at this let-off of Grout. The West Indians stood about, stunned and dumbfounded.

One run came from this stark tragedy. Australia three to win, three balls to go.

Hall, his head low on his chest, trudged back in despair, disgrace and self-immolation. The tumult subsided, waiting for the next ball. In the tense and anguished hush I could hear the evening *Angelus* tolling from a nearby hill and I could imagine Hall hearing a chiding voice in his ear, much as Don Camillo did: 'You asked for ordinary miracles, you know. Not stupid ones.'

Hall stood on his mark, again taking in big gulps of air. Meckiff was now at the receiving end. Hall glared down at him. 'Look out for this one. It will have everything I can give it,' he seemed to say.

Down thundered Hall. Meckiff stood impassive for a split-second and then he swung – trusting all to good fortune – and he connected. The ball flew away, high and handsome, to the square-leg boundary where no man stood. A four, of a certainty! A win to Australia! So roared the crowd; so said the announcer over the radio to hundreds of thousands of listeners; so screamed the press in the maddest scene ever seen in a press-box.

The little things are sometimes the important ones. Because of some oversight, the grass in the outfield had not been cut this morning and a stroke that looked all-over a boundary lost pace in the longish grass – which grows quickly in Brisbane – and was picked up on the boundary's edge by Hunte, who had chased after it as if in the Olympic 100 metres.

So, too, had the Australians sprinted in the middle. Up for one, down for two, a turn for three and the winning run. It didn't matter, then, that the ball hadn't hit the fence. Three were needed to win and Meckiff and Grout were charging down for the winning run.

Never, in all cricketing time, surely, has there been a better throw than Hunte's from the boundary. From some 90 yards away, the ball flew low and unerringly to Alexander. Had it gone just the merest fraction either side of the keeper, Australia would have had the winning run because Alexander would not have had the time to make for the stumps.

But it came perfectly to Alexander's hands and he hurled himself at the stumps as Grout dived for the line like a winger at Twickenham. A roar of an appeal. All looked at the umpire. His hand was up! Grout was out!

Grout arose dishevelled, covered in dust, and slowly walked away.

The two from the stroke made the scores level – 737 runs all. There were now two balls to go and one run to win. One wicket to fall.

I had the strange feeling that what was taking place wasn't real. It was, I thought, an odd dream that would end with a crashing on the floor.

Now came the perfect climax to this mad, surging day. Kline got his first ball from Hall away to leg and both batsmen charged off. From twelve yards away, completely side-on so that only one of the stumps showed to him, Joe Solomon swooped one-handed and threw again as he picked up. Over went the stump, up went the umpire's hand yet again, Meckiff was out and the game was a tie!

This was the miracle superb. Solomon couldn't pause to take aim. Had he taken his eye off the ball as it was coming to him – as so many fieldsmen do when a run-out is imminent – he would have misfielded. And, fielding, he had to throw at the stumps by instinct. Speed was the essence of it all. Nobody was quite there to take the throw (although Worrell was in position for a run out the other end). The throw had to hit the stumps. Had it missed, Australia had got the winning run.

And so the madness ended – a tie, one ball left to bowl after 3,142 balls had been bowled and 1,474 runs scored. A tie had never happened before in the whole history of Test cricket.

It was bedlam in the press-box. All were standing and yelling and clapping at once. Worrell, shoulders drooped in near-exhaustion, was smacked on the back by his fellows and, very quickly, by the invading, cheering and acclaiming crowd. Benaud, with his flair for the proper gesture, walked on to the field, draped an arm around Worrell's shoulders and escorted him to the dressing-room. The crowd gathered there, cheering and calling for the players to show themselves. Ninety minutes later, Hall and his merry fellows were still singing calypsoes in their dressing-room, joined by the Australians.

West Indies

C. C. Hunte c Benaud b Davidson	24	— c Simpson b Mackay	39
C. Smith c Grout b Davidson	7	— c O'Neill b Davidson	6
R. Kanhai c Grout b Davidson	15	— c Grout b Davidson	54
G. Sobers c Kline b Meckiff	132	— b Davidson	14
*F. M. Worrell c Grout b Davidson	65	— c Grout b Davidson	65
J. S. Solomon hit wkt b Simpson	65	— lbw b Simpson	47
P. Lashley c Grout b Kline	19	— b Davidson	0
†F. C. M. Alexander c Davidson b Kline	60	— b Benaud	5
S. Ramadhin c Harvey b Davidson	12	— c Harvey b Simpson	6
W. Hall st Grout b Kline	50	— b Davidson	18
A. L. Valentine not out	0	— not out	7
Extras	4	Extras	23

1/23 2/42 3/65 4/239 5/243   453   1/13 2/88 3/114 4/127   284
6/283 7/347 8/366 9/452   5/210 6/210 7/241
                        8/250 9/253

Bowling: *First Innings* – Davidson 30–2–135–5; Meckiff 18–0–129–1; Mackay 3–0–15–0; Benaud 24–3–93–0; Simpson 8–0–25–1; Kline 17.6–6–52–3. *Second Innings* – Davidson 24.6–4–87–6; Meckiff 4–1–19–0; Benaud 31–6–69–1; Mackay 21–7–52–1; Kline 4–0–14–0; Simpson 7–2–18–2; O'Neill 1–0–2–0.

Australia

C. C. McDonald c Hunte b Sobers	57	— b Worrell	16
R. B. Simpson b Ramadhin	92	— c sub b Hall	0
R. N. Harvey b Valentine	15	— c Sobers b Hall	5
N. C. O'Neill c Valentine b Hall	181	— c Alexander b Hall	26
L. Favell run out	45	— c Solomon b Hall	7
K. D. Mackay b Sobers	35	— b Ramadhin	28
A. K. Davidson c Alexander b Hall	44	— run out	80
*R. Benaud lbw b Hall	10	— c Alexander b Hall	52
†A. T. W. Grout lbw b Hall	4	— run out	2
I. Meckiff run out	4	— run out	2
L. F. Kline not out	3	— not out	0
Extras	15	Extras	14

1/84 2/138 3/194 4/278 5/381   505   1/1 2/7 3/49 4/49   232
6/469 7/484 8/489 9/496   5/57 6/92 7/226
                        8/228 9/232

Bowling: *First Innings* – Hall 29.3–1–140–4; Worrell 30–0–93–0; Sobers 32–0–115–2; Valentine 24–6–82–1; Ramadhin 15–1–60–1. *Second Innings* – Hall 17.7–3–63–5; Worrell 16–3–41–1; Sobers 8–0–30–0; Valentine 10–4–27–0; Ramadhin 17–3–57–1.

Umpires: C. Hoy and C. J. Egar.

2. You Never Know in Cricket

At the time of which I write – late 1926 – Alan Kippax was bringing his young team to Melbourne. New South Wales had just had a creditable win by four wickets over South Australia at Adelaide. Only two experienced cricketers, Tommy Andrews and Arthur Mailey, were with Kippax and he thus had the burden, potentially crippling for any young captain in first-class cricket, of having seven men new to top cricket.

They were: Steele, Campbell (a young slow bowler Hammond was to 'kill' a few years later), Jackson (then only seventeen), McNamee, Phillips, McGuirk and Hogg. It was a year before the first-class advent of Bradman.

With so many new men, a touring skipper needed the qualities of a mothercraft nurse. He had to guide, humour, teach, inspire and understand the varied personalities of his new men, some of them away from home for the first time. In Adelaide, for instance, Kippax had to impress upon one of his young bowlers that it wasn't the thing to put his cap on the ground to mark where his run began, nor was it necessary to call 'play' before each ball was bowled. Kippax had his teething troubles. His men, some wonderful humorists among them, dubbed themselves the 'Portuguese Army'.

The win in Adelaide, however, had pleased the young side and the players had plenty of smiles for the photographer when they arrived by train in Melbourne. The photograph appeared that afternoon and the caption over it was 'Ready for the Fray'. In the same newspaper, a critic wrote that many runs should come from the bats of Ponsford, Woodfull, Hendry, and Ryder, since all of them were in good form. Many runs, indeed!

Kippax won the toss and had no hesitation in batting. After five hours of streaky endeavour, New South Wales were out for a colourless 221. The next day (Saturday) was Christmas Day so the game was put aside for two days. It began again at 11.30 on a bright Monday morning.

As usual, the two Bills, Woodfull and Ponsford, opened for Victoria and a wicket should have fallen early. When Woodfull was seven, Ponsford mistimed a no-ball from McNamee and the ball flew high to Kippax at mid-on. Woodfull, evidently, had not recovered from his Christmas dinner. At all events his reflexes were muddled and he charged towards Ponsford's end. As all schoolboys know, nothing is to be gained in running for a single off a no-ball and, as all schoolboys again know, the only way in which a wicket can be lost off a no-ball (excluding the theoretical ways of interference and such wise) is from a run-out. Woodfull, therefore, for one of the few times in his cricket life, had lost his balance. Moreover, it wasn't his call. Ponsford stood his ground, yelling at Woodfull meanwhile, 'No, no: go back!'

Woodfull stopped and was stranded, halfway up the pitch, as Kippax caught the ball and sized up the situation. As so often happens on such occasions, time to think can lead to trouble. Quick, subconscious action is invariably best, ruling out errors of judgment.

McNamee crouched over the stumps, waiting for the return. McNamee, a lovely, curling off-spin bowler, was a priceless wit but a hopeless fieldsman, rather inclined to grab at the ball. Bearing this weakness in mind and knowing there was plenty of time, Kippax sent him a perfect, slow lob. It would have landed plumb in Mc-Namee's hands.

But the agonies of waiting nonplussed McNamee. The slow, lobbing ball seemed to mesmerize him and it drew him forward. He grabbed at the ball and, at the same time, sprawled all over the stumps, fumbled the ball and then dropped it. In the midst of this horrible muddle, Woodfull raced back to his crease.

I have drawn the circumstances of this incident in detail because the first Victorian wicket should have fallen at 17. It didn't fall until 375! Woodfull made no other error until he snicked a catch to Ratcliffe off Andrews at 133. That was suffering for New South Wales but at stumps the position was even worse: one wicket for 573: Ponsford 334 not out. Hendry 86 not out. The 'Portuguese Army' had been well and truly routed.

Mailey bowled 28 overs that day at a cost of 148. There were only four maidens bowled in the day and Ponsford, who rarely scored behind the wicket, got many runs from a short-arm jab, a stroke which he had learned at baseball, which carried the ball over mid-on's head. His on-side play was faultless, his feet getting into quick and perfect position. In the whole day, he gave not the slightest semblance of a chance.

Spectators trooped to the ground in goodly numbers next day, wondering whether Ponsford would break Clem Hill's Sheffield Shield record score of 365 not out, made for South Australia against New South Wales in 1900–01. But Ponsford didn't break the record. This, next day, was how a Melbourne newspaper described what happened:

> The almost ecclesiastical calm of the Melbourne ground yesterday in those tense moments before Ponsford's wicket fell was an indication of the tremendous interest Australians have in the breaking of records.
>
> As cricket, it was slow, but none would have had it otherwise. The dropping of those single runs into the slot of time, gradually lengthening into the tens that crept up on the record for Shield matches, held by Clem Hill for over a quarter of a century, was sufficient excitement. Impudent play would have been resented. Only a cricket d'Artagnan would have taken artistic liberties in such a duel.
>
> When the fatal ball broke the wicket, it broke the crowd's Sabbatical quiet. Thenceforward, exhortations and witticisms, impossible before, were the portion of the players. The crowd could no longer help their hero.

Ponsford was out for 352. He snicked a ball on to his foot and it rebounded to the stumps. He turned, surveyed the fallen bail, and most seriously uttered with great feeling a remark that the New South Welshmen never tired of repeating in after years. 'By cripes,' said Ponsford, 'I *am* unlucky.'

So, to the bitter disappointment of the crowd and the relief of his opponents – who had come to perceive the genus of amaranth in his bat and his bulk – Bill Ponsford trudged reluctantly back to the pavilion, not to sip nectar and tender thanksgiving to the gods for his 352, but to meditate on how fate had crossed him when only 14 short of a record he had set his heart on.

'The champion', wrote one critic, 'began quietly, too quietly, as he afterwards admitted. He added only 18 in 41 minutes to his overnight score but, for all this, he almost beat the clock with his 352 in 363 minutes, with 36 fours.'

Hendry, a New South Wales player of other years, sacrificed his wicket at 100; Love, another former New South Wales player, was out for six; King went for seven; but then came Jack Ryder and he committed, first, assault and battery on the groggy attack and, finally, sheer murder.

Ryder made 295 – the first 100 in 115 minutes; the second in 74; his final 95 in 56 minutes.

His score in the book read: 1 1 1 1 1 1 1 1 4 4 1 1 1 4 1 2 1 4 1 1

2 1 1 1 1 1 1 1 4 2 1 4 1 4 2 2 1 1 1 4 1 4 4 4 1 1 2 1 1 1 2 1 2 4 4
1 3 1 1 1 1 4 1 6 1 1 4 4 2 4 4 4 1 1 2 6 2 1 2 2 4 2 2 4 2 1 1 4 4 2 1
1 1 6 1 1 3 1 4 1 2 1 1 1 2 4 2 1 1 1 2 1 2 2 1 4 4 2 4 4 4 2 1 4 1 1 6
1 1 2 4 6 4 6.

Six times – a record for such games – Ryder hit the ball over the fence. One hit, off a full toss from Mailey, struck the verandah of the Smokers' Stand; another went into the Reserve and narrowly missed smashing the clock. This caused a sigh of regret in the dressing-room for the story had been current for years that six cases of champagne would be presented to any batsman hitting that clock – though a small item was that nobody, least of all Ryder, knew who had promised the champagne. At all events, Ryder was a tee-totaller.

'Hard luck, Arthur,' somebody sympathized with Mailey in the dressing-room during an adjournment.

'Well, you just can't get wickets if catches aren't taken,' said the whimsical Mailey.

'Catches,' asked the outsider, puzzled, 'I didn't see any catches.'

'There's a chap in the outer who's dropped Ryder twice off me already,' said Mailey.

The crowd roared like a football one as Ryder was hitting his sixes. Two were into the breeze; four against.

Off five overs from Mailey, Ryder hit 62. He was 275 when he faced up to his bosom cobber of tours, Tommy Andrews, who also bowled slows. Ryder hit the first ball for four; the next for six; the next for four; the next for six and, trying to reach 300 in the grand manner, mis-hit the fifth in going for another six and was caught by Kippax.

There is no more enthusiastic sporting crowd anywhere than the Melbourne one when it is whipped up and Ryder certainly did some whipping that day.

The carnage didn't finish with Ryder. Hartkopf, Liddicut and Ellis continued to push the New South Wales attack around and it fell to Ellis to hit the stroke that brought up the 1,000. Jack Ellis was – he still is – a vital, cheerful fellow and as he made the eventful stroke to the outfield he whooped, 'Come on, there's three in it. Three in it and the thousand up! Long live Victoria!'

Fortunately for New South Wales, Ellis and Morton ran themselves out and the innings finished at 1,107 – beating the 1,059 Victoria had made against Tasmania, which had been the world's record score in a first-class match. Kippax led from the field a foot-sore, weary team, their 'eagerness for the fray' (as the newspaper caption had it on their day of arrival) now considerably subdued.

Understandably, the Victorian critics ran to lavish praise of the innings. R. W. E. Wilmot (father of Chester, author of *The Struggle for Europe*) wrote in *The Age*:

It takes a special kind of brain to be a record-breaker in anything, and Ponsford seems possessed of one which believes that records exist to be broken and he is the one to do it. His batting was that of a master. When he hit, he hit hard and that for more than five hours. It was only towards the end of the day that he showed fatigue. The crowd of 22,348 saw wonderful batting, and, though revelling in seeing all those records broken which New South Wales had so sedulously established against Victoria, they could not help sympathizing with and admiring the courageous fight put up by the visitors. One remarkable feature of the play was that the crowd – and a crowd can quite often be cruel – cheered the batsmen, the bowlers and the fieldsmen. There was an entire absence of jeering.

This is what *The Argus* said:

It will be the talk of the cricket world for a long time to come. There has been no other achievement like it in first-class cricket. Enthusiasts, taken completely by surprise, are discussing the likely causes of this startling revelation of the acme of batsmanship. Was it that Woodfull, Ryder, Ponsford and Hendry reached their zenith on the one occasion, or was it that the New South Wales team was of inferior quality? Our opponents were without some of their best players, but who would say that against the same side the same set of Victorian batsmen would compile again more than 1,100 runs? They might not even be equal to 500. Psychology is the safest refuge for all but the *quidnuncs*. It was Ponsford's hour and the glamour of the deeds he performed inspired his teammates. New South Wales may be the next to find the hour and the man.

These were prophetic words. The country lad, Don Bradman, had just been invited to Sydney for a trial. He was to put even Ponsford into the shade – and, just around the corner, also, was the return match between the two states in Sydney.

The *Sydney Telegraph* took a crusty view of the whole affair. It ran an editorial:

In the heyday of Spofforth and Turner, Trott and Giffen, to mention only a few of the great Australian bowlers of a bygone generation, the batsmen were considered lucky if they got into double figures; today they are considered unlucky if they don't make a hundred. After all, you can do only a certain amount of things with a cricket ball. You may bowl fast, medium or slow. You may give the ball certain spin. You may send down a googly. There is a scientific way of meeting every ball and science cannot go wrong on a billiard-table wicket. How easy it is may be gathered from the huge score just completed by Ponsford, who doesn't bother at all about the science of the game but just uses his quick eye and quick foot and punishes everything that comes along.

This was so much balderdash. One wondered what this pundit's highest score had been in any game but the learned man, after suggesting a smaller ball, a narrower bat and a fourth stump, called it an editorial day and, no doubt, pushed off to his club to have a few reminiscent snifters.

The New South Wales players were still leg-weary when they batted on the fourth day. They were all out for 230 and Victoria won by an innings and 656 runs. Kippax was learning captaincy the hard way but he was a light-hearted, philosophical fellow who could see something humorous in most things.

One point must be stressed. Despite the incredible onslaught on his bowlers, Kippax always had his bowlers aim at the stumps. There was no wide or leg-theory and this, undoubtedly, contributed largely to the remarkable fact that Victoria's 1,107 was made in the very quick time of 574 minutes.

This was the Victorian first innings:

Woodfull c Ratcliffe b Andrews	133
Ponsford b Morgan	352
Hendry c Morgan b Mailey	100
Ryder c Kippax b Andrews	295
Love st Ratcliffe b Mailey	6
King st Ratcliffe b Mailey	7
Hartkopf c McGuirk b Mailey	61
Liddicut b McGuirk	36
Ellis run out	63
Morton run out	0
Blackie not out	27
Sundries	27
Total	1,107

Fall of wickets: 1-375; 2-594; 3-614; 4-631; 5-657; 6-834; 7-915; 8-1,043; 9-1,046; 10-1,107.

Bowling

	O	M	R	W
McNamee	24	2	124	0
McGuirk	26	1	130	1
Mailey	64	0	362	4
Campbell	11	0	89	0
Phillips	11.7	0	64	0
Morgan	26	0	137	1
Andrews	21	2	148	2
Kippax	7	0	26	0

A fortnight later, in Sydney, New South Wales made 469 in the return game against Victoria – and then toppled the champions for 35! Ray McNamee, who had 0–124 in Melbourne, took 7–21 in Sydney!

Apparently, the leader writer of the *Sydney Telegraph* wasn't at his desk that week. There was no illuminating article on cricket, which was a pity, because it would have been interesting to know whether he would have advocated a bigger ball, a smaller stump – or whether he just thought that McNamee had produced a performance of which Spofforth, Turner, Trott or Giffen might have been proud.

As to the game itself – as has so often been said, you never know what's around the corner in cricket.

3. A Yorkshire Gesture—1938

Sociologists, not to mention the City Council, may be alarmed to see in what follows a reference to the 'indescribable slums' of Sheffield. The face of Sheffield, I am happy to say, has changed greatly for the better since 1938, when the match was played, and 1946, when I wrote about it in Cricket Crisis.

Cricket Crisis, *dealing mainly with the bodyline era, proved to be one of the best-selling cricket books ever published. This was particularly gratifying, for its birth pains were considerable. I began writing it in 1942 when, as a lieutenant in the Australian Army, I was kicking my heels on the far northern Australian coastline with tens of thousands of my countrymen waiting for the Japanese to show up. This gave me time to write more than half the book which I then committed through the army post to an old editor of mine, A. R. B. Palmer. Possibly the army censor disapproved of its contents. Whatever the explanation, the original typescript has never been seen since.*

Only a man who writes for his living will know the agony of starting from scratch again, but I did so at the end of the war. I have never since written anything other than cheques without keeping a carbon copy. It is a habit which I now commend from the depths of my soul to all young writers.

*

It was a vivid change to Bramall Lane after the peace and quiet of Chesterfield. The leaning steeple of the town looked benignly down on the game against Derbyshire, and stolid, silent be-capped men, who might have interrupted a trip to market and left their cows and pigs outside the ground, sat meditatively around the ground, sucking at their pipes and solemnly wagging their heads in disapproval as the county batsmen advanced to and retreated from the wickets almost before acknowledging the introduction to their guard.

The bowling strength of the county was magnificent, of almost Test-like quality. Copson found bite in the pitch and flicked the ball across from the leg-stump, something he had despaired of doing again in this cricket life after a tour on the hard, unsympathetic Australian pitches. The tall, rangy Pope brothers did much the same thing and Mitchell, brown eyes bubbling behind his spectacles, bowled his leg breaks with an occasional bosie and bowled them as well as ever he has bowled them.

But bowling strength alone is not sufficient. The Derbyshire batsmen went through manoeuvres as crooked as their spire, the game was put into the records book in two days and off we went in our roomy charabanc, chatting, singing and laughing across the peaty moors, bound for our temporary Georgian home in the Grindleford valley. No better prospect than this had happened on our tour. A day off from the game with the green, verdant English countryside beckoning with its trees and meadows and calling with its birds.

If only it didn't rain on the morrow – and it didn't. The sun streamed through the wide windows of the sleepy hotel at the top of the valley; poplars, elms and oaks cut gently swaying filigrees against the bluest of skies and the smell of egg and bacon floated up from below.

Doubtless, the birds were paying homage to the day in rich, limpid tones but this one was not to know for in the room just along the corridor, Brown (basking in the thrill of a glorious double-century the day before) and McCormick were tributing spring with raucous voice. Along the corridor, too, O'Reilly was informing all that his bonny was over the ocean, over the sea, and he wished her brought back to him. If he didn't get her, I reflected as I indulged myself in an idyllic stretch, it would not be for the want either of repetition or volume.

On no other English morning had the team been so happy. Bantering quips and laughter chased across the breakfast table. Gone were the gruff monosyllables that came with each morning of an important game; and gone, also, of such mornings, were the little balls of apprehension that pitched in the stomach.

Yorkshire loomed large on the morrow but what of that? To-morrow could look after itself. Breakfast over, a rollicking band of Australians gathered in the leafy lane. There was no set plan. Apollo was climbing lazily, hazily and unthreatened. We would wander wherever our legs, our inclinations and the long, low line of purple hills in the distance took us.

We went off downhill and made the first of the day's many stops at the wall of the village school. Derbyshire children of ten and eleven, the roses of the hills rich upon their cheeks, were as intrigued with our accent as we were with theirs but the school-bell, ringing, took them off and we continued our ramble, passing a character who took our thoughts quickly back to home, gum-trees, magpies and billabongs.

He was a tramp (a 'swaggie' to us), a lonely, tattered old fellow who ignored our cheery 'good-days' and passed by in silence, deep in thought. But he served a purpose for us. We swung over the bridge singing that essentially Australian song, 'Waltzing Matilda', the words of Banjo Paterson bringing a nostalgic whiff of our bush-land to our noses and memories:

> *Down came a jumbuck to drink by the billabong,*
> *Up jumped the Swagman and grabbed him with glee,*
> *And he sang as he stowed that jumbuck in his tucker-bag,*
> *'You'll come a-waltzing Matilda with me'.*

We swung off the road and down to the river where some swam, Huckleberry Finn style, in paining-cold water. Badcock tickled for trout as he told us he had tickled many a time in Tasmanian streams.

All that morning we lazily followed the course of the quick-running river. We shied stones at rabbits, discovered idyllic falls shut in a wooded little glade, and listened to birds and wondered what they were.

> *To whose falls,*
> *Melodious birds sing madrigals.*

By lunch-time, we had arrived in Sproggett, where we quenched big thirsts with big pewters of cold beer preparatory to lunching, under centuries-old rafters, on cold chicken, the reddest and biggest strawberries in all England, thick, yellow cream and luscious cheese.

We loitered and wandered again that long afternoon, wishing that the day would never end. It was a tired and contented Australian band that arrived back that evening to our Grindleford hotel.

With such a day in between, then, it will be understood when I repeat that the change from Chesterfield to Bramall Lane was a vivid one, vivid in its transition from peace and rural charm and beauty to Sheffield, a city where the fittest triumph, be it in steel, cutlery, business or cricket.

The sun was still radiant next day as our charabanc ran along the top of the moors. We suddenly dipped and in a valley ahead of us hung a pall of mist. 'Sheffield,' said our driver laconically, and in another ten minutes we were in another world. What we had taken to be mist was the oppressive smog of modern industry, a sky belched forth by chimneys as numerous as stakes in a tomato paddock. The somnolent, whispering English woods of sun, shade and birds were behind us. Here was another of those strongly marked English contrasts which are so bewildering – the very rich and the abject poor, indescribable beauty within cooee of indescribable slums; palatial Pall Mall clubs and the midnight soup queue of the Embankment or the tortuous procession of unemployed Welsh miners going beggingly along the Strand.

The battle of life is to be sniffed along the narrow, brown-grey streets of Sheffield. It is the battle of competition and industry, the battle of sun and fresh air against the smoke fumes, and if any beliefs existed that this was an excursion of cricket-peace, those beliefs dissolved as the charabanc swung through the gates of Bramall Lane, one of the historic homes of Yorkshire cricket.

It is easy to mistake the atmosphere that receives rather than greets you on this ground. It seems to bristle with belligerence. The looks bore through you in cold analysis as you go to the nets before the game. At Lord's, going to the nets, one is greeted with cheery nods and smiles and often a call of 'Good luck'. There's none of that at Bramall Lane.

Sheffield connoisseurs of cricket are like the city's cutlery – cold on the surface, sharp in dissection, brimful of good feelings if not cut up the wrong way and always, certainly always, deeply conscious of being Yorkshire and Sheffield through and through, with a reputation to uphold.

The grim looks of the spectators, the postures and gestures of the eleven robust Yorkshiremen with the white rose on their caps, all issue a challenge to the Australians and it runs something like this: 'We are Yorkshire. Tha's playin' wi' cricket fire, laad, when tha cooms 'ere. We're noo abaht to show tha, laad, tha's noot sa good as tha thinks.'

Nothing better suggests the Yorkshire spirit than that piece of doggerel:

> *Tha must see owt and say nowt,*
> *Tha must eat owt and pay nowt,*
> *And if tha dost owt for nowt,*
> *Do it for th'sen, laad.*

One might think that the Yorkshire Eleven is made up of men with granite hearts. It is not so, but in thinking that you could pay them no greater compliment. This (and did not every flamboyant gesture show it?) was the Yorkshire Eleven. All hail, everybody bow and let the trumpets blow! This, the other side, was the Australian Eleven. So what, says the Yorkshireman? Of what use to tell them that this Australian team is unbeaten so far in England.

'Wher'st tha been playin', laads? Why, only in sooth! Stop tha nonsense, get tha umpires oot, and let's gi' on wi' victory!'

The wicket is wet. Sellers, a pair of shoulders on him suggesting a Rugby wall at full-back, wins the toss and smiles as he tells us we can bat. We are for it. McCabe and I walk out, the pair of us in the middle of what is commonly known as a trot, or a patch of lean scores, and I prepare to take the first ball from Bowes. I note with trepidation that the merest touch of my sprig on my mark brings up moisture. There won't be much fun here today for the batsmen.

I shape up for the first ball from the bespectacled Bowes. He lumbers in and – ah!, in that moment, the agony of mind of an opening batsman who takes strike on a sticky pitch, a pitch whose extent of nastiness waits to be probed.

The ball from Bowes is of a length and straight. It hits the sodden turf, takes a seamful of it, and, evidently, not liking the taste, rears violently. A nasty pitch, a cranky one, obviously full of moods!

Bowes comes again and this time pitches on the off. It does not rear this time but, like a rabbit streaking for its burrow, it darts viciously in and hits me on the pad.

Bedlam breaks loose. Bowes shows his teeth, curls one leg behind the other, looks in agony to the heavens and, with hands wide apart, wails an 'Owzat' with a venom that surely sends Duckworth, a prince of appealers, pale with jealousy in the next county.

What does a batsman think in such a split second? His eyes dart to the umpire's face to try and interpret a ray of hope there; his courage sinks to his sprigs if he feels that the umpire must justly give him out, or, if he thinks he has right on his side, his feelings flutter like a spiralling dove.

English umpires cannot be hastened into a decision. A Chester remains mute for the eternity of several seconds and none can read his face. Then he either turns his head away from the bowler, if it is not out (giving him the bleakness of an entire back if the appeal is a frivolous one), or raises one solitary finger to the batsman with the finality of a judge sentencing a murderer. That prolonged in-between period gives a batsman more agony of mind, but it is preferable to the general Australian habit of answering an appeal as soon as it falls from the bowler's mouth.

None of these thoughts crossed my mind with the Bowes appeal. A hazy impression did occur to me that a man who wore spectacles should bear himself with more dignity and respect for his lenses but any other thoughts I had were immediately dispelled by a blood-curdling yell to my rear. The 'Owzat' of the rotund, red-faced wicket-keeper Wood split the heavens yet it was only by a short breath that he beat nine other Yorkshiremen, who faced in all directions and with all manner of gesticulation demanded 'Owzat'. They, for their part, barely beat 15,000 Yorkshire spectators who frenziedly wanted to know of one another if this wasn't, indeed, 'Owzat'.

A self-respecting batsman might well have been cowed by such an appeal and made a move towards the pavilion; but Test experience hardens the soul and the outlook. I stood my ground and the umpire, who had played all his cricket with Lancashire and knew the ins and outs of Yorkshire cricket, answered with a spirit admirably Lancastrian. He roared 'Naht oot,' above the tumult, matching the Yorkshiremen glare for glare.

This, had you not known Bramall Lane, might have been expected to lead to a crisis. Such an appeal and dismissed so contemptuously! But all the Yorkshiremen accepted the decision as if nothing untoward had happened. They hitch their trousers and settle down again, happy in the experience that only the second ball of the day has given them a chance to show their fire and oil their larynx.

There is a frenzy a few minutes later when McCabe is dropped, and the simmer from that has barely subsided when I swing hard at a ball from Bowes. It goes straight to a fieldsman who doesn't have to move an inch – and he drops it! Two dropped catches and a decision against Yorkshire in five minutes! This is too much. The spectators howl their fury and castigation rents the air. People carefully put their capacious lunch baskets on the ground, turn to their neighbours and demand to know what manner of game 'yon laads are playing t'day.'

Bowes looks piercingly at the offending fieldsmen and eight other Yorkshiremen strike poses that suggest never would they have dropped a chance like that.

But it doesn't matter. A few minutes more and both McCabe and I are back in the dressing-room, moving up through the deriding chatter of the members. Yorkshire sleeves are now tucked a little higher to deal with Bradman and Hassett.

The Lane is in magnificent voice. Comment and advice meet every move on the field and the fieldsmen bustle about with intense vigour and enthusiasm, casting malevolent side-glances as they pass the batsmen. The bowlers are full of deadly intent.

Bradman and Hassett are not at all worried. Each is calm, imperturbable, his full attention concentrated upon keeping the ball where it belongs for safety. Bowes never prospered on Australian pitches. They gave him no aid but now he flicks his fingers over the ball and it cuts with a devilish whip from the leg; he flicks them under and there comes a fiend of an off-break.

There is a tremendous roar as Bowes induces Bradman to 'feel' at a ball moving away. Bradman's dismissal at any time in England is a matter of national importance but this time the snick falls short of the clasping hands of first slip. This in itself, however, is an occasion and so as the crowd roars, second and third slip, and even point, dive and leap to lend colour to the occasion.

Bradman is slow to score, very slow, but this innings under such conditions belies his reputation of being a bad-pitch nonentity. He is solidity itself. There are none of those thrilling pulls with a wickedly crooked bat. The pitch is all in favour of the bowlers, risky strokes are out, and footwork is an essential for survival. The batsmen dart forward to get the ball on the full or smother its viciousness at the pitch, or else they play back almost on their stumps with a bat so dead the ball drops at their feet.

Bradman scores a run every three minutes; Hassett is slightly faster and Bramall Lane has a morning of dynamic action to discuss, with thrills and close calls innumerable, as it opens its luncheon-baskets.

Bradman has chewed over much during lunch. His tactics are changed when play begins again. The batsmen move in to attack. Bradman is anxious to get the Yorkshiremen on this pitch. Anything full-pitched is met with a full-swinging bat; a ball the slightest fraction short induces a pull or hook. Both batsmen take abject risks, the fieldsmen scurry here and there and the spectators fall again into critical mood – until Bradman makes a mistake.

He dashes feet down the pitch but misses the ball. Wood clutches it to him like a soldier would his sweetheart after years of service abroad. Wood smites the stumps and bails in all directions, he wails like a banshee, and Bradman is out for 59, one of his best innings in England. The Lane chirps again in high glee.

It is the breaking of the one Australian partnership of merit. Batsmen shuffle in and out like electors at the ballot-box – all except Hassett. He runs down the pitch to a ball from Smailes, his nimble feet bring his body into perfect position, his bat meanwhile goes up and down in a sweet arc, his weight comes at the precise moment from his back to his front foot, there is the delicious sound of sweet timing of leather on willow, and the ball soars higher, ever higher, over the mid-on fence for six. The applause is unstinted.

The next ball Hassett repeats the stroke, only this time the ball flies higher and further to lodge, at last, in the top of the Members' Stand. Two successive sixes! Bramall Lane rocks in delirious delight.

Hassett is a superb batsman, neat and precise in all his movements, his footwork magnificent. Bramall Lane pays him full tribute but, of a sudden, it switches again from credit to calumny. Hassett is doing what he likes with the strike. He is away for a single almost as quickly as ball touches bat and every time Yorkshire changes over it finds Hassett at the receiving end. What the dickens is Yorkshire doing?

Sellers marshals his fieldsmen to stop Hassett and the bowlers know what their job is – but still Hassett defies them. He is making a joke of the Yorkshire fieldsmen. The crowd begins to criticize Sellers, Sutcliffe, Leyland, Verity, Hutton – anybody and everybody. ''Ere, laads, wha's matter wi' thee? Wake up, Yorkshire, wake up.'

Hassett has smelt death in the rain-laden breeze. He rushes to his suicide with glory rampant and twice in an over from Robinson he hits two more sixes. The crowd acknowledges him as if he were a Yorkshireman. Let him hit one more six, they say, and then let the devil himself have him. But Hassett can't get another six. He is out for 94, the innings of a master, and Australia is out for 222.

The wicket is still spiteful when Yorkshire come to bat. O'Reilly is one Australian who could cut batting swathes on such a pitch but O'Reilly, resting, is in mufti on the team's balcony. Knowing that the pitch would be bad, Bradman, McCabe and Barnett, as selectors, probably erred in not switching their team and bringing O'Reilly in at the last moment. He would have been nigh unplayable on this pitch. To stumps that evening, the Yorkshire batting was as substantial as the county pudding. They were 2 down for 50. We leave for rustic Grindleford with heads reeling from the noise and clamour of the day.

There is more rain that night and the wicket is wet next day and even worse. Only Robinson and Wood survive against Waite's offbreaks. Yorkshire are out for 205, 17 runs behind.

The bitter disappointment of the crowd is forgotten as Australian wickets again topple. The pitch is now vile. Only Bradman is at all successful. He makes 42, Australia manages only 132 and Yorkshire need only 150 to lower the Australian colours for the first time of the tour.

The banter envelops us as we take the field. Men and women laugh and joke and call out to one another: 'Good old Yorkshire. 'Ee, but it takes Yorkshire to show Aussies oop.'

Sellers sends in Wood and Verity, two tail-enders to play out time and this they do. Verity, most expert in doing this, refuses to play at any ball that is an inch off the line of the stumps. We journey back again to Grindleford, this time with defeat staring us full face. Our only provision is that Yorkshire will well and truly earn it.

The morrow sees a better wicket. The pavilion doors soon swing to behind Wood's ample body and a piece of freak fielding removes Verity.

'Come one, easy one,' imperiously calls Sutcliffe, that lord of cricket creation, as he slices one typically through the covers. Sutcliffe ambles majestically up the pitch and the modest and effacing Verity, relying on his lord's opinion that it is indeed an easy one, hurries not unduly to the other end. But Bradman, off the mark like a deer, runs for the ball and Hassett, with superb intuition, trails him. Bradman stoops and scoops the ball back. Hassett, who had already positioned himself for throwing, speeds the ball back with one of those typical Australian under-the-shoulder throws and it grooves the stumps. Barnett has the bails off and Verity, with Sutcliffe's 'easy one' still ringing in his ears, is out. Verity leaves in a daze. The quickness of the move dazes also the spectators.

The Pudsey products, Sutcliffe and Hutton, are now together. They are master and pupil, so it is said, but their methods and stroke-making are dissimilar. Sutcliffe's nostrils are dilated with the whiff of battles of other days against Australians. He is loving every minute of it. He feels himself master of the situation and positively purrs. His eyes are not as keen as they were, but his supreme confidence is unchanged.

'Wait thar,' he calls, with almost an Oxford accent. He plays the ball, peers at it, runs three yards down the pitch, crosses the bat across his chest, comes to rigid attention and raises an arm like a traffic cop. 'Wait thar,' says Sutcliffe, bristling with polished dignity from sleek hair, parted in the middle, to immaculate boots.

I think whimsically of Sutcliffe as I cross to and fro between the overs. I played Test cricket against him in Australia and I notice again his emphatic smack, smack on his block with the bat as the bowler runs in and then his shuffle, shuffle across with his feet just before the bowler delivers. No cricketer has had more mannerisms; no batsman has had a better fighting temperament.

I like most the spit and polish of Sutcliffe when he knows he can call the tune. He has been in his element at Lord's, where none can match the outraged indignities he suffers when, with Lord's packed and the immaculate Sutcliffe settled at his crease, somebody moves above the bowler's arm on top of the Members' Pavilion. Up shoots Sutcliffe's arm, daring anything to move between his end and

Buckingham Palace, and he draws away from the pitch to make vigorous, sweeping moves with his bat to the pavilion. All eyes follow the action to light upon some hapless wretch who has dared to move at such a moment in British history. 'Do sit down sir' say the fellow MCC members.

Sutcliffe and his dignity then return stiffly to the job again and he plays the next ball meticulously and pretentiously as much as to say to the still-blushing wretch, 'Had you not moved in your seat, sir, and momentarily distracted me, I would have swept that ball to the boundary.'

Who could match the cool calm of Sutcliffe at Sydney in 1932 when he chopped a ball from O'Reilly on to his stumps and the bails didn't budge? The surrounding Australians almost swooned in agony. But not so Herbert. He looked at us archly as if to say, 'Pray, please, what is all this fuss and ado about?' Sutcliffe was 43 then; he made 194 and not a flicker of his steely black eyes suggested that anything untoward had happened.

The face of the Yorkshire Master is again inscrutable this day. Runs come slowly but he is unworried. There is time aplenty to spare. A single here, a two there and the scoreboard shows how surely Yorkshire creeps upon this victory over Australia.

Hutton, too, is full of fight and confidence. The Australians don't look like a break-through but suddenly Hutton leans into a ball and pushes it to the on. He doesn't quite get over the top of it and it skims along inches from the grass. I get my fingers under it at short-leg and one Yorkshire hero is gone. Barber, a talented batsman, is next. He and Sutcliffe are together at lunch, Yorkshire 3–83, Sutcliffe and Barber each 36. Yorkshire now want only 67 for victory and all the afternoon in which to do it.

We are a quiet and chastened team at lunch. Defeat, as well as the cold roast beef and the perennial salad and hot potatoes, stares at us. The delighted hum of the spectators below floats up to our dining-room.

But suddenly comes an unmistakable sound. It is rain and heavy rain at that. The faces of the Yorkshiremen drop. A bitter fight for two and a half days, victory certain, and now rain!

The shower passes, however, and the thousands stream from their shelters as Sellers and Bradman walk out after lunch to inspect the pitch. 'Good old Sellers,' the crowd calls to the Yorkshire skipper.' 'Poor old Aussies,' they call to Bradman.

Here, now, is the sequel to this tale. You must imagine that setting – two and a half days of intense, tough cricket, with its many ups and downs; the enthusiasm of the keenest cricket crowd in all England; victory just at hand for Yorkshire and that victory waiting to be acclaimed by deep-throated Yorkshire roars and general cock-a-hoopness. Bear this in mind and consider whether you agree with me that this was the greatest gesture seen on a cricketing field.

Sellers walked to one end of the pitch. He took one look there and walked to the other end. Then he turned to the crowd, wrung his hands together and then threw them wide apart.

The game was over! Sellers's gesture was telling the crowd that the pitch was unfit for play and that the match had ended in a draw.

I have seen no more spontaneous act of sportsmanship. Bradman was in an invidious position. As captain of a side facing defeat, he would have felt diffidence in suggesting that the pitch was unfit for further play. Sellers saved him all this. Ninety-nine captains out of a hundred would have been well within their rights in saying, 'It doesn't look too good. We'll have another look, say, at three or four.' Some in Sellers's position, for he had nothing to lose and all to gain, would have pushed for play to start immediately, even if only to establish an arguable position for a later start. Often in cricket is the state of the pitch conditioned by the state of the game and the minds of the captains.

At the very least, for his side and victory, Sellers could have disagreed with Bradman over the pitch and called in the umpires.

But not Sellers. He waved the game off with a magnificent Yorkshire gesture. He gave not a thought to victory, not a second thought to that intensely loyal Yorkshire crowd behind him which cried out in the sheer pain of his gesture. Sellers did not embarrass Bradman by even asking for his opinion of the pitch.

After the crowd had sadly filtered away an hour later, I was finishing packing my cricket bag when I chanced to look down through the dressing-room window. I saw a dear old Yorkshire woman, white-haired, who shook her brolly at me.

'Ah,' she called up at me, 'the pity 'o it, the pity 'o it. We had tha well and truly whacked. If only I could get at tha wi' brolly 'twould be summat, 'twould be summat indeed.'

4. Out of the Old Trafford Pit

An Australian newspaper cutting had been placed on the inside of the Australian dressing-room door the day the fourth Test of 1961 began. On the evening of the second last day, two Australians, Benaud and Lindwall, walked from a cocktail party in the President's Room and stood talking, meditating and looking at the bowler's roughage at the railway end of the pitch. It was a pregnant moment that had its climax on the morrow and its effects, as I saw it, for years afterwards on English cricket.

I thought of all this again one recent Saturday afternoon as I watched ABC television. I usually play golf on a Saturday but if there is anything I abhor, it is golf in the rain. One's clothes get sodden and cling to the skin. The glove gets wet and slippery, the face of the club skids on the wet grass and, all in all, it is a most uncomfortable sporting exercise.

So, this Saturday afternoon, I forsook golf and watched television instead. I was richly rewarded. The ABC re-ran the last day's play of the Old Trafford Test of 1961 and this, without doubt, was one of the most stirring day's Test cricket I had seen. As I had televised and broadcast for the BBC that English summer, as well as writing for English newspapers, it was rather quaint to listen to one's own voice discussing the happenings on television.

It had been an interesting series so far. Benaud had damaged his shoulder and had to withdraw from the second Test at Lord's. If there is one Test in which an Australian likes to lead his side, it is at Lord's but Benaud was not to relish the experience. The Lord's Test became known as the Battle of the Ridge. I still smile when I recall how the MCC officials processed to the middle at the end of this game. It was like a solemn procession opening an Undertakers' Convention as the officials moved with slow dignity and positioned a theodolite on the pitch.

Harvey led the Australians to victory and McKenzie, 1–81 in the first innings, took 5–37 in the second, the beginning of an auspicious career against England. Lawry defied the English attack for 6½ hours for a magnificent 130, although I still remember how Australia, 4–19 at one stage, struggled to get the 70 or so needed to win. Had Peter Burge gone, anything could have happened.

Brian Sellers, the leading personality of north England cricket and an English selector, joined in the general criticism of the sub-standard pitch at Lord's, saying his native Leeds would turn on a 'beauty' for the third Test. 'We know how to make pitches in the north,' proudly pontificated Sellers, whom Australians know as a good bloke.

But Leeds must have lost the recipe somewhere. The third Test pitch was a poor, powdery one, uneven in height and bounce, and Sellers went into retreat, observing a Trappist silence, after the game. Freddie Trueman, after 5–58 in the first innings, cut down his run in the second, bowled off-cutters, and took 6–30. Only Harvey, 73 and 53, could hold up an Australian head.

So the Australians came to Old Trafford for the vital fourth Test, which well could have won England the rubber. Several days before the game I took the chance to pop into Old Trafford and look at the pitch in preparation. I think I hiked in from the British Open golf – wasn't it at Southport that year and didn't Arnie Palmer win it in some atrocious weather? – and I was given a warm welcome at Old Trafford by Secretary Geoff Howard and groundsman Flack. The Lancastrians didn't appreciate the stigma that was left on their pitch after the 1956 Test. This was the one in which Jim Laker got his record Test haul of 19 wickets – ten, naturally, and most brilliantly, in one innings – and I recall vividly the loud guffaw Bill O'Reilly emitted in the press-box on that first day when groundsman Flack used his besom broom to sweep the pitch and clouds of dust rose in the air.

I worked overtime, after that match, for the BBC. I had a summary to do, which was usual, but the producer wanted additional 'spots' for this and that programme and I think, as an Australian, I did justice to Laker over the air and in the English Press for his incredible feat.

Remembering this dusty pitch in 1956 and following on the queer ones in this 1961 series at Lord's and Leeds, I was anxious to drop in on Old Trafford as it was being prepared for this game. Geoff Howard and Flack were most helpful, the groundsman describing his preparation in detail. There was no fear of the dust rising at Old Trafford in 1961.

An Australian editor – some of them at times have an odd con-ception of what is happening 12,000 miles away! – had ordered an article of a sensational nature from his correspondent on the spot in England and, against his better judgment, this correspondent had written (after the fiasco at Leeds) that the Australian team was on the point of disintegration. Benaud, returned to his side, received the cutting from Australia on the morning of the Test. He pinned it, for inspiration to bring revenge, on the Australian dressing-room door.

Unfortunately for England, for he could well have won this Test with his sound technique and calm temperament in a crisis, Cowdrey was declared unfit on the morning of the match. The English selectors dismissed from their minds what had happened here five years before and they dropped Lock, the spinner. They settled, in the main, for a four-man pace attack with Statham, Trueman, Favell and Dexter. Allen was the lone spinner. The English batting tail began high up the vertebrae.

In the light of the poor attendances we have had since at Old Trafford, it is worth noting that crowds of 28,000, 29,000, 33,000 and 34,000 (ground closed) saw the cricket over four days and got remarkably good and interesting play for their money. The game swung this way and that, Lawry making 74 and 102 (Bill Bowes wrote that Lawry was a magnificent player of fast bowling), Booth 46, Simpson 51, O'Neill 67, Peter May a glorious 95, Pullar 63 (the home crowd liked that), Barrington 78, Allen 42; Brian Statham 5–53 (the home crowd exulted over that), Dexter 3–16, Davidson 3–70 and Simpson 4–23. Benaud had 0–80 in the first innings, a keen disappointment for him, but on every day there were outstanding feats – and day after day gave warm sunshine.

It is a strange phenomenon, but no matter what the state of the game, English crowds invariably duck the last day. This, too, looked like being an absorbing one. Australia, four wickets in hand, were only 154 runs ahead. It looked all over an English victory, with a good day's cricket in prospect, but only 12,000 came to watch. Those who stayed away missed about the most sensational final day's play I can remember between England and Australia.

Benaud thought highly of Lindwall's cricket acumen. Lindwall was a master in his analysis of batsmen and, drawing him aside from the evening drink that is always a pleasant feature of a game at Old Trafford, Benaud asked Lindwall to come to the middle with him. On the deserted cricket field, the two famous Australians studied the pitch and, in particular, the marks Trueman had made at the railway end.

'What do you think of the idea of bowling slow leg-breaks around the stumps into those marks?' asked Benaud.

Lindwall pondered. 'To get wickets or tie the scoring down?' he asked.

'Well, either, depending upon the circumstances,' said Benaud.

Lindwall thought again. 'I think there is merit in the idea, Richie,' he said, 'but it would need to be very tight spin bowling. You don't look like having many runs to play with. I would be inclined to give it a go. But it must be tight or –.' And Lindwall shrugged his shoulders.

Benaud got from Lindwall the confidence in his idea that he wanted. What he also wanted that next morning were many more runs. He wanted to win this game, not draw it.

Benaud's hopes seemed dashed in the first few minutes of play. Allen got Mackay immediately and, in a few more minutes, had Benaud and Grout also. Three wickets fell for a miserly three runs. With the score at 9–334, only 157 runs ahead, the Australian balcony seemed as if inhabited by mutes. The depression was obvious. The English ecstasy, on the other hand, was rampant; but, it was to prove, a whit too cocksure.

Davidson took to Allen and hit him thrillingly, in the one over, for 6, 4, 4, 6. May, without giving Allen a chance at the last man, McKenzie, sacked Allen and took the new ball – and the Australians on their balcony breathed easier to see that McKenzie had been spared the spin of Allen.

This last Australian wicket went on to glory. Davidson was unconquered at 77, McKenzie made 32, and they took the score from 9–334 to 432 all out. Had that swashbuckling partnership been broken early, England must have walked in this Test.

Raman Subba Row, a delightful man and a capable opener, joined Pullar with England needing 256 to win in 230 minutes. It was a teasing task, one that needed to be tackled with resolution but one well within the compass of this English team. A good start was important. After that, the batsmen would need to push the rate along. If a scoring rate gets bogged down, important wickets are often sacrificed to catch up with the clock.

Pullar left with the score at 40, with England behind the clock, but then came Dexter to send the ground into convulsions of joy. His 76 was one of the greatest innings I have seen. He took complete charge of the game, Subba Row sensibly carrying out his watching brief the other end, leaving the assault to Dexter. Dexter decimated the Australian attack, cutting, driving and pulling. He lofted Mackay hugely into the crowd at long-on for six, making 50 in an hour. England's 100, then, came in 94 minutes, almost on terms with the clock.

Still Dexter surged on, a batsman of grace, courage and power. England moved swiftly to 150, with only Pullar gone, in exactly two hours. When 100 was needed for victory, nine wickets in hand, there were 110 minutes left for play. It looked to be England's game.

Just previously, Benaud tried his final gamble – around the stumps into Trueman's marks. He had no outfield, a juicy invitation to Dexter which he accepted, almost lofting Benaud for six. Benaud immediately put a man out and had five men on the on-side. The sparsely-patrolled off caught Dexter's attention and he succumbed to it. He tried to force to the off, snicked instead, and Grout caught him.

Now came Peter May. Benaud ostentatiously strung his men around on the leg-side, leaving fine-leg invitingly deserted. May fell like the fly. He dangerously tried to sweep the first ball to leg and left his leg stump open the tiniest fraction. May's bat missed the ball, which spun viciously from the worn part and hit the leg stump. It was a depressing blow for England.

Here, now, was when Cowdrey would have been invaluable, bringing order and calm into an innings rapidly disintegrating into hysteria. The War Horse in a Test sniffs the battle and the tension and, steeling himself, thrives on it. Poor Close, seeming to lose his balance and intent on putting his luck immediately to the test, advanced the English innings further into bedlam. He made an immediate and wild cross-bat swish to fine-leg to a ball outside his off-stump (Close being left-handed) and it fell just short of Mackay's grasping hands.

Mackay had a wrenched muscle. Benaud, not wishing to make his change apparent to Close, told Mackay to change with O'Neill for the next over and he also told O'Neill to drop back another ten yards for Close.

Close played one good stroke in Benaud's next over, which still came from around the stumps. Close moved swiftly down-pitch and hit Benaud sweetly over long-on for six; but fully four more times he played that incredible cross-bat swish. It was uncomfortable watching Close that day and the feeling returned again as I watched the inevitable end on television. Close holed out to O'Neill. It was like the batting of the Australians five years ago, all succumbing to Laker.

Subba Row was clean-bowled, off the rough; Simpson most brilliantly caught Murray, also off Benaud . . . and from being 1–150 the English were all out 201, beaten by 34 runs with 24 minutes to spare. Benaud, with figures of 32–11–70–6, had given one of the most outstanding pieces of intelligent and controlled slow, spin bowling seen in Tests. Under the circumstances, I am sure he would regard it as his best piece of Test bowling.

This was a highly interesting and spectacular Test, replete with drama, suspense and quickly changing trends. Benaud – who gave much praise to Lindwall – snatched it out of the English victory pyre. It was a Test, I think, England should never have lost and I don't think England have yet recovered from this crushing reversal, crushing because victory seemed so much in hand. Had that game been won (the last Test was drawn), England would have won this rubber and so advanced in confidence for future series. More than that. I don't think Peter May, England's most gifted batsman since Denis Compton, would have retired so early. He would have led England in Australia soon afterwards, and not Dexter. I think May's early retirement was in a measure forced by some particularly harsh treatment he received from a section of the English Press. Had he been the winner at Old Trafford in 1961, and not the loser, things might have been different.

Fred Trueman, as I saw him over the years, was no respecter of the batting rights of a pitch. He would never have been out of trouble (and he was originally a miner) on the lease of a digging. Intrusion meant nothing to Fred and his run through was often too close to the line of the leg-stump for batting comfort. Old Trafford, 1961, was one occasion when it hit back at his own team. Another who has to be watched is Snow, of Sussex and England. He almost demented umpire Arthur Fagg at Leeds in 1968 and was fortunate not to have been stopped bowling after being warned. Those big plates fast bowlers wear are very much pitch despoilers if a bowler runs down the line.

The remedy is in a bowler's own feet. He simply must keep off the important part of a pitch in his follow-through. It was Trueman, grand bowler and all as he was and a rich personality, who dug the pit for England's interment at Old Trafford; it was Benaud who had the ability to land with spin into that pit and it was a wise head in Lindwall who helped him to work out the plan. Bitterly disappointed, and understandably so, the Old Trafford crowd accepted defeat most sportingly and cheered the Australians in.

Part Two

GREAT BATSMEN OF THE PAST

In writing of great batsman of the past, I have re-lived many thrilling moments. Victor Trumper is the only one of those I have written about whom I did not know. Hobbs, Macartney and Bardsley were of a different first-class and Test generation to mine but I once was thrilled to walk out with the great John Berry Hobbs to open the innings for the Press against the Australian Navy at Rushcutters Bay, on the shore of Sydney Harbour. Hobbs was a friendly, modest man. I had many talks with him in England after the Second World War.

I played Sydney club games against Macartney and Bardsley and often with them, at the end of their Test careers, in mid-week Sydney games on the Cricket Ground No. 2. They were both tremendous characters – chockful of confidence and cricket personality. Neville Cardus tells a story which typified Macartney's outlook when he met him one London Test morning coming to breakfast. 'My word,' said Charlie, who was also a good trencherman, rubbing his hands together, 'I feel sorry for the poor blighters who have got to bowl at me today.' I have, as I think I have written in the chapter on Bardsley, singled him out because he is a classic example of how a Test cricketer can get to the top if he works at his game.

Nobody could forget Wally Hammond and especially if he had fielded to him at cover in Tests. Lord, how the ball sizzled off his bat! I batted against Maurice Tate once in Sydney when he got the wickets of Kippax, Bradman and McCabe – which means that he was still a great bowler – yet I thought Hammond as a bowler was in Tate's class when he put his mind and his right hand and arm to the job – and his shoulder, because, like Tate, Hammond could make the ball whip from the pitch with his tremendously strong right-side. Hammond, I found, put his all into his bowling – which was reasonable enough, I suppose, because he spent many, many hours at the batting crease – only when he had failed with the bat. As a first slip, he was magnificent. I have seen two clear champions in that position, Hammond and Simpson.

I saw a lot of Ponsford's broad bat and beam in the field when he played for Victoria and I for New South Wales. I also played in the bodyline series of Tests with him, the preceding summer, against South Africa. A great cricketer and a whimsical character, he was, who found relief from Test cricket in fishing. He once got sunburnt soles from this exercise on the Sunday of a Test.

Don Bradman will hold an unchallenged position as long as cricket is played. He was a shrewd, dominating character in most ways and though all conceded his greatness, not many, I think, enjoyed playing with or against him – or under him, although Australian cricketers of a later decade to ours, got on with him much better than we did. I had many games with and against him and once batted almost a day with him against England in Melbourne. He staggered me, once, in Perth by asking me to take Gubby Allen for him on a slightly-wet pitch, saying he thought Allen intended to 'have a pop at me'. This was just before the 1932–33 series began. Bradman would have been the first batsman chosen in any world's eleven. I was stringing along with some two or three others for the final batting position in the Australian Eleven!

McCabe and Compton gave me infinite pleasure, in their cricket and in their company. They were men's men, both playing some of the greatest innings known to the game. In his best Australian side over the past fifty years to play a Computer Test against England, Bradman did not choose McCabe. As Harold Larwood was bound to be in England's team, McCabe would have been the very first Australian batsman I would have chosen. But perhaps computers don't provide for Larwood bowling bouncers!

5. Donald Bradman

====

In the Third Test at Melbourne in January, 1937, G. O. Allen, England's captain, declared at 76–9 in the first innings to force the Australians to bat on a rain-affected pitch. Don Bradman retaliated by sending his tail-end batsmen in first, thus bringing Bradman and Fingleton together for the sixth wicket. Their partnership of 346, a record, set the stage for a remarkable victory for Australia. Now, 31 years later, Jack Fingleton writes about his former captain and team-mate. – Editor, World Sport, London, 1968.

I recently wrote to Sir Donald Bradman, seeking, for the purposes of this article, an opinion from him on the merits of modern cricketers. He surprised me with the depth and the generosity of his reply – ranging over Tilden, Lindrum, swimming, athletics, golf ('what about the implements used? Nicklaus would have been in great trouble trying to drive today's distances with a gutta-percha ball and a wooden shaft') and so on, down to cricket.

It was a fascinating letter, which recalled his batting. His letter was precise and deep-thinking. He brought to bear the same analytical approach with which he first dissected all bowlers of his generation before proceeding to decimate them – the whole lot of them. Let me quote his pertinent thoughts on his own game, though he also played tennis and golf, handicap scratch, to a high standard. Noting how the clock served as a guide in many other sports, Sir Donald wrote: 'A batsman in cricket is not competing against the clock and himself. His feats are subject to what his opponents are doing – a varying set of conditions and a myriad of things of complexity.'

He says his own career covered the smaller ball and larger stumps, and much of it was under the off-side lbw rule. All this favoured the bowler. This, he says, indicates that S. F. Barnes was a greater bowler than his figures suggest. . . . 'and Trumper had to bat against Barnes – I didn't'.

He proceeds with sound, thought-provoking stuff.

I think the modern era tends to have champions of other days thrown in his face, but the error is often committed of comparing only former champions with the rank-and-file of today. What about the rank-and-file of yesterday? For this reason, I often think the modern cricketer is unduly maligned. You may not think our present team for England compares with certain earlier teams, yet I am prepared to say you could find names in some of the earlier fine sides which would be lucky to make the grade in the present team. Are you concerned with style or effectiveness? As Cardus has written, the eagle is more beautiful to watch than a jet plane, but there is no doubt which is the faster. My view is that the champion of any era would have been a champion in any other era. But, having said that, I've no idea how you sort out Dempsey, Louis, or Clay.

I am, understandably, indebted to Sir Donald, who, as a selector, helped choose our side for England, yet I am afraid I cannot go all the way with my former Test skipper. There have been touring 'flops' since cricket time began and of this side of ours soon to tour England, Connolly is perhaps fortunate to get a second chance after his dismal tour of 1964. Joslin gets the greatest cricket tour there is after two abysmal batting failures in his only Test against India – in which he also badly muffed a catch. Sir Donald, I feel sure, will agree that many fine players we both knew in other days performed big deeds without receiving a single tour overseas.

But I must resist temptation. I must not be side-tracked. I have to write of Sir Donald, himself, and I do so with zest because I played with and against him a lot and I can still see him in bold perspective against many of the greats I knew: Hammond, Compton, Woolley, Duleepsinhji, Hutton, Cowdrey, May, Dexter (what a pity the two latter played Tests for so short a time!), Worrell, Sobers, Weekes, Hazare, Amarnath (a lovely stroke-maker), Pataudi jnr., Nourse, Pollock, Ponsford, McCabe, Macartney, Kippax, Jackson, Morris, Miller (up and down but certainly great on his day), Harvey, Simpson and one or two others who touched the top with infrequency. As a youngster, I once opened an innings with the Master, Jack Hobbs, in Sydney. I knew, too, Collins, Bardsley, Taylor, Andrews, Hendren and South Africa's Herbie Taylor.

One's memory, then, covers a glittering field, yet I have not the slightest hesitation in saying that Don Bradman was the most remarkable batsman I knew. Moreover, there would not be a single person of his generation who would not say the same. He bestrode the cricket world as nobody before or since has done. His consistency was incredible.

Dr Grace, who had to contend with indifferent pitches, and J. B.

Hobbs, were outstanding for their consistency, but Bradman stood alone. In all matches, he scored 50,731 runs in 669 innings for an average of 90.27. In first-class matches, Bradman scored 28,067 runs in 338 innings for an average of 95.14: and in Test matches he made 6,996 runs in 80 innings for an average of 99.94. Those are staggering figures and it is pertinent that 63 of his 80 Test innings were played against England, the common enemy. It is to be stressed that he never toured India, the West Indies or South Africa, all with fruitful batting pitches. Nor did he tour New Zealand.

None of his generation, either, toured the West Indies. I flew there in 1965 and had a practice on the Bridgetower ground. The lovely pace of the pitch, its trueness, the clear light, the fast ground and the short boundaries brought Don Bradman immediately to my mind. I thought, then, that he would have written another page in his record book had he toured the West Indies. So, too, had he not withdrawn from the captaincy of our team to South Africa in 1936–37.

Of the 211 centuries Bradman scored in all matches, 41 were double centuries, eight were treble centuries and one a quadruple. He is the only Australian to have made a century of first-class centuries, a wonderful feat when it is considered how few innings he had compared to those others who passed this peak.

I see him, again, as he came to bat in his final Test innings at the Oval in 1948, on the verge of averaging a century in all Tests. Capricious fate saw him out for a duck second ball to Eric Hollies. I think the ovation given him by the crowd, all the way to the middle, where Yardley had his players grouped and called for three cheers for the retiring hero, unnerved him. Bradman was seldom unnerved.

Figures tell the undisputed story of Bradman's greatness, yet they tell only one portion of the story of his tremendous capacity. One had to bat with him, bowl or field against him, or, knowing the game and the art of batting, see and analyse his technique to comprehend the revolutionary dominance he brought to the game. On and on and on he seemed to go, batting into cricket eternity.

Bradman was not, in the sense of Trumper, McCabe or May, a classical stroke-maker as one knows the term. He was of medium build, well-muscled and supple in the wrists, yet there were no pretty passes or deft glides (in the Duleepsinhji manner) to suggest that some magical wand was weaving a spell over the field.

Some bowler, for instance, might think that he had won through to Charlie Macartney's stumps only to find, hey presto, a fiendish flick at the last fraction of time that sent the ball screaming to the boundary. So, too, with Sobers, who has his own type of magic.

Bradman did not deal in such things. There was not a stroke in the game he could not play, but he was common-sense to the tips of his batting gloves.

'Are you concerned with style or effectiveness?' asks Sir Donald of me, and it is a good question. He was such a genius that he could well have indulged himself in the artistic flourishes of batting, but he was too much of a realist to permit himself to do this. He knew two basic things about bowlers; none likes to be met constantly with the full face of the bat; none likes to see what, ordinarily, is good-length bowling transposed into over-pitched stuff by twinkling footwork. His fundamental thinking and love of cricket were, I am inclined to think, basically sadistic. He carried no soft feelings with him to the middle. Music to him was the crash of the ball against the fence: he delighted in seeing the figures revolve merrily against his name on the score-board; he loved to murder bowlers and make the opposing skipper look futile and foolish.

There were, as I have written, no deft passes or pretty glides, but every bowler, every fieldsman, every spectator in Bradman's heyday sensed that he was using not a bat so much as an axe dripping with the bowler's blood and agony. He didn't know pity. He was remorseless and a century rarely satisfied him. It had to be two or three, or even four against Queensland once when he made 452 and still didn't yield. In the middle, he was always planning, deducing and organizing with a concentration that never seemed to flag.

His dynamic and convulsive appeal to the spectator has never been equalled in my time. The roar of absolute delight that circled the ground when his magic name appeared in the vacant slot on the scoring-board was also one of anticipatory pleasure, and Bradman seldom failed his huge 'army'. I was often at the other end to him. Perhaps, with W. A. Brown, we had managed to give our side a good start against the new ball, keen bowling and fielding. If Brown had gone, I might have been 40 or so. In no time, Bradman would be past me, and in no time also the bowling and fielding would be ragged. Bradman soon had them where he wanted them – at his mercy.

He was, at the same time, aggravation to the bowler and despair to the batsman at the other end. He would take guard with a wide smile, survey the field, give his trousers a hitch, settle down and then with a piercing and shrill 'Right' he would be off to his first run off the first ball. Of this, he made a habit. In unnoticeable time, he would be 10, 20, 40, 50 and so on to the inevitable century. He dominated the strike and the batsman at the other end felt like an ineffectual goon. No matter what he did, it paled alongside Bradman's deeds. Bradman made it all seem so easy and he always regarded the clock as another enemy to be trounced.

I heard prominent batsmen of his era, cast deep into the shadows, complain that Bradman got more full-tosses and long-hops than anybody else. They were trying to suggest that Bradman was fortunate. He wasn't. The point was that bowlers were made by Bradman to bowl to him as he wanted. He dictated that. His footwork, his abounding confidence, his skill, pulverized bowlers and mesmerized them. They just didn't know where to bowl to him to keep him quiet.

W. H. Ponsford, who was the magical record-breaker until Bradman cast him from the throne, once told me that Bradman saw the ball quicker than anybody else. Ponsford meant that Bradman judged the ball's possibilities quicker than all others. And this was true. His judgment was impeccable and the co-ordination between mind, feet and bat was like automation at work. His batting, his style, had many facets and it was built on footwork. He believed, implicitly, in the drive, and, often on the run, he drove in an arc from in front of point to wide of mid-on. He regarded the crease purely as a place in which to mark his guard. The keeper he ignored because he never calculated on missing a ball. Bradman was stumped 22 times in his 669 innings and most of those were sacrificial in minor games. He left 'home', the crease, like an arrant night-clubber. When the poor bowler, tired of being driven, dropped the ball short, Bradman drew back and across his wicket in a flash to slash him with pulls he learned on the concrete pitches of his country youth.

Some claimed that he was unorthodox. I don't agree. His batting was based on the soundest of foundations. He stood with the bat between his feet, an unusual stance (and one, incidentally, copied by Keith Miller), and his left hand was further to the right of the handle than is considered orthodox. This grip was doubly effective in that it enabled him to bring his devastating pull-shot quickly down to earth, the bat closing its face quickly over the ball. If he was unorthodox, it was in his outlook. Where others suspected a good-length ball of some explosive content, and were satisfied to play it defensively, Bradman sniffed contempt at it. I don't think there *was* a good-length to him.

His confidence was incredible. He exuded runs long before leaving the pavilion. His judgment was superb; his run-appetite insatiable; his temperament and self-discipline unsurpassed. In Sydney, for example, he was a study when not out during the luncheon adjournment. His pads, bat and gloves would be put on the table, he would wash, take off his pants, put a towel around his middle and sit down to the inevitable light lunch he had ordered of rice custard, stewed fruit, and milk. Each slow mouthful was an essay in method, in digestion, in relaxation, in cold planning and contemplation of the real feast soon to follow in the middle.

To suggest – and he missed nothing of such suggestions – that a particular bowler had his measure, was to invite that bowler's annihilation. We once played a mid-week social game at a hospital in Sydney and I had lunch at his home with Arthur Mailey, who was not at all happy that some scribe had written that morning, apropos of the game, that the veteran, who had taken Don's wicket once or twice, knew how to deal with Bradman.

'They shouldn't write this nonsense,' said Mailey, who was to play against Bradman and knew the effect the article would have upon him. Mailey was right. Bradman absolutely slaughtered Mailey that day. A big crowd had come to see Bradman and he made the day memorable for them at Mailey's expense. He hit him everywhere but into the operating theatre.

So, too, once in Sydney, with Fleetwood-Smith. Some critics had 'set' Fleetwood up and Bradman, who rarely hit sixes, purposely went out of his way that day to hit a gaggle of sixes.

Frank Tyson once suggested in Australia on television that Bradman would not have thrived against what Tyson was pleased to call astute modern captaincy but which some might describe as negative field-placing and bowling. I sensed that Tyson, who would not have seen Bradman at his zenith, was somewhat derogatory of Bradman's genius. As I was appearing at the same time, I told Tyson he would have changed his mind had he bowled against Bradman.

Tyson was apparently suggesting that the modern circle-field, nugatory in its concept and much used these days, would have curbed Bradman. It would have made him grin at its challenge. He knew the circle-field and he played against some astute captains. It was a matter of honour with Bradman to make field-placements and skippers look ridiculous. A captain might take a fieldsman from here and put him there to cut off a flow of Bradman boundaries. Bradman invariably put the next ball where the fieldsman had been – and grinned hugely. The crowd loved this. There was no subtlety in it. It was something blatantly clear. Bradman's footwork in getting to the ball was too brilliant. He could not be confined. In his prime, he would have twisted the spokes of a circle-field in a twinkling but, perhaps, Tyson had most in mind that the slow-over approach which his skipper, Hutton, used would have eased Bradman down. In this, he

1. TIED TEST: Worrell droops with exhaustion, Kanhai explodes with elation, Kline turns away philosophically and one stump leans awry at the end of the greatest Test of all.

2. IMMORTAL MOMENT: One of the most famous scenes in cricket occurs as Joe Solomon throws down the stumps and brings about the first Test tie in all history.

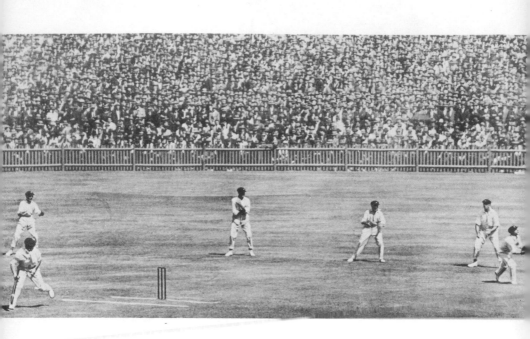

3. HISTORIC CATCH: Sydney, 1925. Hobbs, caught Oldfield, bowled Gregory 0. Australia won by 307 runs.

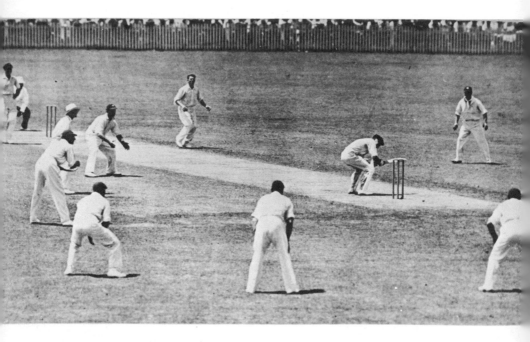

4. HISTORIC FIELD: Six short legs as Woodfull ducks under yet another Larwood thunderbolt.

5 and 6. PORTRAITS OF ENDEAVOUR: (*above*) Bert Oldfield attempts to stump Patsy Hendren in the Nottingham Test, 1930; (*below*) West Indies strive to break through in the second last over at Adelaide. Frank Worrell's field was probably the oddest ever seen in a Test. Sobers is all but grasping Kline's bat. But Kline killed every ball. The Test was drawn.

7 and 8. PORTRAI
OF ELATION: (abo
Richie Benaud bo
Peter May round his le
for o at Manchest
1961, and Australia ke
the Ashes; (below) B
Ponsford, then a sprigh
70, watches an in-swing
all the way in a sligh
different test in M
bourne.

was right. No batsman can carve an attack which won't come to the table.

Comparatively, bodyline did subjugate Bradman although he still averaged over 50 in the series, but that was based on physical attack – in itself a tribute to Bradman's greatness – and it was quickly outlawed. His pristine days were in England in 1930 (when Larwood played) and he made scores of 131, 254, 334 and 232 – 974 in the series, a century before lunch at Leeds, and all made at a fast rate.

Understandably, at forty years of age, he was well past his murderous best when he came to England for the last time in 1948, yet he contrived to make eleven centuries on the tour. Just think of that – eleven centuries in the one summer at forty years of age!

Jim Laker, who once had all ten Australian wickets in 1956 at the Oval for Surrey and got 19 of their wickets in the 1956 Old Trafford Test, never once succeeded in getting Bradman's wicket in 1948. Bradman tallied almost 1,000 runs in games in which Laker played in 1948. Bradman's feet had lost their quickness in 1948; Laker still could not get his wicket.

Bradman was not a hail-fellow with players of his own generation. It is to be admitted immediately that jealousy and resentment often made his position a difficult one, yet there were times when he might have assessed his standing in the game and made more of a gesture himself to his fellows. Yet, he might have reasoned, this could have sapped his purpose. His genius tended to make him a man apart, his soul immersed in batting and (it seemed) in records. He was often a lonely person in his peak years, although he might have thought that the fault was not all his.

Even as a young man, he was an adroit businessman. Offers chased him and he capitalized, as he was entitled to do, on his unparalleled standing in the game and with the public. He seemed to most who played under him in his early captaincy to be dictatorial and it was apparent that post-war players got on much better with him.

Pre-war, he indulged in gestures neither to his players nor his opponents. He ignored the courtesy of bidding his opponents welcome and farewell in the Adelaide dressing-rooms and once he had his innings declared against his former New South Wales side (of which I was captain at the time) by an official over a loud-speaker. His vice-captain, McCabe, his number one bowler, O'Reilly, Fleetwood-Smith and O'Brien were once summoned by the Australian Board to appear before them on a charge of not giving Bradman full support against England. Some Australian officials are odd birds, not deeply immersed in a knowledge of the game, and his team thought that Bradman should have gone along with them to give support.

England had won the first two Tests and we were well down to them in Melbourne in the third Test when the Board issued its summons. We then, surprisingly, got the third Test back and won it. Bradman and I were under the showers at the end of the game and the team were jollying those players who had been 'invited' to tread the carpet. 'What is all this about?' asked Bradman of me. 'Surely you know that four of your players have been carpeted by the Board,' I told him. 'You must go along with them'. 'You know what I think of our Board,' said Don. He didn't go with the players. As we had won the Test, the Board's charges limply crumpled.

Now, in a happy family life and with a charming and helpful wife, Lady Jessie, I think Bradman has mellowed. So, too, no doubt, have some of his comrades of his early cricketing days. Cricket, I think, was more intense, more individualistic, and held the public stage more in those days than it does now. No other cricketer knew the blinding publicity that Bradman knew. His life was seldom private.

Perhaps he never knew that his fellows stood loyally by him in England in 1938 when our Board churlishly refused permission to his wife to travel to England when the playing part of the tour was over. Bradman had the match off, against Derbyshire, when the news of the Board's decision came to us at Grindleford. A team-meeting was called and an ultimatum was given to manager Jeanes, who was also secretary of the Board, that he would have a cricket strike on his hands if Mrs Bradman wasn't allowed to come to England. Almost over-night the Board reversed its decision.

Bradman was a clever, astute captain, knowing all the moves, and he played the game to the full. He was one of the most brilliant fieldsmen ever, unerring in his screaming throw to the stumps, often holding the ball in the deep and challenging the batsmen to run. He is a capital after-dinner speaker, droll in his rich humour. Spectators crowded Lord's in 1948, after his last game there, to bid farewell to the greatest batsman of his type the game has known. For all the thrashings he gave their bowlers – and they included some of the greatest of all time – the English adored Bradman.

One analyses his art again and declares, without question, that he would have been Bradman in any era of the game. He was, and is, a remarkable man. Today, from Adelaide, he holds almost as many business directorates as he still, and will, hold cricket records.

DONALD BRADMAN'S TEST CAREER

In a Test career spanning 20 years Sir Donald Bradman only once finished a series with a batting average below the seventies – such was the power of Australia's run machine. He scored an average of 26.03 per cent of Australia's runs in Tests and 25.47 per cent of his side's total in all matches. Born on 27 August, 1908, Bradman got his chance in first-class cricket at nineteen years of age in the 1927–28 season. He entered the Test scene a year later, batting No. 7 in his first appearance, and became the regular No. 3 from 1930 onwards. Here is a complete record of his 80 Test innings during which he scored 6,996 runs for an average of 99.94.

SERIES	1st Test	2nd Test	3rd Test	4th Test	5th Test	
1928–29 ENGLAND (H) Aus 1 Eng 4	18 1	— —	79 112	40 58	123 37*	England won by record 675 runs on Bradman's debut in First Test. Dropped for Second Test (which England won by eight wickets); he returned to score first Test century (112 in 4 hr 7 min) batting No. 6.
1930 ENGLAND (A) Eng 1, Aus 2, Drn 2	8 131	254 1	334	14	232	Finished series with average of 139.14. Shattered all previous batting records with his 334 at Leeds after coming in at 2 for 1 on first morning: 105 at lunch, 200 at tea, 309 at close. Batted 6 hr 23 min.
1930–31 W. INDIES (H) Aus 4 W. Indies 1	4	25	223	152	43 0	With Ponsford again topped the Australian batting in a low-scoring series. After West Indies had been dismissed for 99 in Fourth Test, Bradman completed first 50 of 152 in 45 min.
1931–32 S. AFRICA (H) Aus 5 S. Africa 0	226	112	2 167	299	— —	An average of 201.50 after batting for more than 16½ hours in series. At the crease 6 hr 36 min in Fourth Test, running out last partner going for 300th run. Did not bat in Fifth Test (injured).
1932–33 ENGLAND (H) Aus. 1 Eng 4	—	0 103*	8 66	76 24	48 71	The 'Bodyline' series. Missed First Test because of illness but in Second hit 103 not out of 191 total after playing on first ball to Bowes for first-innings duck. Fell to Larwood's bowling four times in series.
1934 ENGLAND (A) Eng 1 Aus 2, Drn 2	29 25	36 13	30	304	244 77	In Fourth (Leeds) and Final (Oval) Tests, Bradman and Ponsford dominated the Australian batting, sharing respectively in stands of 388 (4th wkt) and 451 (2nd wkt) which still stand as records for Australia v England.

Season / Series	Test 1	Test 2	Test 3	Test 4	Test 5	Notes
1936–37 ENGLAND (H) — Aus 3 Eng 2 (1st inns)	38	0	13	26	169	Caught first ball off Voce at Sydney for second duck against Allen's MCC side. Shared with Fingleton remarkable 6th wkt stand of 346 in Third Test after Australia had lost 5–97 and batted 7 hr 38 min.
(2nd inns)	0	82	270	212	—	
1938 ENGLAND (A) — Eng 1 Aus 1, Drn 2 (1st inns)	51	18	M	103	—	His finest Test innings was again at Leeds (Fourth Test): a chanceless 103 in 2 hr 50 min. Injured ankle while England amassed 903–7 dec (Hutton 364) in Fifth Test and did not bat in either Australian innings.
(2nd inns)	144*	102*	—	16*	—	
1946–47 ENGLAND (H) — Aus 3 Eng 0, Drn 2 (1st inns)	187	234	79	0	12	After surviving 'catch' to Ikin when 28 in First Test went on to share record stand of 276 for 3rd wkt with Hassett. Record 5th wkt partnership of 405 with Barnes in Second Test; bowled by Alec Bedser for duck in Fourth.
(2nd inns)	—	—	49	56*	63	
1947–48 INDIA (H) — Aus 4 India 0, Drn 1 (1st inns)	185	13	132	201	57†	For the fourth time Bradman ended a Test series with a three-figure average (178.75) and for the first and only time recorded a century in each innings. His 201 in Fourth Test was 37th and last double century of career.
(2nd inns)	—	—	127*	—	—	
1948 ENGLAND (A) — Eng 0 Aus 4, Drn 1 (1st inns)	138	38	7	33	0	Match-winning innings in Fourth Test when he and Morris put on 301 in 220 minutes after Australia had been set 404 to win at 70 an hr. Needing only 4 runs for career Test average of 100, bowled second ball by Hollies at Oval.
(2nd inns)	0	89	30*	173*	—	

* not out; † retired hurt; M match abandoned without a ball bowled.

6. Wally Hammond

The Strand, from my fourth-floor eyrie in the Charing Cross Hotel, is always a fascinating sight by day and night. The commuters in the morning run helter-skelter in one direction. Another few hours and they are scurrying the other way. Yet again a few more hours, when all the lights are gleaming, and it is a hustle for the theatres. I never tired of watching the bustling throng and it was from high up, I recall, that I last saw Wally Hammond. He was unmistakeable as he weaved his way through the traffic and impulsively I called out 'Coo-ee, Wally'.

The pigeons slumbering or courting on the Cross below stampeded in flight. Several policeman looked up. So did some taxi-drivers. So also did Hammond, who waved. A piercing Australian bush call is an odd thing in the heart of London but that, on a July afternoon in 1948, I remember, was the last time I saw Wally Hammond, moving gracefully up the Strand as he once used to saunter from first slip to first slip.

Somebody once wrote that Hammond coming to bat was one of the sights of the cricket world – like a galleon moving along in full sale. Hammond was all grace. In moments of stress on a cantankerous turf, Bradman permitted his body some odd contortions. Once, on a wet Test pitch, he knocked his stumps over from behind against India. I used to think of Sobers as the very epitome of batting grace until one day at Port of Spain when his judgment forsook him against Sincock and his body, with legs plaited, became a convulsive question mark. I never saw anything like that happen to Hammond.

No action by him with bat, ball or in the field ever offended the eye. He was never caught off balance, or, if so, I never saw it and I saw a mighty lot of him in the middle. Once, in a Test, I snicked to slip. Ames had been injured and Paynter, standing back, was the substitute wicket-keeper. Paynter threw himself sprawling at the catch. He succeeded only in clouding Hammond's view, but, behind Paynter, Hammond took the catch inches from the ground, poised, unruffled, yet having only the merest glimmer of the ball.

Frank Woolley, who surely got out of bed on the wrong side at least this once, said in 1938 that there were thirty English batsmen as good as Hammond before the First World War. Maybe, as the politicians often say, Woolley was misquoted. O'Reilly says that Hammond was the best English batsman he bowled against – and they brought Woolley back in 1934 in England purely to negate O'Reilly, which he didn't do. O'Reilly scoffed at the suggestion that Hammond was weak on the leg stump. 'I never discovered it,' said O'Reilly, 'and I probed him there often.'

Hammond was at his commanding best in limitless Tests in Australia. In 1928 29 he made 251, 200, 177 and 119 not out. In Sydney, in 1936, he made 231 not out. No better innings by an Englishman has been played against Australia this century than his classical 240 at Lord's in 1938. It was a sunny Saturday, Lord's was crowded and Hammond, in all his majesty, made it a day of cherishable memory, even for us in the field. To field against Hammond, and especially in the covers as I did, was a rich adventure. No batsman hit the ball harder through the covers, off front and back foot, than Hammond. The ball stung the hands; it scorched the grass.

Yet it was as a killer of promising young Australian spin bowlers that Hammond excelled. He pummelled Fleetwood-Smith back four years in Melbourne although the same bowler won the Test for Australia in Adelaide in 1937 when he upset Hammond's stumps with one that whistled in from the off, so much spin did it possess. This was the ball, in the final analysis, that won that series for Australia after Allen's side had been two Tests up after two.

Hammond put young Chilvers and Campbell, both of New South Wales, out of English tours altogether, so high and hard did he hit them in Sydney games. In 1932–33, he bided his time in the final Test to hit Lee for two huge sixes on the off and so claim a special bonus for his team that was offered by an Australian firm.

Twice in Tests in Australia, when pitches were left open to the weather, he played memorable if small innings on nigh-impossible wet pitches that allowed the ball to rear and spit with spin. Such pitches, unfortunately, are no more in Australia. The critics and the cynics – the two are often synonymous – loved to see the great tested under such circumstances. Hammond had the mettle and the technique for them.

It was a pity he came once again to Australia, after the Second World War. His greatness had almost gone and he quickly fell out with Bradman, the opposing captain. This was when everybody stood aghast when umpire Borwick, who made some odd blemishes in his time, ruled that Ikin had not caught Bradman at second slip.

'A fine bloody way to begin a series, I must say,' grumbled

Hammond, when next he passed Bradman at the crease. The only time words passed between the two again on the tour was when Hammond called as Bradman tossed. It was sad that so many saw Hammond that tour for the first time. He was long past his best.

Hammond went to South Africa later and it was there he died. He suffered shocking head injuries once when his car rolled and his body was jammed in the door. Those injuries left their mark.

Hammond was truly great. There were days, and especially if he had failed with the bat, when his bowling was reminiscent of Tate. He was a superb first slip. One remembers a photograph of him batting in Sydney, making his famous cover drive. His black silk handkerchief peeped out of his trouser pocket, his muscles rippled under his billowing silk shirt. No more classical, no more correct stroke could ever have been played. It was faultless and the picture lives in the memory, so truly did it depict Hammond's grace, power and character.

7. Victor Trumper

On 28 June 1915, Victor Trumper died at Sydney in his thirty-eighth year. His funeral caused the streets of the city to be blocked and he was carried to his grave by eleven Australian cricketers. In London, in the midst of the First World War and all its momentous happenings, the event was featured on newspaper posters, as, for example, 'Death of a Great Cricketer'.

Men said then – and some in both Australia and England still say it – 'There will never be another like Vic Trumper.'

I never saw Trumper bat; I was only a few years old when he died. But so often have I listened to stories of him, so often have I seen a new light come into the eyes of people at the mention of his name, so much have I read of him, that I am prepared to believe that nobody, before or since, ever achieved the standards of batsmanship set by Trumper. Sir Pelham Warner, Warren Bardsley, Vernon Ransford and others saw all the great moderns and near-moderns – Bradman, Ponsford, Hobbs, Hammond, Hutton, Compton, McCabe and the like – yet they cast their minds back over the years and said, 'There will never be another like Vic.'

Many players, it is true, made more runs; but runs can never be accepted as the true indication of a player's greatness. A fighting innings of thirty or so under difficult conditions is lost in cold statistics, yet its merits may far outweigh many staid (and unnecessary) centuries that are recorded for all time. The longer I live, I am pleased to say, the less nationalistic I become. The outcome of a match is interesting but not, on the scales of time, of any great moment. What *is* important is whether a particular contest gives to posterity a challenge that is accepted and won, or yields in classical technique an innings or a bowling effort that makes the game richer, so that the devotee can say years afterwards, with joy in his voice, 'I saw that performance.'

Trumper went to bat one day against Victoria in Sydney on a wet pitch. The first ball from Jack Saunders (a terror on such pitches) beat him completely. Saunders's eyes lit up. His fellow-Victorians grinned in anticipation. Trumper smiled broadly. 'Why, Jack,' he called down the pitch, 'what a thing to do to an old friend. Well, it's either you or me for it.'

And then, by dazzling footwork and miraculous stroke-play, Trumper hit a century in 60 minutes.

At the beginning of 1904, in Melbourne, Trumper faced up to Rhodes and Hirst on a wet pitch. These Yorkshiremen were two of the greatest left-handed bowlers of all time and a wet Melbourne pitch was known as the worst in the world, with balls from a good length lifting quickly around the chin.

Trumper was first in and last out, for 74, in a total of 122. Hopkins made 18 and Duff 10. Noble, Syd Gregory, Trumble and Armstrong made 9 between them!

That innings caused Charles Fry, in one of his unpredictable moments, to rise suddenly from a reverie during a dinner in London and say: 'Gentlemen, charge your glasses. I give you the toast of the world's greatest batsman. Drink to Victor Trumper, first man in, last man out, on a bad pitch and against Hirst and Rhodes.'

Fry knew the full value of such an innings on such a pitch and against two skilled left-handers. His short and unexpected speech brought down the house.

No less interesting is the fact that Mrs Fry (who may or may not have had some knowledge of cricket) shared her famous husband's admiration of Trumper. My information on this point comes from the Sydney *Bulletin* of the period. It appears that Mrs Fry declared in a London periodical that Vic Trumper was an artist and that some day someone would paint his portrait and have it hung in a National Gallery. 'He will be,' the lady said, 'dressed in white, with his splendid neck bared to the wind, standing on short green grass against a blue sky; he will be waiting for the ball, the orchestra to strike up.'

Given this stimulus, the Australian poet, Victor Daley (who wrote topical verse under the name of 'Creeve Roe') broke into rhyme in the *Bulletin*. Here are examples from his seven verses entitled *Trumper*:

> *Ho Statesmen, Patriots, Bards make way!*
> *Your fame has sunk to zero:*
> *For Victor Trumper is today*
> *Our one Australian hero.*
>
> *High purpose glitters in his eye,*
> *He scorns the filthy dollar;*
> *His splendid neck, says Mrs Fry,*
> *Is innocent of collar . . .*

Is there not, haply, in the land
Some native-born Murillo
To paint, in colours rich and grand,
This Wielder of the Willow?

Nay, rather let a statue be
Erected his renown to,
That future citizens might see
The gods their sires bowed down to.

Evoe Trumper! As for me
It all ends with the moral
That fame grows on the Willow Tree
And no more on the laurel.

My formative days in cricket were spent in the Sydney suburb of Waverley. We adjoined Paddington, the club of Trumper and Noble, but we yielded to no Sydney club in the proud possession of internationals and other first-class players. Carter, all the twentieth-century Gregorys, Kippax, Hendry, Collins, Frank O'Keefe (one of our very best batsmen who, denied opportunities, went to Victoria, hit two centuries in a game against New South Wales, and then went to the Lancashire League, there dying soon afterwards) and many other proficient players figured with Waverley and established the high standards of the district. One of the great sources of the club's strength was that cricket, and talk of it, flowed through the life of the district. All the internationals I have mentioned showed themselves on the local oval at practice during the week and played there in the club games on Saturday afternoons.

Saturday evenings and Sunday mornings were given over to post-mortems. We had four grade sides, and promising youngsters, if unable to make grade, were fitted in with the Veterans team where they played under the leadership of men such as Syd Gregory, Australian captain, and Tom Howard, treasurer of the 1934 team to England.

The returning warriors, coming from their games in distant suburbs, would meticulously report in at Bondi Junction on Saturday evenings and at Waverley Park on Sunday mornings – unless, of course, dire personal disaster induced them to go to ground for a week! At those rendezvous, both players and critics gathered and form and happenings were first reported and then dissected and judged. It was a hard and discerning school of criticism. Those no longer able to play were in their element as they passed solemn judgment upon some 'shyster' or 'grubber' – Waverley terms for the lowly cricketer. Few merited the accolade of a 'great' performance. Even 'good' was seldom used. In the main, ranking varied from 'fair' to 'quite good.'

These critics – some lovely characters among them – knew their cricket. When they had disposed of the present they drifted, fondly, to the hallowed ground of the past, and always, I found, the day's reminiscences ended on Victor Trumper.

As I walked home I used to wonder how one cricketer could so capture the imagination above all others; and the imagination, moreover, of men so steeped in the game that they were the severest of critics. Yet even years after Trumper's death they spoke wistfully of him and would brook no criticism. Trumper was unique in that nobody ever criticized him as a cricketer or as a man. In England, in Australia, in South Africa, listening to men who knew and played against him, I never at any time heard a derogatory word said about Trumper.

A mark of a great man is the power of making lasting impressions upon people he meets. Winston Churchill once wrote of F. E. Smith, the first Earl of Birkenhead: 'Some men when they die after busy, toilsome, successful lives leave a great stock of scrip and securities, of acres or factories or the goodwill of large undertakings. F.E. banked his treasure in the hearts of his friends, and they will cherish his memory until their time is come.'

That could also have been written of Trumper. He left no stock or securities. He was a singularly unsuccessful businessman. He ran a sporting goods firm in the city of Sydney but he was too generous with his gifts to accumulate money. Once, on the morning of a Test, he was working in his shop and allowed time to elude him. He hurried into his coat, took down a new bat from the rack, caught a taxi to the Sydney Cricket Ground – and made 185 not out!

It has been said that this was the most brilliant and versatile innings ever played by the Master. The match was the famous one in which R. E. Foster, the Englishman, hit a brilliant 287 in his first Test and Clem Hill was concerned in the most tumultuous run-out in the history of Test cricket.

An admirer of Trumper came into his shop after the match and asked whether he could buy a bat Trumper had used.

Yes, he was told. There was the bat used in the recent Test.

The admirer's eyes sparkled. How much would it be?

'Well,' said the impractical Victor, 'it was a 45s. bat but it is now second-hand. You can have it for a pound.'

Another tale of Trumper – there are dozens – was told me by Vernon Ransford, his comrade in many Australian Elevens.

The Australians were dressing at Melbourne for a Test, against Sherwell's South Africans, when there came a knock at the door. Was Mr Trumper available?

Trumper went to the door and found a young man, a complete stranger, holding a bat. He was anxious to begin in the bat-making business. This was one of his bats and he wondered whether Mr Trumper would use it in the Test.

This usage of material is one of the niceties of 'amateur' sport. A successful player is retained to use the material of a certain sports outfitter. Not only, by his play, is he expected to bring glory and advertisement to the firm's goods, but he must also be well practised in presenting the name on his equipment whenever his photograph is being taken. Thus, when you see a triumphant winner of Wimbledon in a photograph, you have a fair chance of seeing also the name of the racquet used as the hero pushes it to the front. Strictly speaking, of course amateurs are not allowed to associate their names with sporting goods – and knowing editors now sometimes help them to observe the proprieties by blacking-out the name in the printed photograph!

That angle on sport was not developed in Trumper's day. He would have had in his bag several bats that suited him in weight and balance but, nevertheless, he didn't hesitate about accepting the young applicant's gruesome-looking bat. It weighed almost 3 lb 6 oz and it staggered his team-mates.

'Surely,' one of them said, 'you won't use that blunderbuss, Vic?'

'He's only a young chap and he's starting out in business,' replied Trumper. 'If I can get a few runs with this it might help him.'

He made 87 (probably wearying of lifting it!), inscribed it on the back with a hearty recommendation, and gave it back to the delighted young man.

Hanson Carter, the great wicket-keeper, was my first club captain. 'You must never,' he once sternly told me, 'compare Hobbs, Bradman or anybody else with Trumper. If you want to try and classify the great batsmen in the game, put Victor Trumper way up there – on his own – and then you can begin to talk about the rest.'

So, too, with Charlie Macartney, upon whose shoulders the mantle of Trumper was supposed to have descended. He revelled in talking of the things Trumper did. So did Ransford. I sat with him in his office a few years ago when he was secretary of the Melbourne Cricket Ground and he went into rhapsodies regarding the dismally wet season in England in 1902 when Trumper made 2,570 runs.

'If Vic had been greedy, it could have been 4,000,' said Ransford. 'His highest score, despite all the centuries he scored, was only 128. He could, obviously, have turned many of those centuries into double ones had he wished. But he was too generous. He looked around for some deserving character, a youngster maybe, or some player down on his luck, and unostentatiously gave him his wicket. That was Vic.'

Wisden's wrote of Trumper and that tour: 'Trumper stood alone. He put everybody else into the shade. No one, not even Ranjitsinhji has been at once so brilliant and so consistent since Dr W. G. Grace was at his best.'

The English bosie bowler, Bosanquet, clean bowled Trumper with the first bosie he sent down to him. 'Plum' Warner describes it:

It was in Sydney in 1903. Trumper and Duff had gone in first and in 35 minutes had scored 72 runs by batting, every stroke of which I remember vividly to this day. Bosanquet went on to bowl and his first ball pitched a good length just outside the off-stump. Trumper thought it was a leg-break and proceeded to cut it late, as he hoped, for four, but it came back and down went his off-stump. Subsequently, he used to 'murder' Bosanquet but it is worth recording that the first 'googly' ever bowled in Australia bowled out the man who, in spite of all the fine deeds of Don Bradman many Australians regard as the finest batsman their country has ever produced.

It is very doubtful if there has ever been a greater batsman and his wonderful deeds would have been even greater but for in-different health, which, in the end, cut short his life.

No one ever played so naturally, and he was as modest as he was magnificent. To this day in Australia, he is regarded as the highest ideal of batsmanship. He was, I think, the most fascinating bats-man I have seen. He had grace, ease, style and power and a quick-ness of foot both in jumping out and in getting back to a ball that can surely never be surpassed.

He had every known stroke and one or two of his own. When set on a good wicket it seemed impossible to place a field for him. He was somewhat slightly built, but his sense of timing was so perfect that he hit the ball with tremendous power. Most bowlers are agreed that he was the most difficult batsman to keep quiet. I have heard a great bowler remark, 'I could, in the ordinary way, keep most people from scoring quickly, but I always felt rather helpless against Trumper, for he was so quick, and he had so many strokes.'

His brilliant batting stirred cricketing England. His unrivalled skill and resource will never be forgotten. No cricketer was ever more popular, and he deserved it, for he preserved the modesty of true greatness and was the beau-ideal of a cricketer.

On one occasion, after batting brilliantly at Kennington Oval, Trumper 'ducked' an official dinner at night. The fact was, simply, that he didn't want to be talking 'shop' among cricketers and receiving plaudits. He was duly fined for missing an official engagement!

The South Africans had a quick introduction to Trumper. An Australian team called at the Union on the way home from England, where Trumper had had a most successful tour. There were opinions that Trumper wouldn't find the matting pitches of South Africa too easy and money changed hands to say that, in the few matches played there, Trumper wouldn't make a century. He hit a double-century in his very first game on the mat!

The South Africans in Australia in 1910–11 were mesmerized by his skill. This was the team with all the bosic bowlers, but Trumper cut, hooked and drove at will. He had a fascinating stroke against a fast yorker. He lifted his back foot, jabbed down on the ball with his bat at an angle and it streaked away to the square-leg boundary. Somewhat naturally, they called it the dog stroke.

He teased Percy Sherwell, the Springbok captain. When a fieldsman was shifted, Trumper deliberately hit the next ball where that man had been. He was a consummate master at placement. Later, somebody commiserated with Sherwell at having his captaincy, his bowlers and his fieldsmen torn to tatters while Trumper made 214; whereupon the Springbok said, 'Ah, don't talk about it. We have seen batting today.'

Neville Cardus, the Trumper of cricket writing, once wrote, 'The art of Trumper is like the art in a bird's flight, an art that knows not how wonderful it is. Batting was for him a superb dissipation, a spontaneous spreading of fine feathers.'

How unfortunate it is that Trumper slightly preceded the movie-camera age!

Posterity has the chance of seeing all the moderns in action, as it has of hearing all the great singing voices. Sir Robert Menzies, our former Prime Minister, has a thrilling film of Don Bradman – there are a number of copies of the same film in existence – and to see Bradman on the screen is to realize again, instantly, his great stature as a batsman. The speed of his footwork, the flay of his bat, the manner in which he 'smelt' the ball, so over the ball was his head – all this has been caught and kept for the years to come and, in the evidence of the film, there can be no possible disputation over Bradman's status in the game.

With Trumper it is different. All we have, so far as I know, are the several photographic 'stills' of him at the beginning of an off-drive and at the finish and, also, of his stance at the crease. But these do portray his art. The two of him playing the off-drive are technically perfect in every detail – his feet, his shoulders, his head, his back swing, his follow-through with the proper transfer of weight and then, finally, the full, flowing arc of the bat. His stance is perfection.

Those who saw and knew Trumper used to say that Macartney, Jackson and Kippax were reminiscent of him; but that even when they were at their greatest they served only to rekindle memories of the Great Man. He was, obviously, supreme on the field; and a man of kind and generous nature, of consideration for his fellow-man, off the field. He embodied, to those who knew him, all that was good and noble in cricket and life.

'Where would you like your field placed?' 'Plum' Warner, as captain, once asked George Hirst. And Hirst replied, 'It doesn't much matter, sir, where we put 'em. Victor will still do as 'e likes.'

The evidence, then, would seem to be conclusive. Many of Trumper's greatest innings were played in the full face of adversity, the true test of worth. He rose to heights on wet wickets where others tumbled to earth. Although some half a dozen or so players down the years could be regarded as really great, Trumper, as Carter said, merits a niche of his own. He brought to the game an artistry, a talent, and an inherent modesty not manifested by any other cricketer. In short, he possessed all the graces.

8. Jack Hobbs

Melbourne	1911–12	126 (*not out*)
Adelaide	1911–12	187
Melbourne	1911–12	178
Lord's	1912	107
Melbourne	1920–21	122
Adelaide	1920–21	123
Melbourne	1924–25	154
Adelaide	1924–25	119
Sydney	1924–25	115
Lord's	1926	119
The Oval	1926	100
Melbourne	1928–29	142

That is the Test story, in centuries, of John Berry Hobbs – later Sir Jack – against Australia. Twelve centuries, more than those of any other Englishman, against the Great Enemy!

Those centuries, of course, tell only part of the story of the man who, as Australian Test players agree, was the best batsman ever produced by England. You don't judge a cricketer by centuries alone. Quite often such a score is not nearly as valuable to a side as a 40 or 50 made in difficult circumstances – that is, when the strain is on with every pressing minute a test of temperament and resource. And Jack Hobbs was at his very best when the fight was toughest. One other important point: from his first Test match in Melbourne on 1 January 1908, to his last at his home Oval in Kennington, Surrey, in 1930, Jack Hobbs always opened the innings. He got no easy runs, after the sting was taken out of the bowling. He did his own de-stinging.

Furthermore, that long list of centuries could well have been half as long again. In his first Test innings Hobbs almost made a century. He had scored 83 in three hours of correct batsmanship when Cotter clean-bowled him. He later scored 72 in the same series in Sydney. He made a brilliant 62 not out – scoring twice as fast as the re-doubtable C. B. Fry – to push England home to a ten wickets win against Australia in a low-scoring game on a horrible pitch at

Birmingham in 1909. In 1926 he scored 88 at Leeds, 74 in the next Test at Old Trafford, 74 at Adelaide in 1929, 65 in his last Test innings in Australia at Melbourne, and 78 and 74 at Nottingham in 1930.

It is readily seen, therefore, that Hobbs, given just a little luck, could have added another half dozen or more centuries to his list against Australia.

He played in forty-one Tests against Australia and had seventy-one innings for 3,636 runs at an average of 54.23. He played in eighteen Tests against South Africa with twenty-nine innings for 1,562 runs at an average of 60.07. He had only two Tests against the West Indies, for 212 runs at an average of 106.

In all Test cricket, then, with his average not buttressed by games against India, Pakistan and New Zealand, he made 5,410 runs at an average of 56.94. His record number of first-class centuries is 197. He made 61,221 first-class runs at an average of 50.63. Although figures indicate the greatness of Hobbs they don't convey the grandeur of his batting, his faultless technique, and the manner in which he captivated those who could recognize and analyse style. Australians who played against him over the years believe cricket never produced a more correct batsman than Hobbs.

From 1907 to 1930 Hobbs batted against this imposing list of Australian bowlers: Saunders, Noble, Armstrong, Macartney, Cotter, Laver, Whitty, Hordern, Minnett, Kelleway, Gregory, Mc-Donald, Mailey, Arthur Richardson, Grimmett, Ironmonger, Oxenham, Blackie, Wall, Hornibrook, McCabe, Fairfax, and a'Beckett.

In that list there is every conceivable type of bowler – fast right and fast left, medium spinners and swervers, bosie, leg-breakers and off-breakers, cutters, seamers and top-spinners – men who bowled with a plan behind every ball or men who just relied upon their natural ability. And they were, too, players who had shrewd captains such as Noble, Clem Hill, Syd Gregory, Armstrong, Collins, Ryder and Woodfull to set fields to the best purpose.

Hobbs took them all in his century-making stride. In fact, he was 'strung up' only in the final days of his career when Bill Bowes, with a bowling intent not in keeping with his nature, gave the master a dose of bodyline on his native pitch at the Oval. Hobbs remonstrated at the wicket against such intimidatory tactics and, knowing that something alien to the spirit of cricket had entered it, he began to pack his cricket gear for good. He played Test cricket until he was 48; he played for Surrey until he was 52.

During tours of England, I used to think fondly of Hobbs, Tom

Hayward and Ranjitsinhji as I walked on various mornings across Parker's Piece to the Cambridge ground. It was on the Piece that Hobbs and Hayward first played cricket and it was there, too, that the Indian prince first began to reveal his genius to England.

Parker's Piece is a delightful stretch of green parkland but I felt unhappy there one morning in 1948 when I saw a fast bowler producing the most outrageous bumpers from a good length. Sorrowing for the well-being of the courageous batsmen who stood up to such bowling, on such a 'pitch,' I hurried into Fenner's, there to watch possibly the less-terrifying bumpers of Lindwall and Miller on a good pitch.

However, the Piece must have had much to do with the correct moulding of Hobbs's technique. Provided a young batsman has inherent ability, there is no better place to build a solid defence than on a turf that scoots, jumps and imparts abnormal break to the ball. Given too much of it, a batsman could form bad habits, such as drawing away from the ball, but the correct amount at a formative time leads to a sharpening of the eyesight, quick footwork and deft wielding of the bat. Such an experience leads the youngster to notable deeds when he finds himself on better, truer pitches.

Hobbs has acknowledged his debt to Tom Hayward in his early days – Hayward introduced him to Surrey – but it is well to note Hobbs's claim that he never had an hour's coaching in his life. He was a self-made cricketer – observing, thinking and executing for himself.

He didn't copy Hayward's stance at the wickets, although there was a similarity. Hobbs improved on Hayward's stance, which was decidedly two-eyed, with the left foot pointing almost straight up the pitch, the two shoulders round and the face practically full on to the bowler. Hobbs, like Denis Compton, had his face, and thus his right shoulder, a little fuller to the bowler than most top-ranking batsmen and herein, as with Compton, could have been the secret of his remarkable prowess in playing on-side strokes. I think that was the case, although, and in this consideration I include Compton again, Hobbs could not have played the cover-drive and the square-drive – both forward – had his body not been admirably positioned to allow of the correct backswing.

Hobbs was one of the twelve children of a groundsman at Jesus College, Cambridge. His own first job was as groundsman at Bedford School, where he also did some net-bowling against the boys. His life was thus inseparable from cricket, but he had an early set-back when he was recommended to the Essex County Club and found not good enough! Essex turned him down.

Then he tried with Surrey, was immediately accepted and in his second match scored a glorious 155 against Essex. Every run must have given him a special pleasure and, knowing that their club had spurned him, the Essex players must have had some galling thoughts at the end of that game – and forever afterwards through Hobbs's great career.

Fittingly enough, for he was years afterwards to displace the Great Man as a scorer of centuries, Hobbs played his first game for Surrey against the Gentlemen of England, captained by Dr W. G. Grace. The game of cricket was to know no greater stealer of a run than Hobbs and, facing up to Grace, he should have got off the mark with a quick single.

Hobbs, very nervous against Grace, played several balls and then played one a few yards up the pitch. He quickly sensed there was a run to be 'stolen' but just as he began his run the quavery voice of the Doctor came down the pitch: 'Thank you, youngster, just tap it back here and save my poor old legs.'

And Hobbs, suitably impressed by the Old Man, who was a terror to the game's newcomers, tapped the ball back to him. He made 18 in the first innings and 88 in the second.

Hobbs played for Surrey against Darling's great Australian side of 1905. He batted beautifully against Cotter, then at his fastest, and he reached 94 when a thrilling throw-in by Clem Hill from the Kennington Oval boundary hit the stumps and ran him out. It was a compliment Hobbs often returned to the Australians. Perhaps the greatest cover-point ever – quick in anticipation, swift to the ball and unerring in his under-the-shoulder return – he had 15 run-outs on his second tour of Australia in 1912.

No cover-point can ever be considered great unless he has deft, twinkling footwork. As the ball speeds towards him, cover-point must be on the way in to meet it, for a split second thus gained could bring the run-out and, moreover, he should so position his movements in to the ball that he is, immediately, ready to receive the ball and throw it to the desired end with one action. A champion cover-point must possess an additional sense. He must sense what the batsmen are doing, for his own eyes never leave the ball. He must, too, be a 'fox', yielding a single here and there to snare the batsman into a feeling of safety and, when his chance comes, cover-point must be able to hit the stumps from side-on pretty often. Jack Hobbs had the lot – all the tricks.

Hobbs's Test career against Australia was preceded by disappointment. A. O. Jones brought the English side to Australia in 1907 with Hobbs making his first trip. Jones became ill on the eve of the First Test in Sydney and Hobbs seemed certain to get the position. But the selectors did an odd thing, although it was to prove most successful. George Gunn, of Nottinghamshire, had travelled with the team on a health trip and he was asked to play, instead of Hobbs.

Hobbs was not only bitterly disappointed; he thought he had been badly treated, even though Gunn proved the hero of the game, scoring 119 and 74 in a masterly manner in his first Test. Anyway, Hobbs almost equalled the century feat with 83 in the following Test in Melbourne. Gunn headed the Test averages of the tour, 462 at an average of 51.33, and Hobbs was second with 302 runs at 43.14. Together, Gunn and Hobbs put on 134 in the final Test in Sydney. It was a partnership, according to those who saw it, which hasn't been excelled, for classical batsmanship, by any other two Englishmen in Australia.

Hobbs went home to make a 'duck' in his first Test innings against the Australians in England. The Birmingham pitch then was helpful to bowlers. Blythe and Hirst ran through Australia for the meagre total of 74. Hobbs opened for England but Macartney, with the new ball, had him quickly lbw. Marcartney also bowled MacLaren for 5 and Fry for a 'duck'. But in the second innings Hobbs made a brilliant 62 not out, top score for the match – and England won by ten wickets. His stroke play was classical, so much so that Englishmen described it as the best since Vic Trumper's performances of 1902.

That was a time of outstanding batting strength in English cricket. There were so many men of brilliance knocking at the Test door that those inside could barely afford to fail. Yet, with his own place by no means assured, Hobbs was responsible at Leeds for what the Australians thought was a remarkable gesture.

The captain, M. A. Noble, told the story thus:

Hobbs forced a ball off his back foot between short-leg and mid-on. In doing so, he knocked off one of the bails. Believing that it was done in the act of making the stroke we appealed for hit wicket, but the umpire gave him not out on the ground that he had completed the stroke before his foot touched the stump.

Two or three balls later Hobbs made a weak attempt to play a straight one and was bowled. My impression was then – and still is – that Hobbs believed himself legally to be out and deliberately allowed himself to be bowled. It is a most difficult thing to allow yourself to be bowled without betraying the fact to the bowler or someone fielding near the wicket. It was a match of small scores and the loss then of a player of Hobbs's ability probably had a determining influence upon our success in that game.

Another Australian captain who spoke in warm terms of Hobbs's outstanding sportsmanship was H. L. Collins. Hobbs gave himself out at Kennington Oval against the Australians after the umpire had said not out. Few Test cricketers down the years have done that. Most accept an umpire's blunder when it is their way on the principle that they are sometimes given out when they are not.

As I have said, Hobbs's greatness as a batsman lay not only in the fact that he got many runs with incredible consistency but also in the manner in which he made them. He was perfect in the execution of every stroke. His footwork was a model for all players and his style was irreproachable. He was always attractive to watch – a neat, compact figure, faultlessly attired in flannels – whether he was moving along at a fast rate or was on the defensive.

I asked him once which innings he considered the best he had played in Australia.

'Well,' he replied, 'it's a long time since I retired from first-class cricket, twenty-three years, and it was five years earlier that I last played in Australia. Memory grows dim. Quite naturally, I suppose, on being asked which was my best innings, I try to recall which was the best of the nine Test centuries I scored in your country. There was that one in 1912 when I made 178 and along with Wilfred Rhodes put on 323 for the first wicket. England won the rubber by winning that match.

'Then there was the 122 in the second Test at Melbourne in 1921, made for the most part on a rain-damaged wicket: but we lost that match. Both of those innings gave me a lot of pleasure because I felt that I had played pretty well – if I may, with modesty, say so.'

I put it to him that an achievement that will never be forgotten in Australia was the 49 he made in England's second innings of the third Test in Melbourne of the 1928–29 tour.

'Yes,' he agreed, 'perhaps it would be wise to select that innings as England won the match against all the odds. You would be surprised at the number of Aussies who mention that match when they call to see me in Fleet Street. Just the same as folk here speak about the fifth Test at the Oval in 1926 – another 'sticky.' (Hobbs made a brilliant 100 on this later occasion, England winning back the Ashes.)

He continued: 'I well remember waiting in Melbourne for the wicket to dry so that we could continue the match. Australia still had two wickets to fall. I can recall very well how our friends came to the pavilion to commiserate with us, saying what a pity it was the rain came. We thought so, too. We considered we didn't have a chance of getting the runs. That old campaigner Hughie Trumble, then secretary of the Melbourne Cricket Club, told us in all seriousness that 70 would be a good score in our second innings. Well, as you know, we chased 332 and eventually won by three wickets. Our success caused quite a stir at home. I remember that a London newspaper cabled out £100 each to Herbert Sutcliffe and myself.'

It was the opening partnership of 105 between Hobbs and Sutcliffe that enabled England to win that match. Not only was it rich in runs but it defied the Australian attack on one of the worst wickets known in Melbourne. Considering the difficulties, that opening partnership would possibly rank as the most outstanding one in Test history.

The wicket was bad all day, going through different phases. Thirty points of rain had fallen and the English innings began in gentle sunshine, increasing in intensity and drying the pitch in patches so that there were spots off which the ball kicked disconcertingly. It was at its most dangerous period from lunch to the tea interval.

The Australians had no fast bowler in this match, the opening bowlers, Hendry and a'Beckett, being no more than medium-pace, but there was an abundance of varied spin in Oxenham (medium off-breaks), Grimmett (leg-breaks) and Blackie (slow to slow-medium off-breaks).

On such a pitch against such spinners, the English task should have been an impossible one but, right from the beginning, the two great opening batsmen dominated the pitch and the Australians.

For over after over, Blackie bowled around the wicket with a packed leg-side field, but by superb dead-bat play and adept pad-play, together with the most astute judgment in not playing at the ball when it wasn't necessary, Hobbs and Sutcliffe went on for one hour, then two hours and finally came to tea with the score 0–78 – Hobbs 36 and Sutcliffe 32. The whole members' stand rose to them in acclamation.

In effect, the leg-theory tactics of the Australians played into the hands of two such proficient batsmen. Ryder, fast-medium, often hit the body but never seemed likely to hit the stumps. Both batsmen were black and blue on the body – Hobbs was once hit on the head by Ryder – but they never flinched, even though the sharply rising balls yielded many byes off Oldfield's body. Indeed, one ball from Oxenham rose so sharply off a length that it cleared Oldfield's head (the keeper was standing up to the stumps) for two byes. Three successive balls from Oxenham particularly revealed the conditions – one rose high and went from Oldfield's gloves to first slip, the next hit Sutcliffe on the shoulder and the next went for a bye off Oldfield's shoulder.

While Hendry was bowling, Richardson, Blackie, Ryder, Bradman and a'Beckett formed a complete circle of under ten yards diameter around the batsman from silly-point to forward short-leg.

The two Englishmen on that day demoralized the Australian bowling, the fielding and the captaincy of Ryder. They gave their usual superb lesson of running between the wickets. One never let the other down. This was exemplified time after time in their calling and acceptance; many of the runs, of a seemingly dangerous nature at the beginning, being completed at a walk. Once, Hobbs walked out of his crease several yards before Blackie bowled and placed him to the on for two.

The century came in 133 minutes. Just before this the old field-marshal, Hobbs, using the stratagem of signalling for a bat, sent a message to Chapman in the pavilion to change his batting order, sending Jardine in next before Hammond.

It was a shrewd piece of advice. Hobbs went lbw to Blackie at 49, but at stumps England were 1–171 – Sutcliffe 83 and Jardine 18. There were 13 byes in that total. Commenting on this in England, Strudwick said: 'A wet wicket in Melbourne is about the worst of its kind, especially for the wicket-keeper. The ball does all sorts of funny things.'

In short, the old firm of Hobbs and Sutcliffe, making their eighth opening stand of a century against the Australians, out-generalled and out-played Ryder and his men. The next day, with three wickets falling for 14 after the match was all but won, England took the honours by three wickets. Sutcliffe played perhaps his greatest innings, 6½ hours for 135 – but undoubtedly it was that opening stand that won the match.

Hobbs found his first great opening partner for England in Wilfred Rhodes and it was fitting that another Yorkshireman, Sutcliffe, should have been his second. Hobbs and Rhodes made a record 221 for the first wicket against South Africa in Cape Town in 1910: and in Melbourne in 1912 they put on 323 against Australia. This still stands as a record for Tests between England and Australia.

Hobbs was at his best in Melbourne, as his records show. In 1926, after Australia had hit a record first innings tally of 600, one London newspaper announced on its placard: 'Australia 600: Come on Hobbs!' With Sutcliffe, Hobbs batted all the next day, the opening being worth 283. The same newspaper said on its placard next day: 'Thank you Hobbs!'

I am glad to know Jack Hobbs and to have seen him bat though, incidentally, my feelings as a youngster at Sydney were mixed one day when I saw Oldfield catch him on the leg-side off Gregory for none – a catch off a leg-glance, the greatest wicket-keeping catch and shrewdest example of co-operation between bowler and keeper that I have seen.

Good to have seen Jack Hobbs bat? Why, much better than that, I once opened an innings with him. He had retired two years from Test cricket and was in Australia on a writing assignment. We both played for the press against the Australian Navy at Rushcutters Bay, Sydney, and I knew no prouder moment in cricket than when I walked through the gate to open the innings with the Master. I recall very clearly the neat manner in which he tapped a ball off the very first delivery and we finished the run at a walk, so superbly had he placed the single.

On 16 December 1957, Sir Jack celebrated his seventy-fifth birthday in London, being entertained at a no-speeches lunch in a London tavern organized by the Master's club – for he was, indeed, the Master. At the lunch were Sir Pelham (Plum) Warner, George Gunn, who kept Hobbs out of that first Test in Sydney fifty years before, 'Tich' Freeman, George Geary, Patsy Hendren, Jack Crawford, Peter May and others who delighted in the presence of the Master – still erect and well, his eyes full of good humour and love of his fellow man.

In tours of England, one of my greatest pleasures is to see Sir Jack of a Test Saturday in the various press-boxes. His notes on the game appear in a Sunday newspaper so that a Saturday is his sole appearance with us, but it is a joy to see him, to greet him and have a few words. Like his stroke-making, there is nothing uppish about Sir Jack. He is everybody's friend, and I think he appreciates that as much as his great string of records and figures.

'Figures,' an admirer once wrote of Hobbs, 'can convey no idea of the Master, of his full-blooded hooking when he was young, of his driving on light, swift feet, of his peerless square-cut, of his leaning leg-glance, of the natural growth of his talents to a quite regal control and superiority.'

There was all that and success, too, as I have stressed, when the fight was hardest, when the pitch was cranky. Somebody once aptly observed that it was Hobbs who took the description 'unplayable' out of the category of pitches.

Recently Douglas Jardine, who saw many great batsmen at close quarters, was asked to name the greatest. He didn't hesitate. 'Hobbs,' said Jardine, 'is number one every time. He was so good on bad pitches.' The interviewer interposed another name. Jardine looked out of the window – and refused to answer.

9. Bill Ponsford

Many cricketers have had their name blazoned on news-posters *after* the event, but William Harold Ponsford, of Victoria, is probably the only one in history to have his name on posters *before* the event. It happened to him in Sydney early in January 1928, following the most remarkable month known to a cricketer in Australia. And nothing remotely resembling it has happened since.

I am not hot on statistics but I think Ponsford's 1,146 runs in December 1927, made in five innings at an average of 229.20, must be the outstanding batting performance for a month in all time. His innings were 133, 437 (breaking his own world record score of 429), 202, 38 and 336. These scores were the end of a string of eleven centuries in eleven consecutive matches in Australia. The others were 102 in 1925–26; 214 and 54, 151, 352, 108 and 84, 12 and 110 in 1926–27; and 131 and 7 before the flood of runs surged in full force in that December of 1927.

It was all this that led to Ponsford being 'postered'. With a rare touch of business acumen, the New South Wales Cricket Association did something hitherto unknown in the game. It had big posters printed and tied to telegraph-posts in the city and suburbs. They hit Sydney in the eye. Across the top was the one name: PONSFORD. Underneath ran: COME TO THE CRICKET GROUND AND SEE THE WORLD'S GREATEST BATSMAN.

The invitation was cordially accepted. Interest in a cricketer or a team is always gauged at the Sydney nets before a big game begins. If the interest is there, many spectators crowd behind the nets and the hundreds who came to watch Ponsford at the nets were astounded at how wide his bat seemed. The ball never seemed to get past it. The attendance over the match was 67,614 and the gate-takings £4,604. Both were records for a Sheffield Shield match in Sydney but there the records ended. Ponsford made only six runs in the first innings and two in the second. As was sometimes his habit against fast bowlers, he shuffled to the off against Jack Gregory, leaving his leg-stump open to be hit. Gregory also figured in his dismissal in the second innings, taking a sensational catch at first slip.

Nevertheless, it wasn't often Ponsford failed and this was one of the two worst first-class games he knew in Australia, the other being the 1928 Brisbane Test. He had leapt into the headlines in the 1922–23 Australian season when he made 429 against Tasmania – not a Sheffield Shield state but enjoying a first-class status – and that score eclipsed A. C. MacLaren's 424, which had stood since 1895 as the world's record first-class score.

Five years later, again on his home ground of Melbourne, Ponsford improved on his own record by making 437, this time against Queensland and in a Sheffield Shield match. Bradman, however, was now coming over the horizon and Ponsford's record stood for only two years when Bradman toppled it (also against Queensland) with 452 not out in Sydney.

Not even Bradman equalled Ponsford's feat of making two first-class scores of over 400. Aptly, in a sense, Ponsford retired from cricket after the 1934 tour of England, during which he teamed with Bradman to put on 451 in the Oval Test (Ponsford 266, Bradman 244) and 388 at Leeds (Ponsford 181, Bradman 304). These partnerships, in order, were for the second and fourth wickets and are record ones in the Australia–England series. They were the only occasions on which Australia's great record-breakers got together in Tests as a 'firm', although this was something that had been eagerly awaited since Bradman shot into the records' list in the late 1920s.

As was to be the case with Bradman later, Ponsford had his wings clipped by Larwood. The speedy Englishman scattered his stumps for two in the first innings of the first Test at Brisbane and had him caught behind the wicket for six in the second innings. In the first innings of the next Test in Sydney, Ponsford had made only five when a ball from Larwood fractured a bone in his hand. Ponsford played no more in that series. He was left to lament some 'famous last words' that appeared under his name at the beginning of that season in a Melbourne newspaper. 'Larwood,' it had been written by Ponsford, 'is not really a fast bowler.'

There was talk, afterwards, that the lines of communication between Ponsford and his ghost-writer had become jangled. No one who played against Larwood at that period of time would have wittingly written such a false impression and Larwood more than rubbed the opinion into Ponsford.

Ponsford returned to make his favourite Test score of 110 at the Oval in 1930; but Larwood loomed again in the next series in Australia – the bodyline one. Larwood clean-bowled him for 32 in the first Test in Sydney; Voce clean-bowled him for two in the second innings. Ponsford, remarkably, was dropped for the next Test, appearing in the incongruous role of drink-waiter. He played an extremely plucky innings of 85 in the following Test at Adelaide – that match of extreme bitterness – and then was shot out for three, by Larwood, in the second innings. Larwood bowled him for 19 at Brisbane and caught him for nil off Allen in the second innings.

That was the end of Ponsford's Test career in Australia – the selectors clean-bowling him before the final Test – and it is to be mentioned that when he flowered again in England in 1934, Larwood was out of court at Lord's. As was Voce, also.

Larwood, obviously, gave Ponsford much anxiety, and there was certainly substance in the claim that fast bowlers – the best of them, that is – sometimes found a chink in his armour on the leg-stump. They caused his footwork to stutter, which no slow bowler did.

Indeed, it can be fairly said that from the 1920s onward the game knew no better batsman than Ponsford against slow bowling. O'Reilly once told me that he would sooner bowl against Bradman than Ponsford. He gave himself some chance of breaking through Bradman's defence – sound as it undoubtedly was – but the job against Ponsford always struck him as being virtually hopeless. As I saw them, I would have thought the job of a slow bowler against either Bradman or Ponsford was virtually hopeless.

Like all famous Australian batsmen, Ponsford came into cricket of a good class in his middle-teens. He was a few days short of sixteen when he played his first game for St Kilda, in the Melbourne pennant competition. He made an immediate impression with sound defence, an equable temperament, and a marked keenness for the game. Yet, strangely in the case of one who later was to make such mammoth scores, the century eluded him time and again in the pennant games.

He scored well, ranging from the 60s on to (once) 99; but he still had not made a pennant century when he was chosen, at the age of 20, to play against Johnnie Douglas's MCC team of 1920–21. He wasn't a success. He made only 6 and 19 and, the Victorian selectors having a reputation for conservatism, he went back to pennant cricket again.

In the season of 1921–22 he gave the Tasmanians a taste of what was ahead, making 162, and in the next summer came that record 429 against them. Ponsford immediately became news. He moved up into the Victorian Shield team again, this time to stay until he himself called enough in 1934. There was still much good batting left in Ponsford when he put his bat away at thirty-four years of age.

He played his first Shield game against South Australia and made 108 and 17. He played his first Test against England the next season, 1924–25, and, as in the Shield game, began with a century. He says to this day that it was the hardest-earned century he ever made.

I was twenty-four and a very nervous young man. I never seem to remember with much accuracy about dates and scores but that day on the Sydney Cricket Ground, 19 December, 1924, although now so many years behind me, is as fresh today and memorable.

Maurice Tate was a big-shouldered, fifteen-stone giant, with a deceptively short run. He came in flat-footed and swung his arm over. He was not of express speed and I thought I had sighted the ball well. I made my stroke. The ball swung a little, hit the pitch, and fizzed through like a flat pebble ricochetting on a pond. It beat me, beat the stumps, beat Strudwick, the wicket-keeper, and hummed away for four byes.

The next ball, I swore, would not do the same humiliating thing. It did – only this time Struddy took it. The third ball I watched as if it were a bomb. But again it swung at the last moment, came off the pitch with blinding speed, went through me and the wicket-keeper as well and went off for four more byes. 'Tich' Freeman was bowling at the other end. I got a four from one of his leg-breaks and was so relieved at missing a 'blob' in my first Test innings that my confidence, so shattered by Tate, returned and I made a century, which I think was chanceless. We won the match, on the seventh day, by 195 runs.

Thus Ponsford told his story many years afterwards, but he omitted some important details. Batting at the other end was Herbie Collins, the Australian skipper. Those who saw Ponsford make his shaky start against Tate (the sheen had gone from the ball, Ponsford coming first wicket down with the score at 46), will remember how Collins strolled up to him at the end of the over, talked with him, and then kept Tate to himself until the young Ponsford had settled down and got his bearings.

This, so they say, was a classical example of how one man can make a century for another if he has the ability, the intelligence and the team-spirit to protect somebody in trouble.

Maurice Tate, that day (he told me afterwards), almost shed tears of frustration because Collins kept Ponsford away from him. Ponsford made 110 in that first Test innings against England; Collins that innings made 114.

Collins, speaking of the occasion, said he would prefer it if I did not use the actual words of the conversation he had with Ponsford at the end of Tate's over to him, but he said he would always remember Ponsford's gesture when he returned to the dressing-room after his innings. The team made much fuss, naturally, over Ponsford's century debut, but he postponed the slaps on the back and the handshakes and went across to Collins to shake his hand. 'This chap,' said Ponsford, 'deserves most of the credit'.

Which reminds me that on the same ground, which was my home one, I almost made a 'blob' first ball against Larwood and in my first Test innings against England. I had run him away for what I thought was a safe single, but when halfway down the pitch, I saw my running partner with his hand up, countermanding my call. I turned, scrambled, and finally dived, narrowly escaping being run out. One or two of our chaps, in that series, had no great desire to get down to the business-end of Larwood's bowling!

Ponsford made another century in his first Test series of 1924–25 – 128 in the second Test in Melbourne – and he finished the five games with the excellent figures of 468 runs at 46.80. Yet, strangely, he never again scored another Test century against England in Australia. Like many others, he was eclipsed by Bradman's incredible scoring in the Tests in England in 1930 – Ponsford made 330 Test runs at 55 an innings and Bradman 974 at 139.

Ponsford finished his Test career with a blaze of glory in 1934. Whereas on his first trip, in 1926, he made only 37 runs in three Test innings, on his final tour he made 569 at an average of 94.83; and in so doing he shaded even Bradman, whose figures were 758 at 94.75. Yet it is to be repeated – which is an important point in relation to both Ponsford and Bradman – there was no Larwood and no Voce in 1934. Both were stood down by Marylebone as an aftermath to bodyline.

Ponsford was a truly great player. He crouched a little at the crease, the peak of his cap pulled characteristically towards his left ear; he tapped the ground impatiently with his bat while awaiting the ball, and his feet were so eager to be on the move that they began an impulsive move forward just before the ball was bowled. This was the shuffle that sometimes took him across the pitch against a fast bowler, possibly the better to force him to the on-side yet, in the doing, leaving his leg stump peeping out. This aside, his footwork was perfection. I never saw a better forcer of the ball, and that wide of mid-on.

He used an extremely heavy bat – he called it 'Big Bertha' – and an umpire with an inquisitive mind was delighted at Sydney one morning, the morning of the 'Poster' game, to put Ponny's bat to the width gauge and found it wouldn't pass. So Ponsford had to put aside a favourite bat, which, obviously, had spread itself with the constant meeting of the ball full in the belly.

Ponsford could play every orthodox stroke in the game and he added a few unorthodox ones of his own. Those who knew him closely over the years detected a change in his shoulders late in his career – he turned his right more to the bowler – and, whereas he was a strong cutter of the ball in his early days, towards the end he showed a partiality for the on-side. But he never stood two-eyed, as Kelleway and Ryder did.

Ponsford's retirement shocked Australia. He had made 266 in his last Test but I am sure the retirement of Woodfull (and the sapping of all the big scores he had made) influenced him to give the game away.

Woodfull and Ponsford were given a testimonial match in Melbourne in 1934. Woodfull, later to become a leading Headmaster in Melbourne, had announced his retirement and, during the course of the game, Ponsford also announced that he would play no more.

The two Bills, Woodfull and Ponsford, 'Wo' and 'Po', had been batting partners for years for Victoria and Australia and, off the field, were close friends. Woodfull always called Ponsford 'Ponny'; and Ponsford called Woodfull 'Woody'. I never heard either address the other in any other way. Their records, too, were strikingly similar: Ponsford 13,819 runs, Woodfull 13,392, each at an average of 65. Woodfull made 49 first-class centuries and Ponsford 47. In Tests, Ponsford made 2,122 runs at 48; Woodfull 2,300 at 46. Each hit seven Test centuries.

For one so gifted, Ponsford worried a lot over cricket. The ones who glibly think that a player can stand up unceasingly to the demands of big cricket, have never played big cricket themselves. He worried if he heard it raining during the night or during a match, though he was more proficient than most Australians on a bad pitch. He worried, too, whether he would be chosen in Test teams or to tour. Larwood worried him; Bradman, too, I think, worried him because Bradman came so soon after all those Ponsford records which had taken so much out of him and he didn't have the wish to compete with Bradman. Nor, I fancy, after Woodfull, did Ponsford appreciate the thought of playing under Bradman's captaincy.

Accordingly, those closest to Ponsford were not really surprised when he put away his cricket gear and took out his fishing rod. He was always a keen fisherman; indeed, during one Test he could not field because he had fished on the Sunday and sun-burned his feet. In the post-war period, he agreed grudgingly to play in a match with many of his former international comrades but when the time came, he went fishing instead. He just couldn't bring himself to come back to the game, however minor the match. Chasing records, no doubt, had left him with cricket regurgitation.

Ponsford had a strong sense of humour. He was full of satirical fun in the dressing-room, and he made a typical remark in the war period when he was being examined for service and was found to be, of all things, colour blind – a fact which he had never known. He could not distinguish red from green and the puzzled doctor asked him how he had known when the new ball had lost its red sheen when he was batting.

'Well,' said Ponsford, 'I suppose I always knew that a ball was new and red at the start of an innings. When it became worn, I never worried what colour it was – only how big it looked to me.'

Most bowlers will say that Ponsford batted as if the ball were as big as a football and that his bat was much too wide. He would be, for a certainty, the best all-round batsman Victoria has produced.

10. Charlie Macartney

I still recall the intense thrill I knew one Sydney day when, passing between two of the Members' stands, I caught a glimpse of the middle and saw Charlie Macartney. He stood erect in the popping crease, his guard just taken, his bat aloft and twirling vigorously in his hands as if seeking a charge of electricity from the air – and many a bowler and fieldsman often thought it had been super-charged.

Charlie Macartney in the middle was a defiant, dogmatic, domineering imp of a batsman. He had a strong, jutting chin. He had alert, brown, twinkling eyes that roved the field to pin-point the openings. He had thick, hairy wrists – tremendously strong – that enabled him to crack his bat at the ball as if it were a whip. He was chockful of batting impertinence and the very sight of him at the wickets was one of the beauties of the cricketing world. He was artistic in his conception of what strokes could be played; he was a wizard at executing them.

They called Charlie the 'Governor-General'. I asked many of his contemporaries how he got the name but none could tell me. Surely, it arose from the lordly mien with which he came to bat. He entered the field with the air of one about to inspect the ranks, conscious of his own top-rank and not prepared to put up with any nonsense from anybody.

He played his first series against England in Australia in 1907–08, but he was no sensation then, nor was he when he made his first tour of England in 1909. He was then a member of the chorus, not a *prima donna*, and he once batted as low as No. 10. Nevertheless, everybody knew whom Victor Trumper meant when, returning from England in 1909, he said: 'We are to lose the "Governor-General". He's going to New Zealand.'

Trumper didn't mean that he had had a hot tip from the Palace that the second Earl of Dudley, then the Australian Governor-General, was moving on. He was breaking the news that C. G. Macartney intended to live, in future, in New Zealand.

Luckily for Australia, Macartney stayed in Australia and that, possibly, was for the good of cricket also, because Macartney might not have blossomed on the dubious pitches of the Isles across the

Tasman. Even so, he was slow to blossom in his homeland. Some seventeen years were to pass before he reached the zenith of his career. That occurred in England, in 1926, when he was forty years of age.

Australia has had three individual batting triumphs of the highest magnitude in England. They were achieved by Trumper (1902), Macartney (1926) and Bradman (1930); and an interesting point is that in their vintage years, Trumper was twenty-five and Bradman twenty-two. It is curious, therefore, that Macartney should have known his English triumph at forty, an age when a player is fast tumbling down the hill, if he has not already reached the bottom.

In Macartney's case the apparent anomaly was a consequence of what the cricket world missed from him owing to First World War and the various illnesses and injuries Macartney suffered when Englishmen were in Australia after that war. He played in only two Tests against J. W. H. T. Douglas's side in 1920–21 – making a scintillating 170 at Sydney. He did not play at all in the Tests in Australia four years later.

Macartney went to England with the unhappy Australian team of 1912 – the side that went without the Big Six, Trumper, Carter, Cotter, Armstrong, Ransford and Hill – but there was no edge to that tour. Macartney played the outstanding innings of the series, 99 at Lord's, and the manner of his dismissal typified the man and his outlook on cricket. Most Test batsmen, on 99, would creep towards their century like a cat-burglar towards his objective. Not so Macartney. He tried to hit F. R. Foster into St John's Wood Road.

'And I should have done, too,' said Macartney afterwards. 'Damn full toss. Made a mess of it.'

In his halcyon days, Macartney's stroking was pungent, crisp, deliberate. It was not always so. His cricket seems to have undergone violent evolution, for he was noted as a stonewaller when he entered Sydney grade cricket. A critic of those days, Frank Iredale (who had Test experience behind him) wrote that Macartney had an ugly, defensive style. That amazes those who saw him at his greatest, but that it should have been written of him is proof that his batting underwent a vivid metamorphosis.

In the beginning, he was a better left-hand bowler than a right-hand batsman. Whereas he averaged only 18 in Tests in his first tour of 1909, he was second in the bowling with 16 wickets, averaging 16. At Leeds, where he was to win immortality 17 years later, he took 7–58 in the first innings and 4–27 in the second. Nor did he have any accepted position in the batting order. He went up and down, like a painter on a ladder. He was chosen against A. O. Jones's team in 1907–08 as an all-rounder and batted No. 7. About this time, Duff was lost to Trumper as an opener – no doubt they were Australia's best opening pair of all time – and Macartney opened with Trumper in the next Test. He was moderately successful and again opened in the last Test; but in 1912 he found his position-by-right in the batting order and to the end of his Test days he batted first-wicket down for Australia.

I asked him once which batting position he liked best. Back cracked the answer, snapped in his usual aggressive manner of speaking: 'Opening up. If you get on top of an attack early, you are on top for the rest of the innings. And if the first ball of the Test asks to be hit for six, why you just hit it for six.'

That was his pugnacious philosophy, but he was expounding it long after his Test career had ended. It's not a philosophy one would recommend to a young batsman beginning a Test career as an opening batsman. I know how selectors would react if a batsman was out trying to hit the first ball in a Test for six!

Macartney held that every ball had a look on its face as it came down the pitch to him. 'It was labelled,' he said, 'either 1, 2, 3, 4 or 6. I leave out the 5. Too damn far to run.'

He left out, too, it will be noticed, the defensive stroke for none. Charlie didn't believe it even existed. He held that every ball bowled was punishable.

I once opened an innings with Charlie and I walked out on air. A grand old character named Jimmy Searle, every finger and thumb broken and knarled from years of wicket-keeping, was the New South Wales coach and Jimmy ran mid-week matches on the Cricket Ground No. 2. His team would play against the various Junior teams of Sydney. Many a Test player came up through these games and they were all the more enjoyable for the young in that Macartney, Kelleway, Kippax, Oldfield and other retired or active Test players would often turn out for the 'Colts'.

This particular day I was transported into delight, awe and reverence as I walked out with the great Macartney to open an innings. It was, for me, a most sacred occasion.

'I'll take strike, son,' said Charlie. 'And keep your eyes open for the first ball.'

I did, indeed. I thought the Great Man meant that he would be off for a quick, stolen single and I was doubly anxious to do his bidding. I was just leading down the pitch when the ball came back like a meteorite. I fell to earth; the bowler fell to earth; the umpire did likewise. We were all prone on the ground, as if in an air-raid, as the ball crashed into the pickets.

I picked up my dishevelled self and walked down the pitch to Mr Macartney. 'It's always a good idea,' he told me, tapping his forehead in the middle, 'to aim the first ball right here at the bowler's head. They don't like it. It rattles 'em.'

It was the same man who rattled Macaulay – and England – at Leeds in 1926.

Unknown to the English, the Australians that year held a very high opinion of G. G. Macaulay, the Yorkshire spinner and seamer. He didn't play for his county against the Australians (he played instead in a Test trial), and the Australians were apprehensive about him when he was chosen for the third Test at Leeds, Macaulay's home ground.

It was seldom Macartney feared a bowler, but he did Macaulay. 'This bloke,' said Macartney, on the eve of the Test, 'could go through us. There's no better bowler in England. I want permission to "murder" him immediately.'

Collins, the captain, was ill and Bardsley was the Australian skipper for the Test.

'You don't often talk like this, Charlie,' said Bardsley.

'No, but I know just what Macaulay can do to us if we don't nobble him first.'

So Bardsley agreed to let Macartney have his way against Macaulay.

It is well to know this background because it gave rise to one of the most brilliant innings in the history of cricket.

There were storms during the night and the groundsmen switched to a new pitch next day because the original one had been flooded under the covers. The Australians gathered in an anxious band around the pitch while the English were having trouble in the pavilion finalizing their team – and also discussing with Carr, no doubt, what he should do if he won the toss.

The three Australian selectors – Bardsley, Macartney and Ryder – locked themselves in a bathroom while they finalized their team. They, too, had to discuss what they would do if they won the toss. Carr won the toss and put Australia in. That decision by Carr was to become one of the most criticized in Test history this century. I don't think Carr ever lived it down – although he would have been very consoled had he known that Bardsley would have sent the English in had he won the toss.

What made Carr's decision seem illogical was that, although he sent the Australians in, the left-hand bowler, Parker, had been dropped from the English side. Perhaps the Englishmen gambled on losing the toss!

The sun was out as the match began but it soon withdrew, which didn't help Carr. He probably thought that sun on the wet pitch would cause it to 'bite'. It never did.

Bardsley was out first ball of the match – something that had happened only once previously when, 31 years earlier, MacLaren fell to Coningham in Melbourne. Sutcliffe caught Bardsley low at first slip off Tate. I can well imagine how the excitable Yorkshiremen would have greeted that!

In strode Macartney. He glided Tate's third ball through the slips for two, but then, horror of horrors for England, he snicked the fifth ball of the opening over to Carr in the slips – and the English skipper mulled the catch! Poor Carr! That became the most publicized missed catch in all Test history by the day's end. Australia, instead of being two down for two in the first over, didn't lose the next wicket until 235.

Had Carr taken that catch, it was not inconceivable that Australia could have been all out by lunch. And the missed catch, following upon Carr's decision to send Australia in, made Carr the most miserable cricketer in all England at the day's end.

It is so simple to drop a catch and, more often than not, it is the simple ones that are missed. Some say Colin Bland, the Rhodesian, is the most brilliant fieldsman cricket has known but I can never forget how Bland, in Melbourne once, put Redpath down off a juicy little sitter to short-leg just after the innings had begun. Redpath went on to almost a century.

The best a fieldsman can do is practise, practise, practise catching so that his fingers, loose and supple, will time the ball and close instinctively on the catch when it comes. If his fingers are stiff and taut, stiff with anxiety and endeavour, the ball rejects the fingers and out it pops. Possibly, Carr tried too hard, or perhaps he didn't properly sight the ball against the dark background of the crowd.

Macaulay, playing his first Test against Australia, opened the bowling from the pavilion end. His first delivery was a no-ball, which Woodfull hit for a single. Up came Macartney. He took guard, studied the field, twirled his bat, cocked his front foot to the bowler, as was his wont, and hit Macaulay for two to the off. The next ball he slammed almost for six, over mid-off. The 'murdering' of Macaulay had begun.

The Leeds crowd, which had uttered an agonized 'Oh' when Carr dropped Macartney, now began to exclaim 'Ah' as Macartney unfolded his artistry. He smacked Macaulay for two more fours next over and in 40 minutes, Australia had 50 up – 40 to Macartney. The 100 came up in 79 minutes, Macartney's share being 83. In only 103 minutes, Macartney scored a century, the first batsman since Trumper to hit a Test century before lunch. (Four years later, and also at Leeds, Bradman was to hit a century before lunch, a century before afternoon tea and end up with 309 before stumps.)

At lunch, Macartney was 112 and Woodfull 40. After lunch, the 'Governor-General' went on and on, using his bat like a merciless flail. A field that had closed in on him in the first over of the day and had been expelled in the second, didn't close in again for three hours. Macartney dominated the English attack and none so more than poor Macaulay.

At 151, Macartney lofted Macaulay to Hendren and was out. The crowd rose and cheered him all the way in. In the pavilion, Archie MacLaren said: 'We have been looking at Victor Trumper all over again!'

That was the only wicket Macaulay took. He bowled 32 overs (8 maidens) at a cost of 123 runs. Macartney set out intentionally to 'murder' him, because he feared him, and the sad fact was that Macaulay was never again chosen to play for England against Australia, despite his tremendous feat in top-scoring for England at No. 10 with 76, his sensational partnership of 106 for the ninth wicket with George Geary saving England from defeat.

So, too, in thinking of Carr's decision to field and Carr's dropped catch – no matter how sympathetic one could feel towards him – there is also the thought of what could have been Macaulay's career, in Tests against Australia, had Macartney been dismissed for two runs at Leeds in 1926 and not 151.

Sir Pelham Warner, who knew many of the great years in cricket, had this to say of Macartney's innings:

> I say without hesitation that I have never seen a greater innings. Not even the immortal Trumper could have played more finely. And what higher praise can I give to any batsman, English or Australian?
>
> After his dropped catch, he made but one false stroke, a mis-timed hit on the off-side just before he was out. He simply pulverized all the bowling, with the exception of Tate's. Such stroke-play I can never hope to see again. His timing of the ball was perfection itself, and every sort of stroke came in rapid succession.

It mattered not what length the bowler bowled; runs simply flowed from his bat at an amazing speed. As quick on his feet as a Genee or a Pavlova, his steel-like wrists and powerful forearms reduced the bowling, always excepting that of Tate, to impotence. No Grace, no Ranjitsinhji, no Trumper, no Hobbs could have surpassed his batting!

This score by Macartney was the middle of three Test centuries in succession. He charmed a Lord's crowd with 133 ('By cripes,' he was reported to have said when he came to breakfast the morning of his Lord's century, 'I feel sorry for the poor coots that have to bowl at me today') and he followed his Leeds 151 with 109 at Old Trafford. And in those three Tests he also bowled 86 overs – not bad work for a man of forty!

Of his innings at Lord's, one well-known English critic wrote:

Everybody at Lord's was talking about Macartney's innings – it was so far above everything we had seen on the cricket field this season. How he makes his shots and where he gets his power from is a question everybody asks and nobody answers. He is gifted with a rare degree of limb-quickness and sight-keenness and is possessed of an immense belief in himself. His feet are those of a dancing master. His eye is like that of a hawk. His confidence is colossal. 'Little Mac' has no respect for reputations or conventions. He doesn't wait to play himself in. He is not dependent upon the loose ball for runs. He thinks in fours.

Leeds was for Macartney (as it was to be for Bradman) a happy scalping-ground. Yet possibly his most remarkable innings in England was in 1921 when he hit 345 against Nottinghamshire at Trent Bridge. He was missed in the slips at nine, and then stayed at the wicket for four more hours. That's not a bad lacing of the clock – by almost a hundred minutes!

Seeking a comparison, it could be said that had Macartney batted at the same rate as at Nottingham and for as long as the South African, Jackie McGlew, did against the Australians at Durban in January 1958 – 572 minutes for 105 – Macartney would have rattled up something like 860. It is colossal – impossible – but interesting!

Bert Collins, the Australian captain of 1926, said he saw Macartney play a nigh-miraculous stroke in 1926 at Nottingham. The ball was on its way and Macartney had taken his bat back for a cover-drive along the ground. The ball, however, changed direction off the pitch and Macartney, as quickly, changed direction in his down-swing. He hit the ball clean out of the ground, into the street behind the pavilion, over long-off!

In that innings of just on four hours, Macartney hit four sixes and 47 fours. Australia made 675, and Notts, demoralized by a bat 'as crooked and as wicked as original sin,' could manage only 58 and 100 – losing by an innings and 517 runs.

In 1926, at Old Trafford against Lancashire, Macartney played a dazzling innings of 160. It sent the spectators into rhapsodies. Many of his runs were made against the great Australian fast bowler, E. A. McDonald, who had an engagement with the county. Then, with the ball, Macartney had 27 overs (16 maidens), taking 4–15 in the first Lancashire innings, and in the second innings taking 1–19 off 19 overs.

How good was Macartney as a bowler? I have a pretty fair idea of that as I played club cricket against Macartney in Sydney. In the opinion of one English critic, Macartney was the best left-arm bowler Australia sent to England. This was before Australia had Bill Johnston, a really high-class left-hander; but they were different types, Macartney spinning and Johnston using the new ball. Macartney clean-bowled – clean-bowled, be it noted! – MacLaren (twice), Fry, Hobbs, Hirst, Warner, Rhodes and Chapman in Tests. That's a pretty distinguished haul to be clean-bowled.

Macartney had a graceful, slow run to the line of about seven yards. With his powerful wrists, he put a terrific amount of spin on the ball and he had a luring, curving flight with adroit changes of pace. Perhaps his best ball was one that came from the off with speed from the pitch. I found that he invariably delivered this ball (he bowled around the stumps) from wide on the line. He cut his biggest finger across the seam with a quick flick, and this, with the angle of delivery, gave it an almost incredible whip and seeming break from the pitch.

Once, in a Sydney grade match, he clean-bowled Tommy Andrews with it, and Andrews, who had made two tours of England with Macartney, should certainly have known his wares.

'You won't get me with that one again, Charlie,' said Andrews, before play began again on the second day. Macartney grinned.

'Now, Tommy,' Macartney called down the pitch when Andrews came to bat, 'you're sure you know it?'

'Yes,' said Andrews, 'I'm ready for you this time.'

'Right, off we go,' said Macartney – and in that very over he clean-bowled Andrews again!

Bert Oldfield told me that story. He kept wickets to Macartney in club, inter-state and Test matches and rated him very highly as a bowler. In addition, 'Little Mac' was a brilliant fieldsman, with sure hands and a quick flick of a throw to the keeper.

In all Tests, Macartney made 2,132 runs at 41 an innings. In all first-class cricket, he made 14,217 runs at 47 and took 366 wickets at 21. A remarkable feature of his career is that, of his 48 first-class centuries, not one was scored at Melbourne. Twenty were made in Sydney and only one in Adelaide. But England saw the best of him, not Australia.

Charlie Macartney had no coaching when young. He watched the giants of his youth and then applied his own methods. In the summer he never varied his habit – not even when he was playing in a Test – of arriving at Chatswood Oval (in Sydney) at 6.40 and leaving at 7.50 on five days a week. Some 17 Gordon members went to this early-morning practice and Macartney found that the pace of a composition ball skidding off a dewy pitch was ideal for sharpening up his eyesight and his strokes. It was the strength in his wrists that enabled him to play so late – a short, sharp backswing and then a convulsive whip at the ball that led you to believe you were watching magic.

Not only was Macartney the terror of cricketing bowlers. There was also apprehension on the Chatswood bowling rink of a Saturday when Macartney was batting on the local oval, over the railway line from the bowling club. Macartney rarely failed to lift a few out of the ground, clean over the double railway lines and on to the bowling clubhouse roof or on to the bowling green itself.

Because of his audacity, because of his all-round competence, the little Governor-General will never be forgotten by those who knew him.

One of the most graphic cricket pictures I have seen is not of any play but is of Macartney walking down the steps of the Members' Stand at the Sydney Cricket Ground on his way to bat. The members have stood to receive him, they are loudly clapping him and on their faces is the most delightful look of rapt anticipation.

And, on the other side of the Ground, the Hill would be rising to him, also, saying: 'Here comes the little Governor-General.' Macartney, himself, in the picture, looks to the middle and you can almost hear him telling himself: 'The first ball will have a look on its face. I feel pretty sure it will be 4.'

In the late 1940s, the compiler of the Australian *Who's Who* wrote to Macartney to seek details of himself. Macartney's answer was typical: 'I have no desire to appear in any publication of this kind, and I fail to see that any good purpose will be served by my name appearing. If you desire, of course, to publish my cricket history, well and good, but I would rather let it rest at that. I have gone over the particulars supplied on the attached, and they appear to be correct, but I have no record of figures, nor am I concerned with them. My only interest is in the manner in which runs are compiled and how wickets are taken, and in the good of the game.'

Those sentiments summed up the delightful cricket career and story of C. G. Macartney. The very sound of his name was cricketing music. To see him standing in the middle, as I did when a young boy that day on the Sydney Cricket Ground, was to conjure up a tingling vision of artistry soon to be unleashed.

11. Warren Bardsley

The last time I sat and spoke with Warren Bardsley I did so with some trepidation and much listening. For several good reasons one usually did the listening when 'Bards' was about, but on this final occasion (he died soon afterwards) he was holding forth in the Visitors' Gallery of Parliament House, Canberra. And Speaker Archie Cameron, a likeable man but a very stern one, cast more than one look in our direction.

A debate was in progress and from the Press Gallery I had seen Warren and his wife come into the House. I slipped down to join them because I was very fond of Bardsley. 'A good speaker, this bloke,' said Bardsley in a loud whisper. Speaker Cameron turned towards us. Years before at Liverpool, England, Bardsley had been 'pinked' (as he termed it) by a fellow Australian and one-time Test mate, Ted McDonald. This hit on the head had left him somewhat deaf and, like most others similarly afflicted, he was apt to raise his voice in conversation.

Speaker Cameron was no sporting man. Not long before he had, somewhat churlishly, forbidden the loan of Parliamentary cups and saucers for Prime Minister Menzies's match against the West Indians at Manuka Oval and he would not have known Bardsley. Moreover, the same Archie Cameron had ordered the removal of a photograph of Phar Lap from the barber's room at Parliament House, an action that shocked horse-loving Australians, to whom Phar Lap was the Bradman of racing.

But Warren saw not the Speaker and was not deterred from commenting on one of the debaters. 'This bloke's on a good length, Jack,' he said in a loud whisper. 'Who's he!' I had visions of the Serjeant-at-Arms presenting us with the Speaker's compliments and asking us to continue our conversation in the lobbies but, instead, there came a note from the Prime Minister inviting us to his rooms. The Prime Minister knew Bardsley and, like me, was fond of him, and especially of his stories.

At the present time, in these days of hustle, it would be difficult, I think, to have a recurrence of Bardsley's record as a cricketer; yet in the story is an indication of the long and often tortuous path that must be trod if a cricketer of modest beginnings is to reach the heights – as Bardsley certainly did.

Bardsley was not a man of brilliance. He came into first-class cricket when Victor Trumper was shedding his genius over the cricketing fields of Australia and, naturally, inspiring large numbers of youngsters. All wanted to be Trumpers. Bardsley, on his part, soon realized that he could never be a Trumper. But he also realized that he could, by hard work, become a first-class tradesman.

Even as a youth, Bardsley had both feet firmly on the pitch. He analysed his assets and put Trumper beyond his aspirations. The parks and the ovals of Sydney in the early days of this century were strewn with the stumps of ambitious young fellows who, in attempting to emulate Trumper, paid the penalty of trying to achieve the impossible.

Sensibly, Bardsley decided that he would get out of cricket only what he was prepared to put into it. There could be no short cuts. His early policy, and indeed the policy he was still following at his career's end, was hard work, plus close thought that deepened into concentration. Thus he became one of the best left-handed batsmen in Australia's history.

He toured England for the first time in 1909, becoming the first player ever to make a century in both innings of a Test; and he toured England for the last time in 1926, laying another stone of immortality for himself by batting through the whole of Australia's first innings of the Lord's Test, making 193 out of 383.

Only a purist in orthodoxy could endure and succeed (as Jack Hobbs also did) over so long and so vital a period. It was a period which saw the discovery of the bosie, the exploitation of short, fast bowling on the leg-stump, the acute leg-side field placing (Fred Root of Worcestershire), and the perfection of swing bowling.

Every now and then cricket will throw up a freak who lasts only as long as the keen edge of his eyesight. I once played with a rich character in Waverley named Hughie Davidson who, for a short period, kept wickets for New South Wales with distinction. Davidson was also an inter-state hockey player and, so far as the seasons were concerned, all he changed was his clothes. In batting, he would advance his front foot up the pitch, stoop low, and play murderous hockey sweeps to leg. These shots were as remarkable and as full-blooded as the oaths they drew from the bowler; but their raffish success decreased as Davidson's years increased.

Bardsley prospered so long because he was correct in everything he did. He stood at the crease as upright as a guardsman. Most opening batsmen like to think they can change course for a swinger by holding the bat low on the handle, but Bardsley held his bat exceedingly high. His right hand disdained a batting glove. His flicks with the bat, while awaiting the ball, were meticulously straight back. He never allowed any waverings or hysterical flutterings out towards point. This backswing, perhaps the first essential towards success, was always a model for the young. Back and down and always along the line of flight of the ball.

Appropriately, Bardsley was born in Nevertire, north of the Macquarie River in what was, in a sense, the Never-Never of New South Wales. He was named after the nearby town of Warren and his cricket career began when the family transferred to Sydney when his father became headmaster of a school in a suburb known as Forest Lodge.

The elder Bardsley had a deep, old-fashioned love of cricket, and he saw in Warren a means of achieving a more personal link with the game than he himself had ever known. He must have been a shrewd man. He didn't fuss over Warren, driving him to the game, but merely provided the implements and the opportunities. Like the good schoolmaster he undoubtedly was, he had, too, eyes for others, and his period at Forest Lodge coincided with the youthful rise of Cotter, Kelleway and Oldfield, all Test men. Another Bardsley, Ray, was to play for New South Wales so that with Warren, too, it could be said that no other Australian headmaster – or possibly English – gave so many riches to the cricketing world as did Bardsley senior.

'Tibby' Cotter was killed at Gallipoli in 1915. He was one of the greatest of fast bowlers and Bardsley always retained the vivid picture of his knocking the middle stumps of Hobbs and Fry out of the ground at Leeds in the Test of 1909.

Cotter was the terror of the school playground. The lads played on an asphalt pitch during recess and Bardsley was one of the very few who showed an interest in batting when Cotter was bowling. The bounce off the asphalt was high and there were always broken palings in the fence at the rear while Cotter was at school. Bardsley declared that once, in a school game, they had to put six long-stops to Tibby.

'As I afterwards saw Tibby breaking stumps, breaking fingers and breaking ribs,' Bardsley once told me, 'I was always glad I played with Tibby in grade, state and Test cricket, and not against him.'

Cricket was not only a summer game for those lads. They also played during the winter, and in that period Bardsley rose every morning to do physical exercises – he wanted a strong body and supple wrists. Exercises done, he would go to a park to join Cotter, Kelleway, Oldfield and others in an hour's cricket before breakfast. If there happened to be a game in a paddock as Bardsley was coming home from school, it wasn't long before he had wheedled himself into that as well.

Giving thought to improving his stamina and footwork, he took up boxing. He even took up jiu-jitsu. To strengthen his wrists further, he squeezed a tennis-ball on the way to and from school. These were the incidentals. Of prime importance, as he came to young manhood, was the time he spent at the nets. He once calculated that he must have spent quite a few years of his life at cricket nets.

'My aim,' he once told me, 'was to have eyesight and footwork in perfect working order and co-ordination by the time I got into the middle. If you have to find these things in the middle, you have no right to be there. You must be in perfect physical shape and form long before that. You have to work for these things very early in the piece.'

A famous pianist, Warren once pointed out, never achieved the top without years of solid grind and daily practice. Thus, as a pianist worked at his instrument, so Bardsley worked with a bat.

This complete addiction to work at the nets was a feature of Bardsley's generation and, I think, mine too.

I once met an official of the New South Wales Cricket Association who had managed a side on what we call our southern tour. This was a modern side, travelling by air, and he was staggered at the little interest his charges took in net practice at Adelaide and Melbourne. They seemed, he said, to have no sooner left the dressing-room for the nets than they were back again.

He contrasted that attitude with a New South Wales side he knew in Bardsley's time, when travel was by train and the journey to Adelaide was broken in Melbourne for a few hours. The players asked the manager to get all the cricket bags down to the Melbourne nets so that they could occupy the spare hours there. Then, on the day before the game against South Australia in Adelaide, the players spent both the morning and the afternoon at the nets.

In case it should be thought that the New South Wales players of the period of which I write stood more in need of practice, let me name them: Collins, Bardsley, Macartney, Kippax, Andrews, Taylor, Kelleway, Gregory, Hendry, Oldfield and Mailey – every one a Test player of distinction. These were the men who hustled their manager – and it was a hustle – to get their bags off the train for a few hours at the Melbourne nets.

I am sufficiently modern, I hope, not to be over-critical of our present-day cricketers but I do think they have grown away from net-play. Some, indeed, want to get more out of the game than they are prepared to put into it. I can't say whether it is a matter of disposition, or of too many tours, or of too much air-travel; but I do know that I admired Bardsley when he told me of the attention he gave to detail. He left nothing to chance.

When Bardsley went to England for the first time in 1909, he would rise early on the first day of a match and go down to the ground before breakfast. He did this because he wanted to feel that he knew the ground when he walked out to bat.

He used to tell of the surprise he got on the opening day of the 1909 tour. He walked on to the Trent Bridge field before breakfast and couldn't see a pitch anywhere. He asked the groundsman, 'Where's your pitch for today's game?' The groundsman staggered him by replying, 'I'll pick one out in a minute and go to work on it.'

That story gave me the impression that Bardsley thought present-day players were molly-coddled by well-prepared pitches (he would not have thought so on a few occasions in England in 1956!), and I had, too, an idea that his disdain for records might have come in the mellowness of his retirement. Certainly he himself had a pretty voracious appetite for runs as he was climbing the ladder.

His first three innings in 1909 yielded 63, 76 and 63 not out – a splendid start for a man of twenty-four years on his first trip – but he wasn't satisfied. He wanted a three-figure score and when it came, against Essex, it was sorely needed. He opened with Hartigan. Two wickets were down for eight when Ransford, another young left-hander having his first trip, joined Bardsley. In three hours and twenty minutes these two young men added 355, and in a way that clearly suggested that two more left-handed scourges had come to flay English bowlers where Hill and Darling had left off.

Ransford went for 174 and Bardsley flopped on the ground and gave himself over to pleasant thoughts as Trumper walked down the pavilion steps.

'Let me see,' mused Bardsley. 'I'm nearly 200 now. There's almost another three hours to stumps. With a bit of luck I should be about 400 by tonight.'

That spot of reasoning – worthy of the latter day Bradman – was soon jolted into nothingness.

He moved safely past two hundred and at 217 pushed one out to the covers and called to Trumper, 'Come one.' Off sprinted Bardsley but when he got half way he saw that Trumper hadn't left his crease. Bardsley was run out by the proverbial mile. He was still brooding over why Trumper had left him high and dry when Victor returned to the pavilion after making 74 in sixty minutes.

In a hurt voice Bardsley said: 'That was a bad show, Vic. There was an easy single in it and it was my call and everything. Why did you leave me stranded?'

'Now look here, Warren,' said Trumper. 'You had made over two hundred. How many more did you want to make? There are, you know, a few others in this side who like an innings.'

Bardsley said he learnt the lesson and ever afterwards felt contempt for batsmen who went on and on after runs when the soul had gone out of the game and runs were of no account.

He ran into more trouble at Glasgow. The batting order took a sharp about-turn with Bardsley batting No. 10 and Armstrong No. 11. Bardsley hit a century and then a note was brought to him from the captain Noble. All it said was: 'Get out!' So Bardsley did as he was told – he hit a high catch intentionally and walked off.

'What the dickens did you do that for?' exploded Armstrong. 'Don't you think I'd like a bit of a hit too?'

Bardsley showed him the note. That brought him further trouble in the pavilion. 'When I send you a note,' said Noble, 'it is obviously meant for you and not to be made public property!'

There were times when Bardsley thought there was more trouble for him in the pavilion than in the middle.

On another occasion he was batting with Noble and had just reached his century with a boundary. As he walked back past Noble he looked at his skipper, expecting words of commendation. Instead, Noble merely looked at him and said, 'Well, and how many sixes are you going to hit now?'

Bardsley took the hint and was swallowed up by the pavilion in no time.

Noble was known as a captain who brooked no nonsense. He ran his side as a unit, not for individuals, and those who played with him would not have had it any other way.

Bardsley once told me he thought there was much less selfishness in cricket in his day than in mine. I remained noncommittal (not necessarily disagreeing) and he went on to tell me the story of Sammy Carter and Trumper. They were watching Trumper from the pavilion and he moved to 95.

'Whoever is next had better get his things together,' called out Carter. 'Vic won't be long now.'

That meant that Trumper would get himself out as soon as he

reached the century. All this, from the basic spirit of the game, is commendable. A criticism in England against the Australians of 1948 was that they regarded every match as a Test; they never relented. On the other hand, a criticism against the Australians of 1909 was that they were not 'stern' enough. You can't please everybody!

After that first trip to England it was written of Bardsley: 'Of all the men new to England, none made so big an impression. More orthodox in method than many of Australia's greatest batsmen, his wicket always a terribly difficult wicket to get, so accurate was his footwork, so beautifully straight his bat, whether in back or forward play. But Bardsley was always full of strokes, a beautiful cutter, wonderfully skilful at forcing and 'running' the ball to leg; above all he had the temperament for playing long innings in big cricket.'

That was written of Bardsley at the start of his career: it could well have been written of him, also, at the finish, for he changed his technique over the years by not even a flourish. His last great Test innings was in 1926 when he scored 193 not out at Lord's, and that on a pitch that was dry at one end and wet at the other, calling for a different batting technique at either end. A hose had been left running over-night.

Some of our legislators had tart tongues where Bardsley was concerned. Still giving everything he had, he was plugging along for his club in the late 1920s when I began playing with Waverley. Everything he did in the middle was a lesson for the young player and yet, I recall, the up-and-coming were warned against him. He was, they said, a sour old Test player – one to be avoided.

Bardsley had high cricketing standards. He spoke out of the left side of his mouth with a gruff voice that belied the inner man but, like many another, he could not be bothered any longer with the game when he felt pin-prickings. This is one reason why many of the rich heritages of the past have not been handed down in Australian cricket. Unlike English cricket, which gathers the old gaffers to the game with links of affection and respect, Australian cricket too often puts off the old name for the new, and the average old-timer, after the first twinge of regret, is not greatly put out over it. If he feels that he isn't wanted he simply finds a niche in golf or bowls, and thus becomes lost to cricket for ever.

Bardsley was once so highly regarded that he was made sole selector for New South Wales. He staked his reputation by choosing a young doctor, H. V. Hordern, just returned from studies in the United States. The Australian selectors followed Bardsley's lead

and Hordern took 5–85 and 7–90 in his first Test against England, and
that against a side including Hobbs, George Gunn, Rhodes, Mead,
Hearne, Foster, Woolley and Douglas. Hordern thus equalled the
record of the Kent bowler, F. Martin, who took twelve wickets in
his first and only Test. I must learn, some day, what happened to
Martin, because even after such a burst he was not chosen for the
next Test at Manchester.

Hordern, whose nickname was 'Ranji' (possibly because he was so
swarthy), was a slow bowler, expert in the bosie, and took 32 wickets
in that series at an average of 24. Because of the demands of his
profession and the war he never again played for Australia. But
Bardsley must be given high marks for so quickly recognizing his
merit.

Now, it has to be admitted that some old cricketers are thorough
bores. You find them at most grounds, always eager to revive the
past at the expense of the present. Bardsley was certainly not one of
these. He dipped often into the past, but always in a fond manner. I
never found him sour or embittered.

I saw him once when Morris, another left-hander and an outstanding cricketer for any generation, was having a sad run of
outs.

'I can almost cry when I see Morris failing,' said Bardsley.
'He's one of the very best cricketers. All his Test centuries shout
that. But he's fallen into the horrible habit of playing the ball on the
move. He's shuffling now as he plays. He's lost grip of himself. I
could put him right in five minutes. Doesn't anybody tell him these
things?'

I couldn't answer that. A wise maxim in Australian cricket is
never to give personal advice unless it it sought.

Bardsley, like all the others, adored Trumper; but only a little
way behind was Cotter.

'By cripes,' he once exclaimed, 'Tibby was a real corker. Strong,
big. Never got tired. He broke more stumps than any other fast
bowler I knew. We were always running out of stumps down at
Wentworth Park. Tibby loved to break stumps and he loved to
pink a batsman. Every fast bowler does. Gregory, McDonald,
Larwood – the whole ruddy lot of 'em. Just as soon hit a batsman as
the stumps. And no harm in that either, I suppose.

'We were playing North Sydney one day and Tibby was in great
form, knocking stumps over in all directions. In came Stud White
and first ball Tibby smashed Stud's fingers against the handle of the
bat. A sickening crunch. They took Stud off to hospital. Never forget

Tibby's remark. "Well," he said, wiping his hands, "that's one of the —— out of the way." About an hour later Stud came back to bat again with his fingers heavily bandaged. Very brave man, Stud. Tibby took one look at him and snorted, "Give me that ball. I'll break the bastard's neck this time." Tibby reckoned that when he "pinked" a batsman he should remain "pinked".'

Bardsley, as I remarked earlier, was himself 'pinked' in Liverpool, England. He tried to hook a short one from McDonald, when the latter was playing for Lancashire, and received a hit on the ear. Another inch or two and it would have hit his temple and, possibly, he might have rested for all time in English soil – as was the fate of McDonald himself.

Bardsley had a delightful quirk in conversation. Whenever I induced him to tell me of his best innings he would always start by saying, 'Well, to cut a long story short.' I have no doubt that many a bowler, after looking at his broad bat for many hours, would have liked him to cut his innings short.

Which was his greatest feat in Test cricket? He himself favoured the time – as well he might – when in 1909 he got a century in each innings of the Oval Test. Tests, then, were only of three days' duration, and S. F. Barnes was at his peak.

'Some people believed Barnes to be the best bowler in the world,' said Bardsley. Not, you will notice, that Bardsley said this himself. He modestly put it on to other people, as if he, himself, had some doubt in the matter.

He liked to recall, too, the occasion in 1926 when he played through the innings at Lord's for 193. He was congratulated on that feat by Dr H. V. Evatt, then a rising young barrister.

Bardsley's acknowledgment was typical. 'I'd swop it for one of your degrees,' he told Evatt.

'Well,' said Evatt, 'give me the 93. You keep the 100 and the not out and you can have any degrees I've got!'

Once, in a manner that I hoped was disarming, I said to Warren, 'What about F. R. Foster?'

I perceived, even years afterwards, a slight wince. That English left-hander had been a blight on Bardsley's early career – very much as Bedser was with Morris. Foster came to Australia in 1911–12 and, swinging the ball late across Bardsley's body (left-handed opening batsmen rarely get this ball, a common one to a right-hander), he clean-bowled him four times in the Tests. Bardsley was dropped from the fifth and final one, but after his preceding innings, so they said, he merely dropped into the dressing-room on his way back from the middle, took Bill Whitty, our left-handed bowler, and led him to the nets at the back where he had him bowl almost unceasingly to him. It was said that Bardsley in that season wore Whitty more into the ground than did the English batsmen, but it was indicative of how Bardsley set out to overcome his problems. Not that he did with Foster.

Bardsley played with or against many of the richest characters in the game. He told me how he once faced up to a 'pair' against George Hirst.

Hirst had sent his stumps flying for nil in the first innings and Warren said he didn't feel very happy about things as he faced the same bowler in the second innings. But, to his great surprise, Hirst threw up a full-toss, which Bardsley tucked away for three.

'As I finished at Hirst's end,' said Bardsley, 'I smiled at him and said "Thanks". I thought that he had presented me, a young player, with a full toss to get me off the pair. But Hirst glared at me. "Doon't thank me", he said, "bloody ball slipped!" And then he clean-bowled me again, for three.'

Like all his fellows, Bardsley idolized Vic Trumper. In Melbourne once, when Trumper was captain of New South Wales, there were loud cheers from the Victorian room when their skipper won the toss. He sent New South Wales in on a Melbourne glue-pot, as bad a pitch as cricket knows.

Trumper said to Bardsley, 'Come on, Curley, put them on. You and I are for it. Stay there half an hour and I'll always remember you.'

Bardsley continued the tale: 'Well, to cut a long story short, we were still there at lunch-time. Vic was 50 and I was 70. The South Africans were here for a Test series and saw that game. One of them said later, "If you can do that on a glue-pot, what will you do against us on a good pitch?" '

In England in 1921, when Australia won three Tests and drew the other two, no fewer than 29 men played for England in the series. They played 14 bowlers and never once, according to Bardsley, played G. M. Louden, of Essex, the best bowler in England.

The story goes that plenty of duck-shoving went on when Bardsley and Collins batted against Louden. Bardsley would try to give Collins the strike; Collins, in turn, would try and manœuvre the other into it. All the Australians were agreed that Louden was the best bowler they met in England in that year.

Why didn't England pick him for the Tests?

'Well,' said Bardsley, 'all we did was tell the truth. We told everybody that Louden was England's best bowler. They thought we were leg-pulling and just didn't pick him!'*

One could go on and on about Bardsley but I must remind myself to cut a long story reasonably short. The last time I saw him was when a cold, wintry wind was blowing in off the Pacific and we were burying in the cemetery upon the Waverley cliffs the remains of Dr Rowley Pope – friend, adviser and medical comforter to every Australian team to England for many, many years. Many famous Australian cricketers were grouped around the graveside and as the ceremony concluded I asked Warren what were his thoughts.

'I was just thinking what a great bloke old Doc was,' said Bardsley. 'I was thinking of him and then I just happened to see so-and-so across there and I thought, Poor old so-and-so. By cripes, he's looking old. And then I thought, well, I suppose some of them are looking at me and saying, Poor old Bards. By cripes, he's looking old! That's just the trouble. We are all just poor old so-and-so's.'

But not really. You couldn't pity men with memories as rich and as happy as Bardsley. Yarning with him was one of the most pleasant experiences I have known in cricket. Perhaps it was because we had so much in common – the feelings of a Test opener as he waits for the first ball.

In Test matches, Bardsley made 1,487 runs against England at an average of 33; 982 against South Africa at 61; and in Australia's Sheffield Shield games he made 4,171 at 60. These would be outstanding figures in any era, and the fact that they were made when the ball was red and the bowlers and fieldsmen were on their toes make them (to me, at least) all the rosier.

* I told this story on BBC Television in England in 1956 when somebody asked whether it was true that Australians tried to play certain individuals into a Test team against them. I offered it as proof that we were much too simple for such a cunning device! Later that summer, when I was playing in a village game at Amersham, Louden came and introduced himself to me.

12. Stan McCabe

The cricket genius of Stanley Joseph McCabe merged without fuss or bother into three epochal events – Sydney (1932), Johannesburg (1935) and Nottingham (1938). At each of these three citadels of cricket he played a Test innings of immortality. Bill O'Reilly reminded me only recently – in 1971 – that we alone participated in all three Tests in which McCabe triumphed and I know that O'Reilly, like myself, hesitates to say which one of McCabe's innings was the greatest.

Unlike many other immortal innings which do not reveal their value on paper, McCabe's three innings immediately stand out when set down in relation to the team's total. They clearly tell how he monopolized the scene. At Sydney, against the almost unknown and full fury of Jardine's bodyline tactics, McCabe made 187 not out in a total of 360: at Johannesburg, in deplorable light and on a badly worn wicket, he made 189 not out of his team's 2–274: at Trent Bridge, he made 232 of Australia's 411 after five other acknowledged batsmen of the side, including Bradman, had fallen for only 151.

In all these games, Australia had its back to the wall, a point worth particular notice because it was in such circumstances that McCabe shone out. At Sydney, with Bradman out from the Australian team through illness, McCabe came to the wickets with the score 4–87. Larwood had taken three of the four, and bodyline had paralysed most of the Australians in the few prior games in which it was exploited. At Johannesburg, he came to the crease when Australia needed 382 runs to win with nine wickets in hand on a tattered pitch that had already produced 898 runs. At Nottingham, on the Trent Bridge pitch, when McCabe attacked the English bowling with one of the most brilliant and vicious innings known to the game, Australia was facing ignominy with 5–151 in answer to England's mammoth total of 8–658 (declared).

Obviously, then, McCabe's genius shone its brightest in a crisis. He played all his Test cricket – apart from South Africa, for which tour Bradman was not available – in the shadow of Bradman, and a considerable part of it in the time of Ponsford. This is but another way of suggesting that had there been more crises it is reasonable to assume that there would have been more epics from McCabe. Knowing his temperament, I often sensed that the glory of McCabe was dimmed by the dominance of Bradman. He failed often when he came to bat with big totals on the board.

An instance of this was in the conciliatory and appeasing year of 1934 when the Australians toured England. Larwood and Voce, being dubbed (unfairly) the bad boys of the bodyline donnybrook, were stood in the corner for the whole of that Test summer. They had, however, so upset the mental poise of Bradman and Ponsford in 1932–33 that these two batting giants did not find their international batting feet again until the fourth Test of 1934. Until that game, Bradman's Test figures were 29, 25, 36, 13 and 30 – his leanest patch in Test history – and Ponsford's were 52, 5, 12 and 30 not out. During the preceding three Tests, it was mainly McCabe who held the Australian batting together with 88, 65, 34, 19, 137 and 33 not out.

Then came the Leeds and Oval Tests. Bradman and Ponsford hit form and confidence together and for hour after hour, McCabe, the next batsman in, doodled and fidgeted in the pavilion while Bradman and Ponsford put on 388 at Leeds and 451 at the Oval. McCabe followed these paralysing partnerships and made only 27 and 10.

Exceedingly better and more understanding is the English habit of today. When a long partnership is in progress, the next batsman in is changed from interval to interval. Only those who have experienced it know how dismal it is to sit in the pavilion for hour after hour with the pads on, gloves and bat handy, and with the limbs, at first tensed and eager for action, becoming colder and colder through inactivity.

Such inactivity chilled McCabe's ardour. He came to bat one day in Cape Town after Brown and I had made a record 233 opening stand against South Africa – and McCabe was out first ball! Many batsmen delight in walking to the wickets after the bowlers have been thrashed, but McCabe didn't belong to these. He preferred to sniff battle as he walked out, not bowling corpses. He liked to do his own taming, his own mastering, and he was never one to chase big scores when they were there for the mere staying at the wickets. In such circumstances, he lost interest.

In this outlook, McCabe differed from most other batsmen of his time, an era of innumerable batting records. He differed materially, too, in that he never allowed the stultifying atmosphere of limitless Tests to dim the glittering light of his brilliance. Outwardly, at least, it cost Hammond no appreciable effort to bundle up his beautiful artistry and leave it behind him as he walked out in a limitless

Test to do battle with his tradesmanlike ones, twos and occasional fours. Hammond's batting times in limitless Tests in Australia never suggested his brilliance. McCabe, on the other hand, batted the same in all types of matches – picnic ones, Sydney grade games, Sheffield Shield or Test. His batting was based on attack.

McCabe usually batted number four or five, and when his time came the game had assumed a definite character. If his side was in trouble, McCabe reasoned that his job was to extricate it by attack; if his side was on top, his duty was to force home the advantage by aggression. Thus, whatever the state of the game, McCabe always played the same and it was typical of him that, unlike the vast majority of batsmen who are lured by the magic of three figures, he never got into low, safe gear as he approached the century. Rather did he try and accelerate. He never held that this particular Mecca should be approached by slow, deliberate footsteps of deference.

This complete disregard of a century was characteristic of his cricket outlook. It first became noticeable at St Joseph's College in Sydney, where he attended as a boarder, and in which team he was a useful performer with bat and ball. It was his captain, Clarrie Cullen, who gained newspaper publicity with his string of centuries. McCabe barely rated a mention. His greatest sporting renown at school was won when he disregarded a chronic appendix, played in a Rugby final and distinguished himself with thrilling diving tackles.

From school, he returned to his country town of Grenfell. Like Bradman, O'Reilly and Allsopp, the latter a glorious crowd-pleaser of those days, McCabe was essentially a country product and learned his batting on a concrete pitch. This is always a better nursery than a dubious turf pitch. The ball conforms to an even pace and height off a concrete pitch and it was thereby that McCabe, like Bradman, learned to pull and square-cut with a brilliance which lit the cricket world wherever they went. On spacious country grounds, also, across which magpies, parrots and kookaburras flutter and from which sleepy, blue mountains are glimpsed far off in the distance, there crept into McCabe's batting a light-heartedness of spirit, an outlook on the game not always easily gained on city grounds hemmed in by space, industry and critics.

McCabe might have been born to blush unseen, or even bud late in first-class cricket, had not opportunity come to him in the guise of an Easter visit to Grenfell by a city team, captained by E. A. (Chappy) Dwyer, later to become an Australian selector. Dwyer immediately formed a high opinion of McCabe. Tales of his prowess were carried back to Sydney and McCabe further embellished his good name when

he came to Sydney in one of those magnificent Country Week carni-
vals, sadly no more, which put life-blood into Australian cricket.

This was the week marked off on the calendar of all aspiring young
country cricketers. Cow-cockies from the coastal belt; jackeroos and
boundary-riders from the hot, parched plains of the far west; cattle
drovers and timber-cutters from the tropical north; wheat-growers,
squatters, musterers, shearers, fruit-growers and pickers from the
Riverina – from all parts of New South Wales they converged on
Sydney in heightened spirit for a week crammed full of cricket,
cobbership, movies, dances, sight-seeing and general excitement.

Spirit alone was left to these footsore, magnificent young Australians
at the end of their week. Another day or two and they would be
riding far over the ranges again after sheep and chuckling to themselves at memories of the Big Smoke, as countrymen affectionately
call the city. With becoming modesty, it never entered their minds
that they would be remembered in the city, and thus there was a
sensation one day in the placid south-western New South Wales
town of Grenfell when a telegram came for Stan McCabe, asking
him to Sydney to play with the Sheffield Shield team.

There is not much secrecy about telegrams in the average Australian country town. They soon become common property, not,
necessarily, through the agency of the person to whom they are
addressed, but because any link with the outside world is considered
to be news belonging to the community. An invitation to one of their
towns-people to play first-class cricket not only made Grenfell history. It made decidedly hot news.

It was a talking point in the town whether the correct McCabe had
been chosen. There were four brothers, three of them outstanding at
cricket, and many wondered whether the selectors had made a mistake and chosen Stanley instead of his older brother, Leslie. Stanley
Joseph himself thought that the one they wanted was Leslie. Leslie
said Stan.

Somewhat diffidently, then, Stan McCabe returned to Sydney and
he joined the Sheffield Shield team. He didn't set the Harbour on
fire, nor the Yarra nor the Torrens when he toured interstate. Bradman came to the top fold with a tremendous flourish, making a century in his first Shield game. McCabe, like his nature, slipped in
quietly and unobtrusively. He did just well enough to hold his place
in the first season – a few runs here and there, an occasional wicket
with medium-pace and, always, a smart, neat fieldsman.

The following season was 1930 with a team to be chosen to tour
England. The headlines were being monopolized almost entirely by

Bradman in making 1,586 runs at an average of 113.28. He had the incredible world's record that season of 452 not out and, set alongside Bradman's feats, McCabe's scores of 35, 46, 77, 3, 69, 70, 70, 50 not out, 15, 60, 81 and 29 seemed lean. They showed, however, that McCabe was consistent; that he got his runs brightly and that he might indeed have approached Bradman's five centuries for the season had he attached more importance to three figures.

McCabe slipped into the Australian touring team in as quiet a manner as he had into the New South Wales side. He hadn't made a single first-class century and this made him seem a most surprising choice for the English tour, although good judges appreciated his worth. Most of the attention was focused on the dropping of Ryder, who comprised with R. E. Jones (New South Wales) and Dr C. E. Dolling (South Australia), the touring selection committee. There was intense drama in the manner in which Ryder had his cricketing throat cut by his fellow selectors. Ryder had captained Australia the year before against Chapman's team and was considered certain to lead again in England. He had had a good Australian summer and nobody was more shocked than Ryder when his two fellow selectors told him they didn't want him for England. They would make only one concession to Ryder. They would hold the team's announcement over until Ryder batted in the second innings next day against New South Wales.

It says much for Ryder's temperament that, under this intense stress, he made a century. His fellow selectors remained unconvinced. The team was announced and Ryder wasn't in it.

The publicity surrounding Ryder diverted attention from McCabe's choice. He was only nineteen. Bradman was twenty-two.

Four years before, Kippax had the colossal average for the season of 112. Kippax was a batsman of exceeding charm and on the eve of the 1926 team being chosen for England, Kippax made a Shield score of 271 not out. The touring side was announced next day but, like Abou Ben Adhem, Kippax's name was not on the list. Victor Richardson, who had carried the South Australian batting on his manly shoulders for years and who was an outstanding fieldsman, also missed out in 1926.

Opportunity is sometimes more than half the winning of the battle for recognition. Bradman, Jackson and McCabe were more fortunate than Kippax and Richardson and others in the time they came to the game. Those who waxed successful just before and after the First World War still held the stage in 1926 and most didn't pull on their retirement slippers until after that tour. The door of opportunity, therefore, was ajar in 1930 but, even so, the selectors of that time did well in their discernment and courage to choose the youngster McCabe.

McCabe followed in the distinguished footsteps of Clem Hill, who was nineteen when he made his first trip to England in 1896. S. E. Gregory was twenty when he made the first of his eight trips to England and Trumper was twenty-two. Ian Craig was seventeen when he went to England in 1953, but he possessed neither the technique nor the maturity to succeed.

Bradman squeezed all the other Australians out into the cold in 1930. McCabe was not an outstanding success, yet he made moderate scores when runs were needed most and he batted with bright courage. His first seven innings in England yielded only 51 runs and much doubt as to the wisdom of his choice. Woodfull sent him to open one day against Oxford and he made 91. Against Cambridge, he made 96, his highest score of the tour because he was destined to return home with still no first-class century under his belt.

His highest Test score of 1930 was 54, and his subsequent Test innings in Australia against the West Indies and South Africa – in neither series did he score a century – didn't prepare the cricket world for the first of his three epics.

It was Sydney of late 1932 and the first Test of the bodyline series. Woodfull and Ponsford had opened for Australia in a sound, orthodox manner against orthodox fast bowling; however, when Larwood switched across to his leg-side tactics, Australia's star took a quick dip towards the horizon. Four wickets had fallen for 87 with Bradman not playing when McCabe came to the middle. Australia's batting was in a pickle.

When he was five, McCabe played a ball from Larwood to Voce at gully slip. The ball flew high off the bat and touched ground just a few inches short of Voce's grabbing fingers. In such a manner does fate toy with history, granting or denying favours by the flimsiest of margins. A. W. Carr opened the first page of an immortal chapter when he dropped Charlie Macartney at Leeds when he was two in 1926. Had Carr taken that chance, cricket would have been infinitely poorer by the loss of an innings which yielded a century before lunch, a century out of the team's total of 131 in 100 minutes, and an innings everywhere acknowledged as unexcelled in the history of the game for sheer artistry and brilliance.

So, too, had Voce grabbed that near-chance from McCabe when he was five the game would have been robbed of one of its gems. In this innings, McCabe first had to master an English attack which included Larwood at the very apogee of his greatness. After he had assumed control, McCabe switched to defiance, taking the crowd of 50,000 enthusiastic countrymen from the depths of despair to the heights of happiness.

How the crowd surged into ecstacies that day at the temporary slaying of the giant Larwood! To this stage, Larwood's deeds had been a fiery challenge, not only to Australian cricket, but also to Australian manhood. He flowed in a wonderful current of rhythm to the delivery crease like a wave gathering itself smoothly up before crashing down on the beach. Larwood's speed, best demonstrated as the ball flew through to the keeper, and his physical danger to the batsman were such as to strike awe into the hearts of those watching even from the outside. McCabe first had to check him and then cheek him.

With Victor Richardson, whose share was 49, McCabe put on 129 for the fifth wicket, the most impressive of all Australian partnerships of that series. Yet is was on the following Saturday morning that McCabe reached his dizziest heights. With Grimmett, who made 19, McCabe added 68; and with Wall, who made four, McCabe added 55 for the last wicket. This was an amazing partnership. McCabe shielded Wall from the strike and, in between, crashed four after four that sent the record crowd into a delirium of joy and disbelief. Never have I heard such a long and sustained bedlam on a cricket field.

When stumps were drawn at the end of the first day's play, Australia were 6–290. When the innings finished before lunch on the next day, Australia had totalled 360, with McCabe 187 not out.

Considering the bowling odds he had to face, I am inclined to think that this Sydney innings was McCabe's greatest, yet as soon as one feels like becoming dogmatic, there obtrudes the thrilling and recurring vision of McCabe's epics at Johannesburg and Trent Bridge. I batted for a long period with McCabe at Johannesburg and here he had to face pitch disabilities unknown to him at Sydney and Trent Bridge. At each of the latter places, he batted on a glorious pitch, the type of true pitch a batsman dreams about. At Johannesburg, on the contrary, he batted on a dusty, irritable pitch that had already witnessed 898 runs. Of all wickets, even a wet and sticky one, perhaps none is more difficult than that off which a ball either shoots or jumps.

McCabe ran to a flowing century before lunch, joining Macartney and Bradman in the feat; in the afternoon, if possible, he was even more brilliantly devastating. He pulverized the South African attack into the dust. The Springboks had plenty of bowlers to take advantage of the spinning pitch. Langdon and Nupen were splendid medium-paced spin bowlers and Mitchell and Balaskas found that the pitch greatly exaggerated their leg spin and allowed them several heights of bounce.

McCabe never put a foot or his bat in a false position. To me, at the other end and most conscious of the difficulties of even keeping one's wicket intact on such a pitch, McCabe's batting bordered on the miraculous. He made 100 in 91 minutes; 150 in 145 minutes and in that tally was the amazing number of 24 boundaries.

In the middle afternoon, lightning flashed with frightening vividness in the mineral-laden Johannesburg air. Peals of thunder rolled over the old Wanderers ground, yet not even the wretched light of the impending storm could dim McCabe's brilliance.

With Australia still 125 runs behind and three hours left to play, Herbie Wade, the Springbok skipper, paid McCabe the extraordinary tribute of appealing against the light, from the field. It was apparent that the pending storm would stop play at any minute. There was thus no fear that South Africa could be beaten, but Wade was nonplussed, mesmerized and indeed stampeded by the profuse profligacy of McCabe's boundaries. Some said there was a flavour of unsportsmanship about Wade's appeal. Wade was a magnificent sportsman. I knew from close quarters that McCabe had woven a spell over him.

Trent Bridge differed again in its circumstances. McCabe, here, had to contend with strictly orthodox tactics on a perfect pitch.

I was standing next to Don Bradman on the dressing-room balcony that day when he called inside to some of our fellows engaged on varied dressing-room activities. 'Come and see this. Don't miss a moment of it. You will never see the like of it again,' said Bradman. I recounted this incident in *Cricket Crisis*, published in 1946. Not even the most ordinary journalist would have missed such a generous tribute from Bradman, and I've seen it reprinted over and over again.

The Trent Bridge circumstances were similar to those of Sydney in that McCabe had to shepherd the 'rabbits' away from the strike. Not even the peerless and graceful flow of boundaries (he played his shots with less effort than any other batsman I have known), showed more genius in McCabe's innings than the deft manner in which he dictated the strike, circumventing Hammond's captaincy and the wiles of the English bowlers and fieldsmen to keep him away from the strike. McCabe's score was 232. Those of the others who joined

him at the wicket were Ward 2, Hassett 1, Badcock 9, Barnett 22,
O'Reilly 9, McCormick 2 and Fleetwood Smith 5 not out.

McCabe took the complete strike during eight of the last ten overs
of the innings. In a last wicket stand of 77 in 28 minutes with Fleetwood-Smith, McCabe scored 72. He hit 34 fours and one six, and 16
of the boundaries came in the ten overs just mentioned.

The writers at Trent Bridge that unforgettable day seemingly
scoured their Thesaurus to do McCabe justice. 'The glittering, un-
dimmed morning star of the first Test . . . and what of the visionary
monster Larwood now? . . . This Siva with a necklace of skulls . . . a
matter for history in Test cricket . . . here is a cricketer who is a true
son of sport. . . . The heart and youth of Victor Trumper beat again
in the cricket of McCabe . . . with the grace and verve of a lithe-
limbed ballet dancer . . . cheers rolled like thunder as he stood there,
the noblest young Roman of them all, whipping England's bowlers as
with the scourges of the Seven Furies, with all the calmness of an old
warhorse before the battle, with all the abandon of confident
youth. . . . Test cricket has seen no more immortal innings.'

So did the English writers strive to do justice to McCabe at Trent
Bridge. It was trite for cricket writers that McCabe's career saw fit to
bestow one epic innings upon each of three great cricketing lands –
Australia, South Africa and England, in turn. No wonder O'Reilly
and I preen our reminiscent feathers when we recall that we alone
played in the same team as McCabe on all three occasions!

Emphasis on his three epics is not to suggest that McCabe knew no
other big moments in Test cricket. He had a Test century at Manchester in 1934 with 137; he played brilliantly for 149 in a Durban
Test in 1935; and he recorded a Test century of charm in Melbourne
in the last game of the series against G. O. Allen's team in 1937.

McCabe, as I suggested earlier, was never one to measure success
by the yardstick of three figures. I never met a batsman who cared
less about centuries and he was never one to cast miserly and anxious
eyes at the score-board to watch his approach to the century. Had
McCabe been century-hungry, due caution would have given him a
much longer list of first-class and Test centuries, for dismissal often
came to him in the seventies, eighties and, indeed, the nineties.

I once saw him given out at 93 in a Test against England in Sydney
by Borwick, whom we thought not a very competent Test umpire.
Even from the balcony of our dressing-room, it seemed a bad decision. There was a distinct snick before the ball hit his pads, but not
one of the huge crowd was given the slightest suggestion by McCabe
that the umpire had given a bad lbw decision. McCabe moved away

quickly from the crease with a little characteristic skip he had. About 99 per cent of Test batsmen – and I include myself – would have permitted themselves some peevish act of disapproval – perhaps not to the extent of throwing their bat down! – but they would have shown understandable disapproval at being given out in the Test nineties in such a way by hesitating somewhat, by slapping their bat against a pad, by glowering, or letting off some steam to the first fieldsman they passed. Many a spectator, too, has heard the crashing sound of a thrown bat in the dressing-room when a warrior returns from a bad decision. Not with McCabe, on this occasion in Sydney. His quiet reply to the inevitable question in the privacy of the dressing-room was: 'I think I hit it.' To such a question, many a disgruntled batsman would explode: 'Hit it? Of course, I bloody-well hit it!'

There was another occasion when he showed out in true colours. At Scarborough, in 1934, Sutcliffe hit a ball to square-leg and called Wyatt for a run. The ball hit the umpire's foot (which doesn't make it 'dead') and went off at a tangent to a fieldsman, who returned it smartly to McCabe, who was bowling. Wyatt was stranded yards down the wicket. McCabe quietly caught the ball and walked back to his bowling mark. Wyatt, very relieved, scrambled home. There was no fussy ostentation about McCabe, nothing blatant to show spectators that he was 'playing the game'.

If McCabe, with me, will always stand on a particular pedestal, it is no easy matter to assign him his position among the top batsmen of his time. Possibly it could be said of him that he wasn't a reliable Test batsman, in the real meaning of the term. Whenever, for instance, I saw Leyland and Paynter walk to the Test middle, I knew instinctively that there would be no pap and nonsense, that each would have to be dug out by the roots like a century-old oak. Test cricket, to these two and their like, was Test cricket first, last and in the middle, and each Test ball would be met with resolute determination and concentration, a bat taken back straight and put down straight to the ball with a head above it crammed with admirable north of England canniness.

It was not in McCabe's nature to look upon cricket as such a life-and-death business. Bowlers did not get him out in Test matches so much as he got himself out, taking risks. He could never, for instance, resist the challenge of a hook stroke. It is a strange thing to write, but I don't think he had any great liking for Test cricket. He could not bring himself to play the cautious, canny type of play which Tests so often demanded, and he begrudged the nervous toll a series exacted from him.

Once in Adelaide, Robins set an exaggerated field to give McCabe a single so that Robins could get at the other batsman. Most batsmen would not have been worried by Robins's field. They would have bided their time, looking for twos and an occasional four, but McCabe jumped immediately to the challenge and tried to hit Robins over the fence. He missed by a few feet. He was caught, at 88, as the ball almost cleared the fence.

Bradman upbraided McCabe in the dressing-room for playing such a risky shot. McCabe, who was vice-captain of Australia, quietly heard his captain out. 'Well Braddles,' he said, smiling, 'if a similar ball comes up in the second innings, I will still try and hit it for six.' Robins got him again – at 55.

Like the advice from Polonius, McCabe always was true to himself. His generous nature did not allow him to regard cricket in any other light than a game that should be played chivalrously and cavalierly, whether it was a Test, a Shield game, a grade game in Sydney or an up-country game. Some of his Sydney grade innings were incredibly brilliant.

Nothing in cricket gave him more enjoyment than his many tilts with Clarrie Grimmett. They were warm friends, and always the same leg-pulling would go on as he came to the middle.

'I'll give you the cane today, Grum,' McCabe would call down the pitch, as he was taking his guard.

'I don't think you will,' the Fox would smilingly say from the other end, 'I have a surprise or two for you.'

In truth, it did seem that Grimmett bowled better against McCabe than any other Australian batsman. A little skip, a little hop, and over in its low trajectory would come a ball from Grimmett, full of spin and guile and pitching, for a certainty, on the blind-spot and forcing McCabe back on to his stumps.

Grimmett might have come out of these duels overall with slight honours, but mainly because McCabe carried the attack to him. McCabe might send him soaring over long-off or long-on, but Grimmett would motion his field back and back and McCabe always accepted the challenge. There were days, of course, when McCabe triumphed and gave Grimmett a lacing, but it was not uncommon to see Grimmett trap him, and then Clarrie would double up in mirth and twit McCabe as he left.

'You sly old fox, Grum,' McCabe would call gaily as he walked away, 'but wait until the next innings. I'll get you then.'

That was how McCabe loved to play his cricket, a bit of fun in it and not too serious, not feeling that the Sword of Damocles hung over his head constantly at the wickets. He was always ready to take risks, blatant risks. Many Australians claimed they preferred to see McCabe play a century innings than Bradman. This was purely a matter of opinion. Each was a powerful force in cricket and each played his own individual and essential role. It is to be remembered that Bradman's genius was much more consistent and on longer view than that of McCabe's. It is possible, also, by over-indulgence, to become blasé about the choicest wines.

McCabe and Bradman will be remembered by those who played with and against them in different categories. McCabe is assured for all time, because of his three epics, of the highest ranking in the batting art.

The batsman McCabe idolized was John Berry Hobbs. He told me once that he learnt more about batting when fielding to Jack Hobbs at cover at the Oval than in the rest of his career. 'His footwork was magnificent,' said McCabe – and Hobbs was then in his 50th year! McCabe was not extravagant in his own footwork. He didn't dance down the pitch, for instance, as Bradman did. McCabe barely took more than two paces at the best of times but his feet were always correctly placed. Nobody in any era could have played the pull and hook better than McCabe. He played them effortlessly.

McCabe never thought he was much of a bowler. With a grin, he would say how much he would like to bat to his own bowling and smile ruefully when he recalled how Duleepsinhji got 'stuck into' him. 'Duleep used to sharpen up his bat when I took the ball,' said McCabe. He was being too modest. He could fizz his medium-paced deliveries off the pitch and could bowl a baffling medium-fast bosie. Four times he took the wicket of Wally Hammond in Tests, a feat for any acknowledged bowler. He also got the wickets in Tests of Hobbs, Robins, Duleepsinhji, Leyland (2), Tate, Jardine, Larwood, Ames, Allen, Walters, Woolley, Worthington (2), Peebles, Wyatt and Wellard. As my friend, Ian Peebles, would be bound to say: 'there are some noble batsmen in that list.'

News of his tragic death, falling over a cliff at his Sydney home, came to us in London in August, 1968, on the Sunday of the final Test at the Oval. I wrote, with infinite sadness, his obituary notice for *The Times* next day and concluded it thus: 'His manner and character never changed. He abhorred humbug. He was the warmest and most loyal of friends, and there was neither conceit nor deceit in his nature.'

On this Monday, at the Oval, I thought the Australian team, at the very least, would have honoured his memory by wearing black arm-bands. They didn't. As I returned to the Oval, after lunch, I saw the Oval flag at half-mast. 'At last,' I told myself, 'they are paying tribute to Stan.' I found out, subsequently, it was for Princess Marina.

13. Denis Compton

One day in Melbourne, Wrong-Grip Jake, as they called Jack Iverson with his finger-flick spinners, was turning Denis Compton inside out. It happened not only to Compton on that tour of Australia. Cyril Washbrook, a pretty competent professional batsman, never worried much about trying to decipher which way Iverson was turning the ball (it came mostly from the off with a leg-break action). Washbrook sometimes used to open his shoulders with mingling hope and despair. This was after Washbrook's (then) record benefit match and he was at the end of his career.

Compton was worrying his way along most tenuously against Iverson and at the end of one over, David Sheppard, his batting partner, called a mid pitch conference on Iverson. Denis rounded it off. 'You keep playing Iverson the way you are, David,' said Compton, 'and leave the antics to me.'

The story typified Compton. He was full of humour and antics. And chockful of ability. Indeed, looking over the years and the names, I think I would just as soon have watched a century innings by Compton, one of his best, as by any other batsman I have known. He played every stroke and threw in a few special ones of his own conception and execution; his footwork was magnificent and, when he would begin a long run out to a slow bowler before the ball was bowled, of his own conception and execution; and against the bouncers of Lindwall and Miller in England in 1948, he revealed courage of the highest order in pulling the ball fearlessly off his uncapped brow.

Denis hit a century against Australia in his first Test, at Nottingham, in 1938, and a young inexperienced man of nineteen who got a century in his first Test against a bowler like O'Reilly had to be a good batsman. He made a century in each innings of a Test in Adelaide. But Compton is not a batsman you deal with in figures, brilliant as they often were, particularly in the immediate post-Second World War years when he (and also Bill Edrich) peeled off century after century for Middlesex. What his scoring mostly did then was to emphasize what brilliance we missed from him in Australia in what, but for the war, would have been the 1940–41

English tour. Compton would then have been at his zenith. His soccer days with Arsenal (he was a war-time international in this game) left him with damaged knee cartilages. This cut short his career and, largely through inactivity, put weight on his solid frame.

Compton, as I have said, is not a man you deal with in figures. I don't think he worried much about centuries (many will have a vivid memory of him holding his bat aloft over his tousled hair to acknowledge applause for a century), but derived his cricket pleasure from accepting challenges and playing all the shots. He wasn't a greedy man in the middle. He had no designs on hogging the strike but accepted it as it came. He figured in more running mix-ups than possibly even Geoff Boycott but with Compton it all looked like part of the entertainment and it certainly added excitement to a Compton appearance. There was bound to be some hectic helter-skeltering between the wickets with Denis, like an absent-minded professor, forgetting all about the accepted rules of run-calling. There was nothing personal in it.

'Yes,' he would admit with a smile, 'I'm afraid I did "do" one or two of my batting partners at various times. Nothing personal in it, you know. More or less a case of tangled interpretations of what constituted a run. Once or twice, perhaps, I might have suffered a rush of blood to the skull on a hot day. But nothing personal, mark you.'

Perhaps his most 'personal' run out was when he was batting with his brother, Leslie, at Lord's one day and Leslie was run out. It was Leslie's benefit match! 'Surely,' said Denis, deprecatingly, 'you would expect a brother, and a younger one at that, to know his brother's calling.' What Leslie thought and said isn't printable!

Compton played the bouncer better than Hammond. Indeed, he had more shots than the man from Gloucestershire, who concentrated upon the off-side with his peerless cover-drive. I have never seen better pull-shots – and my memory covers all of McCabe's three epics – than Compton's at Old Trafford and Trent Bridge in 1948 against Miller and Lindwall. Strangely, for all the fuss the Australians made against bouncers from Larwood and Voce, Bradman never attempted to curtail the incessant bouncers that Lindwall and Miller were allowed to bowl in England in 1948 and there were innumerable times when they served up as many in an over – although without the packed leg-side field – as Larwood and Voce in Australia.

Len Hutton, with his damaged and shortened left arm, was at a big disadvantage. Compton was not. His pulling of Miller at Trent Bridge late one afternoon – Lindwall had retired injured – was as devastatingly and courageously brilliant as anything I have seen in cricket. Compton did not have a big back-lift with his pull-shot. Indeed, he could not have done so against the speed of the Australians. He hooked with a short-arm jab and he hooked off the very tip of his nose – after he had been hit on the head at Old Trafford by Lindwall, he continued to hook off his very head-bandage.

After all that had gone before, I was not at all comfortable watching all these head-high bouncers the Englishmen had to withstand from Lindwall and Miller. Compton never flinched nor winced. He was over-flowing with guts.

Compton was a peerless driver of the ball, in a wide arc. His footwork to the ball down the pitch was lovely to watch and, as I have mentioned, he threw in that little bit extra when he started to move out before the ball was bowled. This was not 'antics', but it often led to much merriment. Compton's reasoning was that he could destroy the length of a slow bowler by walking out to him before he bowled and, if he had miscalculated and walked into trouble, he could scamper back to his crease. Hence the merriment. I can't recall ever seeing Compton being stumped in this exercise.

He had two particularly brilliant strokes of his own devising. One was the leg-sweep and he played this type of shot, which has many derivations, better than anybody. I often thought it could with Compton be termed a backward drive. Compton's bat went out high towards the bowler with its face open. His left foot also went down the pitch. Then he brought his bat down . . . not across . . . and through with the ball. Nobody played this shot finer past the wicket-keeper than Compton.

Whereas many, and to off-spin bowlers, seem to play the sweep as a desperation swish shot when they are bottled up – and it costs many their wickets – Compton always looked safe in playing it. No doubt it sometimes cost him his wicket but his guard would have been on the leg stump and his back leg, therefore, would have guarded that stump – particularly if against a leg-break bowler – and he seemed to choose the right ball with judgment.

His other speciality was a forward drive just in front of or behind point. His front foot would go well across the pitch and, with perfect timing and the snap of strong wrists coming in at the last fraction of time, the ball would sizzle past point.

Denis Compton was a glorious batsman. England hasn't produced the like of him since. Some might be strong on this or that side, but

Compton had no batting weakness and had a flair in his stroking
that made him reminiscent, to Australians, of Macartney and
McCabe.

In his young days, he was a good slip fieldsman. One day at
Headingley, Leeds, his name could well have been posted in big
black type had his bowling been supported. With a slight rolling
amble, he bowled over the wrist left-handed slow spinners and
Norman Yardley threw the ball quickly and unexpectedly to Compton for one or two overs of his so-called 'Chinamen'. Crapp dropped
Morris at first slip; and Godfrey Evans, of all people, dropped Don
Bradman. This was the game which Australia sensationally won on
the last day with the Australians making 403–3. Had those chances
been taken, this might have been a day of glory for England and
Compton. 'Godfrey over-slept that morning,' said Compton.

Compton has a rich sense of humour, at its best when his fancied
horses come home. He rarely gets upset but he was lost for words at
the Oval in 1948 when, after being caught off a mistimed pull,
Bradman told him: 'We played for that. I remember you put a ball
up in that spot when you batted against us here in 1998.' Even
Denis thought that was a bit rich!

One day in Melbourne in 1971 he was most amused when a
woman walked up to Jim Swanton and said: 'My word, Mr Compton, but you have put on weight since your playing days.' Denis
Compton, in his thinking, is not quite in accord with modern players.
He doesn't think they get much fun out of the game. When Middlesex, after a run of outs, had a good win, Denis went into the dressing-
room of his old team and asked them to have a celebratory drink
with him. He was astounded at the orders, not even a beer among
them. 'Why,' said Denis, 'one chap even ordered a glass of milk.
Things were different in my day.'

Part Three

SIX BOWLERS

To write of six bowlers is not to restrict to that number the great bowlers I knew and played against. Nor would Ian Meckiff be included in such a list. I have included him because he personified a period of extreme contention through which Australian cricket passed. Also, I did not think much of the manner in which he was 'called out' of big cricket. A little paragraph on Learie Constantine illustrates an important point on the action of bowlers. Learie used to watch his hand overhead as he delivered, to make certain there was no crook in his arm. Coaches of bowlers should make certain that the young player begins with an action beyond suspicion.

Ian Peebles recently wrote a splendid book on this contentious subject of dubious actions, a subject, indeed, which once gave the game one of its most heated controversies and which led to Sir Donald Bradman and W. J. Dowling, the two leading cricket officials in Australia, flying to London to discuss the upheaval. Peebles had the simple solution to the trouble – that once the arm reached the horizontal in its delivery, it should be straight until the ball is delivered. As far back as 1953 in England, I recall Keith Miller batting at the Oval and making a throwing action to the umpire after Tony Lock had bowled to him. The incident went almost completely unreported. It was not until some time later that a gaggle of extremely dubious actions in Australia, and particularly in South Australia, gave rise to much discontent and discord. Lock was one of the many, incidentally, who modified his action.

I played innumerable games with – 'with', I am relieved to say – Bill O'Reilly. Don Bradman gave him the accolade as the greatest bowler he knew, the supreme compliment. I enjoyed writing about the 'Tiger', as I did also about Clarrie Grimmett, his wonderful sparring partner, as O'Reilly described him. I always thought that each bowled his best in partnership with the other and if Test cricket knew a better pair of spinners than these two in concert, I will be surprised. I met the great Syd Barnes often in England. His temperament was similar to O'Reilly's: he sniffed hate at the batsman – not a bad sling in the armoury of a bowler. I have gone back into history to dig up his wonderful feat in Melbourne and, in this, I had the advantage of talking to some of those – now all, alas, dead – who faced Barnes in that great match.

One must observe restrictions, unfortunately, in a chapter like this. Tate and Bedser were wonderful bowlers who deserve recognition. Tate's early feats in his tours of Australia were outstanding and Bedser, a tireless worker, was magnificent against the Australians in England. He bowled at his best against Arthur Morris, one of the best openers any country has known. In recent years, I have been consistent in criticizing those ridiculously long runs that fast-medium bowlers, for the most part, have permitted themselves and have been permitted under the rules. This long walk-back and run has contributed much to the tedium of modern cricket. The action doesn't flow. The batsman is frustrated. The spectators fiddle and twiddle. It is interesting that three of the greatest fast bowlers of all time – who were *really* fast – did not take lavish runs. They were Larwood, Lindwall and Miller and I group them in one chapter.

It is also interesting, I think, that Bedser lost his Test place in Australia in the mid-fifties because he got through an over too fast! His quick delivery of an over didn't fit in with Len Hutton's plan of keeping a tight rein on the batsmen by cutting down the number of overs per hour. This belief still holds sway in English and Australian camps with both sides choosing three fast and medium-fast bowlers. That third such bowler wasn't wanted when O'Reilly and Grimmett were in action, but the modern trend of one-day matches has made the slow leg-break spinner almost unemployed, more's the pity. Cricket – and captaincy – will be all the better when the spinners return. One of the most pleasing features of the 1970–71 series between England and Australia in Australia was the manner in which Ian Chappell, a new skipper, in the final Test, generously bowled O'Keeffe and Jenner and set attacking fields for them.

14. Bill O'Reilly

The cricket story of William Joseph O'Reilly is one of a man big in heart, in stature and in ability. None but the big in heart merit Test bowling fame and particularly if he is a spin bowler – as O'Reilly was – and if he bowled – as O'Reilly did – in an age when the art of producing doped and over-prepared wickets had reached its height.

One could not deal mathematically with O'Reilly. It could be said that in so many games he captured so many wickets at such a cost, but this knowledge leads nowhere in an analysis of the bowling powers of this Australian giant. The record book is too easy an escape for the stumped or unknowledgable critic, and, moreover, it tells only a portion of the story, as all averages do. Figures don't tell whether a bowler was at his best in a time of crisis or whether he handed his marble in; they are mute on dropped catches and utter not a syllable on moral wickets, when a bowler breaks clean through a batsman only to miss the stumps by a fraction. And O'Reilly, as others know as well as himself, had many of these in his time and many a wicket did he get, also, for the bowler at the other end by first worrying the batsman into desperation.

For all that, O'Reilly's figures are worth knowing. In four Test series against England, and at a time when English batting was of a very high standard, he took 102 wickets from 7,846 balls at a cost of 25.64 each; in two series against South Africa, one not a full one, he took 34 wickets off 340 overs (six and eight-ball overs) at 18.97; in two tours of England he took 260 wickets at 14.52; in Sheffield Shield he took 203 wickets off 1,342 overs at 17.43; in 15 years of grade cricket in Sydney, played on Saturday afternoons, he bundled out 921 batsmen at under ten runs apiece. How many wickets he took in the country, from Tibaburra to Griffith, is not known even to O'Reilly.

Figures, however, tell only a meagre portion of the story of O'Reilly. He was a mystery bowler. He made good by stealth for his art was not clearly apparent to those watching from outside. Larwood was different. The merest tyro knew immediately that Larwood was a great bowler, such was the terrific speed with which the ball hurtled through to the keeper. So, too, was the genius of Tate apparent. He whipped the ball off the pitch and, behind his arm, one could see the ball move sharply in the air and off the pitch. Mailey's profligate breaks were as obvious as day, and Grimmett was another whose wiles were apparent to the spectator.

These bowlers and others took a spectator into a game with them, but not so O'Reilly. He covered himself up, he hid his intentions with long, flaying arms, the 6 ft 3 ins, of him bobbing and jostling on his unusually long run to the stumps. He was a flurry of arms, legs, fire and steel-edged temper – a temper which glared and opened fire when anything fortunate befell the batsman. His cynical and noisy laugh when a batsman snicked him discomforted many. O'Reilly was never one to spare anybody's feelings, particularly those of a batsman.

Much of O'Reilly's technique was visible to spectators, but when a batsman facing him was cramped uncomfortably on the defensive, when he was lbw or bowled, and particularly when he popped up a catch to the short-leg field, many on the outer were not too certain what had happened or why. For that matter, many an O'Reilly victim was not certain of what had been going on under his nose.

That is the sense in which O'Reilly was a mystery bowler. One could count on the fingers of one hand the batsmen who succeeded in recognizing his wares to the extent of rough-handling him. He dismissed every batsman of world class in his day and the manner of dismissal left no possible doubt whatever.

Bats did not go forward to meet O'Reilly with full-faced impunity and certainty. They wavered out, much like a peroxide-blonde entering the surf without a bathing cap, for one could never be quite certain against O'Reilly that the ball he was playing for a leg-break might not, indeed, be a bosie or, just as embarrassing, a top-spinner.

This general atmosphere of mystery made O'Reilly the most discussed bowler of his day. Some said immediately that he was the greatest bowler of his time. Others conceded – and the record book did not suggest rashness – that he was fit to rank with the bowling immortals. Then lined up the doubting Thomases, among them leading critics – who didn't have to face O'Reilly, be it remembered – and they found it difficult to say whether O'Reilly was a great bowler or a flattered one. Their argument against him was that when he wasn't getting wickets, he did not look a world bowler.

O'Reilly, on his day was without doubt the world's leading bowler but his day was never one when the pitch had not been stirred from its doped sleep. Length and variation of pace alone stood to O'Reilly on such days. Of what use was it to deceive a batsman with spin if a glazed, doped surface wouldn't allow a ball to spin? At such times, O'Reilly plugged away, waiting for a glimmer of life to come into the pitch. It was there one day in Melbourne in 1933, for instance, and O'Reilly tied the Englishmen into knots with his quick spin from the leg.

O'Reilly's father, as W. J. was to become himself, was a school-teacher, and O'Reilly was born in the never-never at White Cliffs, right up in the nor-west of New South Wales. The father moved, in time, to the little rustic school at Wingello, about a hundred miles south of Sydney and just thirty miles further along the railway line from Bowral, the drowsy little town that nurtured Bradman before giving him to a doting sporting world. Just across the little railway-station at Wingello is the modest school, an equally modest church, a store that stocks most things, and sparse houses which tail off into the bush down the road and which lodge railway fettlers and the other workers of the district.

The houses, even now, are roofed country-fashion with corrugated iron, which gives off the sound of rain in winter and blistering heat in the summer. In summer, also, come dry westerlies to whip up the dust and dry off the pastures ... and it was then, in O'Reilly's youth, that Wingello became a fit preparatory school for an embryo Test bowler destined to spend interminable and toiling hours in the sun.

The Australian boy of the outback who seeks sport in the high noon of summer must have a well-developed sporting appetite. O'Reilly had that appetite, and he was further blessed – although he wasn't to think so at the time – in being the youngest of four bowlers. The dignity and the size of his elders taught the young O'Reilly to mind his place; not to give himself airs and graces; to accept a menial job, such as bowling.

The family had little sporting equipment. They had no ball but, with great ingenuity, they unearthed a tough, gnarled Banksia tree-root. They took it in turns to work on the root with a chisel and in time it came to resemble a ball. It saw out the entire cricketing life of the O'Reillys at Wingello.

With an improvized bat, also, the brothers made their daily jaunt past the creek to the paddock that had been cleared of timber. And, W. J. being the youngest of the four, his invariable legacy was the ball, the hard work. Long and intimate association taught him all there was to know about the root-ball. It had a knot either side of it and, as O'Reilly's long fingers twined around each knot in turn, he came to know them as the off and the leg-break knot. He experimented and persisted with them, telling himself as he trudged off to fox his Banksia root in the mulga across the creek that his day would come against his brothers. Time wore down the ordinary wood of the root-ball; time and usage had little effects upon the knots and so, as they became more pronounced, the young O'Reilly got more spin on the ball.

He had his first official game of cricket when ten years old. Wingello could not make up a team by itself and so, with reinforcements from the next village, the side set out for battle with more dogs than pieces of cricket equipment. The dogs would have many a rabbit-chase on the way and in this fashion the Wingello team of boys made its way on foot down the seven long dusty miles to Tallong. They walked there and back.

O'Reilly doesn't think he was successful. By far his most vivid memory of the match was being bitten by a Jumping Joey ant, which is a memory not easily erased.

Around this time, the young one was often finding himself in disgrace in the home paddock with his brothers. He was hazy concerning the reason for many a cuff he got but possibly the truth was that his bowling had now come on apace; he was often rattling the kerosene-tin wicket of his brothers, and they didn't like being shown up. The day of the underdog was indeed dawning, even if only in the bush.

His next game of consequence – and it is to be noted how few sporting chances a lad in the bush received in those days before cars – was a few years later when he was invited to play for the Governor's team against I Zingari at Sutton Forest. He doesn't remember his feats but he thinks he must have bowled well because the former Test slow bowler, Dr H. V. Hordern, took him aside and gave him some bowling hints.

O'Reilly now began to play against Bradman. He played in that game which gave Bradman his first notoriety, when Bradman batted over three days, yet O'Reilly could well have had Bradman out early.

O'Reilly's first slip was a world war one soldier who allowed himself the liberty of having the company of a pipe while fielding. It was no ordinary pipe. It was a big meerschaum and, with a high wind blowing, first slip was having some trouble in keeping his pipe alight. In the midst of his endeavours in this direction, Bradman early snicked a catch from O'Reilly and first slip wasn't ready for it. It hit him plumb on the gold watch-chain on his vest. Fieldsmen usually thought it safer to keep their valuables on them.

Bradman rose to the top quicker than O'Reilly, who was a country school-teacher when Bradman wrote his first cricket book just before the 1930 tour of England. Bradman wrote at length on the ability of O'Reilly as a bowler.

Grown out of his father's country school, O'Reilly went to St Patrick's College in Goulburn, where he was a sporting all-rounder rather than a cricketer. He went to Sydney at seventeen for a teacher training course and oddly, for a youth who sought out the game under the country's bleakest conditions, O'Reilly didn't bother to play the game in this city of cricket plenty.

Athletics was his love. He had a New South Wales record in the hop, step and jump and nothing could wean him from athletics in those years. He might well have gone on to become an Olympian had there not been a Saturday morning when he went as an onlooker with a student friend who was playing in the Moore Park junior competition.

The side was a man short and O'Reilly agreed to make up the number. He took the field in borrowed gear and, as a gesture towards his willingness to help out, the skipper gave him a beneficiary over.

O'Reilly was a sensation. In the first instance, his long, Kangaroo-like run gave everybody the giggles but the smiles soon switched as wickets began to tumble. The coir matting on which he bowled gave his breaks tremendous purchase and the batsmen couldn't put their bat on him. His fellows acclaimed him. He simply had to play again.

And he did, but he didn't forsake athletics for cricket. He played cricket in the mornings and did athletics in the afternoon, although his athletics career was now tainted with doom. To the accompaniment of crashing stumps, his fame spread through the parklands. It reached senior clubs and there came an invitation from the North Sydney club to play grade with them the next season.

O'Reilly went into grade and the change from matting to the spin-responsive turf pitches of club cricket suited him admirably. He was fast on the way to notoriety, playing for a second New South Wales team, when the bush claimed him again. O'Reilly thinks – and many will agree with him – that had he stayed in Sydney, he would have gone to England with the 1930 side.

He had qualified as a teacher and his posting was to the back-blocks. In quick succession, he taught at Griffith, Rylstone and Kandos, small centres, and in this second bush immersion he set himself a task.

It was to perfect a bosie, a ball he didn't have the confidence to bowl in Sydney. On that delivery his very fame was built. It is a ball which needs intense practice and often, in the wooing, it is capricious enough to kill other natural talents. By hard and persistent seeking, O'Reilly won his bosie and retained, also, his old leg-break and top-spinning loves.

The Education Department helped the cause of cricket and the game in Australia when it recalled O'Reilly to the city. He returned as the 1930 Australian team came home from England, and with such venom that in only one year he was in the Australian team, playing against South Africa.

When the Australian team was playing the second Test of that series, O'Reilly went south with what was virtually a second New South Wales team. Many of the first side were in the Test team. Dr Reg Bettington was captain of the touring Shield team but well and all as O'Reilly bowled in Adelaide and Melbourne, he was dropped from the side when the Test men returned. Bettington, a very good slow bowler and hard-hitting batsman, who had played with great distinction for Oxford, was kept in the team. But, feeling that O'Reilly was a Test man in the making, Bettington went to the selectors and asked unselfishly to be dropped for O'Reilly.

And O'Reilly, dropped from the New South Wales team a week or so before, was in the Australian team for the third Test against South Africa. And he never afterwards lost, nor looked like losing, his Test place.

O'Reilly was like Bradman – he had complete confidence in his own ability. The first time he appeared among the élite at the Sydney Cricket Ground nets, O'Reilly was approached by Mailey who suggested that O'Reilly should change his grip on the ball.

Mailey was Mailey. His advice would have been gospel to most rising young bowlers, who would have hastened to do his bidding. But not O'Reilly. He had a mind of his own. That grip had come to him in the bush and it was going to stay with him. Politely, he told Mailey that he had always held the ball that way and, if Mr Mailey did not mind, he would continue to do so.

That was not impertinent. If somebody had gone to Mailey years before and suggested he should have changed his grip, Mailey would undoubtedly have done what O'Reilly did. Individual art is created. Little moulding is needed. Champion qualities are either inherent in an individual or they are not, and he prefers to work out his destiny on his own lines.

Mailey twined his fingers around the ball and cracked his fingers like a whip as he delivered. O'Reilly cupped his fingers around the ball and rolled it out with spin. Mailey was not renowned for his length; O'Reilly was. Mailey was a slow bowler; O'Reilly was

9, 10, 11 and 12. BOMBS AWAY: (*top left*) Harold Larwood, who emigrated behind enemy lines; (*top right*) Bill O'Reilly, who breathed fire over all cricket grounds east and west; (*bottom left*) Ian Meckiff, who was sentenced for life; (*bottom right*) Clarrie Grimmett, who regarded batsmen as purely temporary obstacles.

13, 14, 15 and 16. MASTER BOWLERS: (*top left*) Maurice Tate, the perfect bowling action; (*top right*) Sydney Barnes, 189 wickets in only 27 Tests; (*bottom left*) Keith Miller, as liable to bowl off four yards as twenty; (*bottom right*) Ray Lindwall, fast bowling for the connoisseur.

17, 18, 19 and 20. ODD MAN OUT: Charlie Macartney (*bottom left*) is the only right-hander. The others are the dominant left-handers of their generations: (*top left*) Gary Sobers; (*top right*) Graeme Pollock; (*bottom right*) Warren Bardsley.

21. THE HEAT IS ON: Greig leans across the threshold of the pitch as Bedi bowls to Inverarity in Australia.

22. THE HEAT IS ON: Lawry avoids plastic surgery as he draws away from Peter Pollock in South Africa.

medium pace and between the two was a fundamental difference in all things, even to temperament. Mailey never seemed to mind how many runs he gave away; O'Reilly resented the meagrest single.

I knew no bowler who resembled O'Reilly. At medium pace, he bowled his stock leg-break ball, his bosie and a top-spinner. If the pitch took spin, he could turn the ball the width of the stumps but generally his spin was modest yet deadly enough to miss the bat by a fraction or nip its edge for a catch.

He concealed his bosie most artfully. There was some mixture of top-spin in his bosie that made this ball bounce higher from the pitch and this was the ball which brought many catches to his leg-trap.

O'Reilly was not distinctive only in the variety of balls he could bowl. He had other rich gifts, none more tantalizing than his long, odd, bobbing approach to the crease. Edmund Blunden, the author and poet, under whose captaincy I once played for Authors versus the Publishers at Westminster Square, described O'Reilly's run-in aptly when he said that his bowling began long before he got to the wickets. A batsman likes to see a bowler run in evenly to the crease. It doesn't disturb his vision. But with O'Reilly a batsman's line of sight went up and down like a see-saw as O'Reilly came jolting along, like a kangaroo in the legs and a windmill in the arms. And then, finally, the ball erupted at the batsman from a mass of whirling arms.

'I have never seen a bowler,' Constantine once told me, 'who seemed to suggest by his action that he wished to goodness he was a fast bowler, a fast bowler who would sweep everything in front of him. That, all other things being equal, is the ideal bowling temperament to possess.'

Nothing in O'Reilly's make-up was more vital than his temperament. Hot blood, always close to the boil, surged through O'Reilly's veins. His 'paddy' was quick to show if he thought he was being wronged by fate, umpires, batsmen or cricket legislators – and I think at no stage of his career did O'Reilly think that his bowling brethren were anything else but the victims of oppression. Possibly the grudge that grew with him in his Wingello paddock never left him. Throughout his career he contended that bowlers were the playthings of the game, the legislators and the gates. In his view, the bowler was the male Cinderella of the game, always doing the interminable grafting work for his elder brothers, the batsmen and the legislators.

Such things worried O'Reilly. He fumed in Sydney one day when Richardson wouldn't bowl him before lunch at Bradman. It was a

testimonial game and a Saturday and no risk could be taken of
Bradman being out before lunch. O'Reilly differed in his bowling
outlook, for instance, from Fleetwood-Smith who never worried that
doped and over-prepared pitches robbed him of spin. Fleetwood was
the playboy of Test cricket. It was nothing for him to squawk like a
magpie or whistle brightly as he ran up to bowl in a Test. In all the
Tests I played with him, only once did I see Fleetwood-Smith do
credit to his superb ability – in Adelaide, in 1937, when he spun a
Test win for Australia out of a seemingly hopeless position.

O'Reilly's outlook on the game was completely different. Cricket,
to him, was a job of work that had to be done, and his broad shoulders seemed to attract responsibility. No job was ever too big for his
cricketing heart but that didn't mean he couldn't allow himself a
complete loathing for the type of first-class pitch on which he had to
bowl.

Veterans have assured me with glints in their eyes that Turner,
Spofforth and others of preceding generations could spin a ball on
any pitch in the world. I doubt it. I could not conceive anybody turning the ball by spin (not body-break, mark you) on pitches I have
seen over the first few days of a Test match at Adelaide, Melbourne,
Sydney, Trent Bridge, the Kennington Oval and Cape Town. The
grass from those pitches had been shorn like hair from a convict's
head.

Spin is abortive unless it has something to grip. It must have resis-
tance. But on many of the Test pitches on which O'Reilly bowled (he
would have been unplayable on the many poor pitches in England
in 1968), he was forced to fight the batsman with length bowling for
hour after hour until the pitch came to some growing life again and
responded to spin.

Those were the occasions when a carping critic would say of
O'Reilly that when he was not getting wickets he did not look to be
in the highest world class. What spin bowler did under such circumstances? Grimmett, possibly the greatest slow bowler the world has
seen (O'Reilly was not a slow bowler), was dropped from the
Australian Eleven in his homeland in 1932–33 and not even considered in 1937, a year after a most successful tour of South Africa
which made the Springboks think his slow magic was not of this
world. And Freeman, who once took 304 wickets for Kent in a
county season, never worried Test batsmen on Australian pitches.

O'Reilly hated these pitches and he impersonally hated the batsmen who thrived on them. He started every such game with hate, and
it showed in every ball he bowled. If his aged father had come to bat

against him on such a pitch, O'Reilly would have recognized his inexorable enemies, the bat and pads, before knowing his own flesh and blood and he would have shown him no mercy. There was no mercy in his bowling make-up – and certainly not to youngsters playing their first game in Sydney club cricket. From the field, I often felt for some poor tyro who came in to face O'Reilly when 'the Tiger's' dander was up. He was known throughout his career as 'the Tiger' and for good reason.

He was an avid, raucous and consistent appealer. In his first Test against South Africa, he thought he had a batsman caught behind by Oldfield but O'Reilly was too shy (this is what he said!) to appeal. Oldfield said he didn't appeal because O'Reilly didn't. The umpire afterwards expressed surprise that no appeal was made. He would have given the batsman out – and this would have been O'Reilly's first Test wicket! On the spot, he decided he would never err in future by not appealing.

It was in Adelaide, also, that he had a pretty warm difference of opinion with the English batsman, Charlie Barnett, who made a sarcastic aside to an umpire over an O'Reilly appeal. O'Reilly heard the remark and the pair barked at each other for some time. They were still trading words when drinks came. O'Reilly had the last word. 'You do your bloody job, Barnett,' he said, 'and I'll do mine.'

A sense of humour most marked off-field was hung up on the pavilion peg with his street clothes as O'Reilly dressed for cricket. Mailey was the first to see the funny side of things when some gasping batting fish, hopelessly unable to tell which way the ball would break, streakily snicked it between his legs and the stumps. Grimmett, too, enjoyed himself hugely by keeping in some rabbit and tantalizing him with his tricks. O'Reilly didn't hold with such things. The pitch was no place for fun or dunderheads, and he greeted indecent, inelegant or fortuitous strokes with a noisy cackle that rubbed deep into a batsman his good fortune and inefficiency.

He once wrote an article on bowling for his club report. It told you much of himself and I quote from it:

You can never become a good attacking bowler if you do not develop a bowling 'temperament'. A happy-go-lucky, good-natured and carefree outlook is of no use whatever to an ambitious and competent bowler. He must be prepared to boil up inwardly on the slightest provocation, and opportunities are so common that there is no need to cite even one.

Conceal that desirable temperament from the public, but reveal it in all its force and fury to your opponent, the batsman. Spectators often imagine that a bowler is introducing sting or devil into his bowling when he is, in reality, merely working off a little of the surplus blood pressure caused by a 'bowler's temperament'.

O'Reilly did not practise what he preached in this for his fury was apparent to all when he missed the stumps by a fraction, when he was no-balled, or when somebody had scrambled him away for a lucky four. Then O'Reilly really boiled and it was there for all to see.

There was possibly method in such blatancy. If often gave him a psychological advantage over a batsman. He bluffed and bullied many a batsman out. When O'Reilly worked himself up into such a dander, no batsman could take risks against him. At such a time I have fielded within several yards of Bradman, Hammond, Nourse, Ponsford, Compton, Hutton, Sutcliffe, Edrich, Taylor and others at short-leg and not felt I was taking an unusual physical risk. I knew nobody could hit O'Reilly hard to leg when his Irish was up; and I know of no other bowler to whom I would have paid a similar fielding honour.

One could not retrieve one's mistake against O'Reilly if he didn't pick his bosie. His pace would not allow of that and O'Reilly's bowling was always on the three-penny piece. He aimed both his bosie and his leg-break at the middle and leg stump.

His length was magnificent. It was mechanical and it was possibly because of this that batsmen on the short side (Hassett, who made a century in each innings once against O'Reilly in Sydney; Wallace, of New Zealand, in the only pre-war time he faced O'Reilly) found him slightly less difficult than players of taller build. These two and Yardley, who collared O'Reilly at Fenner's one day in 1938 to execute the prettiest on-driving I have seen, were in my mind earlier in this chapter when I wrote I could count on the fingers of one hand the batsmen who have really dealt harshly with O'Reilly.

His mechanical length would have been a fraction on the short side to smaller batsmen, and this, I think, enabled Hassett and Wallace to swing him to the on as they did. W. A. Brown, in 1944 in Australia, did much the same thing against O'Reilly but his fangs were then blunted.

On their day and not on his (Hutton at the Oval in 1938 for 364, for instance), others might have subdued O'Reilly but, even then, few took risks against him. His many duels against Bradman, all on Australian pitches, finished about even. Bradman caned him in

Adelaide in 1939, but O'Reilly called the tune later that season when he caught Bradman on a re-laid Sydney pitch that took spin. Bradman gave O'Reilly more respect than any other bowler – Larwood, over a period, not excluded. Bradman says O'Reilly was the best bowler he met.

Hammond devised the best method of combating O'Reilly. He knew O'Reilly's strong point was pitching to a batsman's legs, aiming at his blind spot and thereabouts. In Australia, in 1936–37, Hammond took guard against O'Reilly on his leg-stump and sometimes even batted wider than that. This meant that O'Reilly, attacking Hammond's legs, was wide of the stumps and Hammond devised what we called a 'cow-shot' to sweep O'Reilly. On this angle, also, it is interesting that O'Reilly didn't like bowling at left-handers, such as Leyland and Paynter, because it meant he had to use his bosie incessantly to attack their legs.

The Englishmen, at home in 1938, generally batted on their leg-stump to him and I think this robbed O'Reilly of some of his hostility. He was not then the bowler he was in 1932–33 or in South Africa in 1935, when he had Grimmett with him. Not even yet has O'Reilly forgiven our selectors for not choosing Grimmett for England in 1938.

I think he reached his bowling peak in 1932–33 and possibly never recovered from the burning-out Woodfull gave him in that series. He bowled 383.4 eight-ball overs. His heart that season, indeed always, was too big. No captain asked him to bowl in vain. He was a captain's delight in that he never sulked or needed cajoling if another spin bowler in the side was given preference in bowling to a worn spot. O'Reilly could have used that spot as well as anybody and, because of his untiring efforts when everything was against him, richly deserved such a crumb, but he was first to realize a skipper's difficulties and generously gave way to others.

He and Grimmett had some delightful feuds in South Africa in 1935 in trying to feed on the tail. In one game, O'Reilly grew sick of the sight of Bruce Mitchell, who constantly faced him while Grimmett was getting the tail at the other end. At Cape Town, when Grimmett was getting the tail once again, the last batsman skied a high one to mid-off and O'Reilly called down the pitch to Grimmett, as O'Reilly took his cap from the umpire: 'That's one wicket you won't get, you little ——.' But mid-off was Fleetwood-Smith, who rushed to get a stump as a souvenir. The catch fell to earth, untouched. Grimmett then got the last wicket, after all!

I asked him once for his general opinions of pitches and those he bowled against. This is what he told me:

South African pitches: I loved them. Possibly it was because the South Africans were easier to bowl against than the English. The pitches took spin and were faster than English ones.

English: The memory of that Oval wicket in 1938 will take a lifetime to efface. When they were not overdone with marl, I liked them, although they were always slow and one had to push the ball through on them all the time. You will remember ordinary county pitches did not remain 'sticky' for long. Half an hour or so.

Australian: The subject is tiresome. Covered pitches are anathema to me and so are the people who decree them. Batsman administrators! Good on the fourth day for bowlers if bowlers have any energy left by then. More 'drongo' (an Australianism for indifferent) batsmen get centuries in Australia than in any other place in the world.

Ponsford: Greatest batsman I bowled against. Also the greatest concentrator. Like the elephant, he never forgot. I can never remember him taking a liberty with a good ball. Others did.

Bradman: Sat on the splice until he had me, and then proceeded to show how I should be dealt with. Always gave me the impression, in his supreme confidence, that he might do something not according to Hoyle. Have had him lbw to a good length break on middle and off to leg.

Hammond: Grand player in all but the push away off his toes to leg for a single, Woodfull's masterpiece. Do you remember the 'cowshot' he brought to light here in 1932? I think he evolved that for my benefit. I got him several times using it.

Hutton: Has all the shots and one day will be persuaded to use them. A marvellous player, but not good enough to hold an all-time Test record.

Nourse: A really good player, splendid in his footwork – but, do you know, I have almost forgotten all about Nourse. It was an extra good trip we had to South Africa, wasn't it?

O'Reilly's criticisms are like his bowling, full of pep and to the point. He has written splendidly and with the highest authority for the *Sydney Morning Herald* for many years now and most would say that he is a pungent critic, a little too much so for modern players. He had one secret ambition that he never realized – to captain an Australian team in England. He was an inspiring leader, an aggressive one with no half-measures, and the English would have loved his speeches – witty, a splendid flow of English, though delivered in a rather nervous voice, and with humorous satire.

Off the field (he never believed in the slightest word of thanks to short-legs who took risks for him as well as catches), he was the ideal touring companion, ready to give a travelogue as the ship sailed along the Red Sea, full of history, conversation and good-fellowship, with an infectious Irish sense of humour.

I recall one big moment he had when he travelled in a Johannesburg hotel lift with Gracie Fields, the only two in the lift. Gracie had only arrived in South Africa a few minutes before and clamoring hundreds greeted her as she got out of the lift.

'Who's the big fellow?' asked somebody.

'Oh, that's Mr Gracie Fields,' said another.

And O'Reilly took a bow.

His best moments of all were in Ireland in 1938, when the O'Reillys for miles around gathered to honour their Australian cousin. At Belfast, they held the game up while they walked to the middle with O'Reilly, chatting of this and that. A huge, cherubic grin never left O'Reilly's face in Ireland. England doted on Bradman, adulating crowds cheering him on and off trains and following him up Piccadilly and the Strand – but O'Reilly was King in Ireland. It was the only time I heard him congratulate a batsman on hitting him for four!

He loved to conduct community singing on tour, which meant he was conductor every time there was some singing. He towered over the singers, dominating them like a Beecham. And he was always having something Irish.

'We will now have Mother Machree,' he would announce. 'I want you all to come in together on the downbeat three. Now, then. One, two . . .'

'Shure –' I'd begin to sing.

O'Reilly would glare. 'Another peep before the downbeat three and I'll Mother Machree you,' he would threaten. 'Now, we will start again with Mother Machree and on my downbeat of three. One, two. . . .'

'Shure —' I'd start again, and Barnett would branch off brightly on 'Bonnie Charlie'.

'Beecham' would put down his baton, roll his sleeves and there would be a free-for-all. When he had established order, he would take up the baton again.

'Now that's its been established who's the best man here,' he would say, 'we will now have some singing. And we will have something Irish. We will have Mother Machree.'

And this despite the fact that for the past hour or so we had been having 'something Irish'! A great man was the O'Reilly, a veritable giant in the game of cricket.

The old flame fired again in the Sydney press-box in 1969 when both Hall and Griffith warned Redpath that he was leaving the crease before the ball was bowled. Griffith had run Redpath out in Adelaide, holding the ball instead of delivering it. Some Australians took a dim view of Charlie Griffith, thinking him the white sheep of West Indian cricket. When Griffith didn't deliver in Sydney but this time warned Redpath, who should never have been caught napping again after Adelaide, Simpson and O'Reilly indulged in a warm debate on the merits of proceedings.

O'Reilly rightly contended that the onus was on Redpath to see that he didn't leave the crease before the ball was bowled. In a rather waspish voice, Simpson said to O'Reilly: 'How many batsmen did *you* run out like that in your time?'

Without hesitation, O'Reilly shot back: 'I never found in my time that the batsman in runs was over-keen to get down the other end against me.'

I stood up, sitting next to O'Reilly, smiled and held out my hand. 'Why, you old so-and-so,' I said, 'I'm mighty proud of you.'

15. Syd Barnes

Write the name of S. F. Barnes, of Staffordshire, England, and set against it this bowling analysis: 11 overs, 7 maidens, 6 runs, 5 wickets. There you have the finest piece of bowling ever seen in Test cricket, for it was performed on a true pitch at Melbourne and the wickets were those of Bardsley, Kelleway, Hill, Armstrong and Minnett.

I first saw Barnes in London in April, 1953, at a Cricket Writers' Dinner at the Skinners' Hall. He had turned 80 years a few days before, yet he was a proud and erect figure as he stood up with Jack Hobbs (70), and Ian Craig (17), to take wine with the chairman, Charles Bray. Barnes signed his autograph in copper-plate writing, his hand as steady as his bowling was reputed to be. Soon after that he turned out in a Testimonial match in which the sides were captained by Walter Robins and Bill Edrich, and before the game began Barnes said to his captain, Robins, 'You had better give me an old ball. I might run through the other side with a new one and spoil your match!'

Barnes was to bowl the opening over of that match. He felt so well after the one over that he promptly bowled another. That at 80!

I met him again later in the tour at Stoke, and we had just settled down to a good old cricketers' 'yarn' when an official came up and said that our Prime Minister, Mr Menzies, was anxious to see him. I am still in the process of forgiving the Prime Minister!

There was a mix-up over the 1901 English side to Australia. The MCC could not get a satisfactory side together and passed the job over to Archie MacLaren with their blessing. Yorkshire made the task no easier by withholding Hirst and Rhodes, and MacLaren, as a brave and knowledgeable man should often do, backed his own judgment – he did so by plucking Barnes out of the Lancashire League. Barnes had played a few games for Warwickshire as a fast bowler, but he was a spinner when MacLaren spotted and selected him.

Barnes had played only two Tests in Australia when he was being acclaimed as the finest hard-wicket bowler England had sent abroad. A few years later M. A. Noble singled him out as the world's finest bowler, and to this day Sir Pelham Warner plumps for him as the greatest bowler he has ever seen.

Barnes's first Test wicket was that of Victor Trumper; he caught and bowled him for two in Sydney. Also, he clean-bowled Clem Hill in the same innings. Barnes took 5–65 in that innings (he got only 1–74 in the second), but in the next Test, at Melbourne, his name was being spoken everywhere because he took 6–42 and 7–121 (he got Trumper and Hill in both innings). Melbourne was to be his best Test ground.

Misfortune hit him hard in the next Test at Adelaide. He suffered a knee injury, withdrew from the match, and didn't play in another Test until the July one at Sheffield in 1902. There he took 6–49 in the first innings, and 1–50: yet, unaccountably, he wasn't chosen in the immortal next Test at Old Trafford, which Australia won by three runs. Barnes didn't play against Australia again in England until 1909, and he missed another trip to Australia.

It is interesting that Noble should have placed Barnes on a pedestal for, in fact, Barnes learnt a lot about swing bowling from Noble. Barnes began, as most bowlers do, as a fast bowler, but he soon learned that there was more to the business than sheer speed. He experimented with finger-spin, both off and leg, and it was as a medium-paced spinner that he was singled out for the Australian tour by MacLaren. Barnes possessed a very shrewd and deductive cricket brain. He closely watched the other leading bowlers of that day and quickly applied some of their technique to his own bowling.

Monty Noble, in particular, captivated him. Here was an off-spinner of the old and original school (very similar to the latter-day Jim Laker) who possessed all the variations of the art. Noble would gain tricks of flight by delivering the ball at various heights – gaining this by dipping or straightening his right leg at the moment of release – and he had an out-curve as distinct from the ordinary off-break. If a breeze came in from fine-leg, Noble was in his element as he curved, floated, and dropped the ball with side-spin and over-spin. He brought to the cricket field much of the technique of the baseball pitcher.

I don't know whether modern Test bowlers have a union in which they swop the tricks of the trade – I think not – but Syd Barnes found that Noble lived up to his name, for the great Australian all-rounder and captain gave him many tips on bowling.

Barnes not only wanted off-breaks and leg-breaks from the pitch. He wanted movement in the air as well, and in England he studied the great English left-hander, George Hirst. The normal swing of a right-hand bowler to a right-hand batsman with the new ball is from leg to off. Similarly, a left-hand bowler will swing in from off to leg – as Hirst did.

Barnes practised with his leg-break allied to a certain body action at the moment of delivery and, hey presto! he found movement in the air similar to Hirst's natural swing.

But observe these important differences in the technique of Barnes and let me illustrate them by referring to Maurice Tate, one of the greatest of all bowlers. Tate was a glorious mover of the new ball, mostly from the leg and with tremendous whip off the pitch. His swing (as distinct from swerve, which comes from spin) was gained by holding the ball in the normal fashion with the line of stitches facing the batsman. This swing comes late in the ball's flight, and the ball, off the pitch, continues on in the direction of the swing – that is, towards the slips. A nightmare of a ball, too!

When Barnes swung in the air from the leg, by spin, the ball turned back from the off. When he swung in from the off, with his leg-break action, the ball gripped the pitch with its spin and turned from the leg. In the case of Hirst – and Alec Bedser, with his in-swing, being a right-hander – the ball, on hitting the pitch, continues out towards the leg-slips. Thus Barnes's swerves broke from the pitch in directions different from the normal swings.

'At the time I was able to bowl these,' Barnes once told me in a letter, 'I thought I was at a disadvantage in having to spin the ball when I could see bowlers doing the same by simply placing the ball in their hand and letting go; but I soon learned that the advantage was with me because by spinning the ball, if the wicket would take spin, the ball would come back against the swing. . . . I may say I did not bowl a ball but that I had to spin, and that is, to my way of thinking, the reason for what success I attained.'

In Barnes's first Test innings against Australia, Charlie Macartney was at the bowler's end when Barnes clean-bowled Trumper. 'The ball was fast on the leg stump,' said Macartney, 'but just before it pitched it swung suddenly to the off. Then it pitched, broke back, and took Vic's leg-stump. It was the sort of ball a man might see if he was dreaming or drunk.'

Those who have played against Barnes – unfortunately, there are now not many left – have told me that he was accurate and kept a perfect length. He had variations of pace and flight and could regulate the spot at which his swing became effective. He could also regulate the amount of break. Moreover, he used the width of the crease, first over the stumps, then from halfway, and then from the edge.

'But I never bowled all out at the stumps,' he maintained. 'I liked to study the batsman and then bowl at his strokes. I intended him to make a stroke and then I tried to beat it. I tried to make the batsman move. It is amazing how often a batsman will make a mistake if you induce him to use his feet.'

I asked him about that December morning of 1911. 'Naturally, I was very pleased,' he said, 'but I did not consider it the highlight of my career, for I knew that it was possible to bowl well with little or no result. On the other hand, one could bowl not nearly so well and reap quite a harvest of wickets – you know as well as I do that there is a very small margin between success and failure.'

And then, after a pause: 'Still, I think I did bowl well that day.'

Of course he did. I looked up the files.

They had bands at Test matches in those days – they did in Sydney right up to 1931 when the Springbok captain, Jock Cameron, asked the band not to play as he could not concentrate while the music was in the air.

The band in Melbourne was playing comic opera tunes as the Englishmen were led out by Johnny Douglas. The early morning was dull and close and around eleven o'clock there were a few drops of rain. The weather looked like developing into a thunderstorm. But Clem Hill, winning the toss, feared neither the light nor the moisture-laden atmosphere – lending swing to a new ball – nor even the pitch. 'Bad luck, Johnny,' he said to Douglas, 'we'll bat.'

There was a slight mist as the umpires walked out. Bardsley had been put through a pretty rigorous physical test and had been pronounced fit, although, after a battering from Foster in Sydney, he was well strapped up as he walked out with Kelleway to open the innings.

Kelleway was very wary in playing the first over from Foster. Then Barnes prepared to bowl to Bardsley. Barnes, in collaboration with Douglas, took a long time to settle his field. He was most pernickety in this matter.

At last he was satisfied and over came the first ball. It was on a good length and Bardsley shaped at it very cautiously. He missed, and it hit him on the leg and went into his stumps – an in-swinger that would have had the Australian lbw had it not bowled him.

Another left-hander, Hill, was next, and he took a single from the first ball, a fact to be noted because it was a long time before another run was scored from Barnes.

Hill faced up to Barnes again for his next over, and a torrid one it was. There was an immediate and loud appeal for lbw but it was rejected, and Hill, defending desperately, saw the over through.

Kelleway faced Barnes for his next over. He missed completely an in-swinger on his leg stump that straightened up and he was out lbw Australia: 2 for 5.

In came Armstrong and he saw Hill in all manner of trouble. Barnes gave him one that was an off-break to him, and followed with an in-swinger. Then came one a little wider, going away, which Hill allowed to pass. The final ball of the over pitched on Hill's leg stump and hit the top of the off-stump. Australia: 3 for 8.

As captain, Hill had put Trumper lower on the list so that he could bat with the sheen gone from the ball. But Trumper came now with the ball still almost new. Meanwhile, spectators were busy recalling an earlier tour by Warner's team when Australia batted in Sydney on a perfect pitch under a thundery sky, and Hill, Trumper and Duff were out for 12, leaving Noble and Armstrong to stop the collapse. This time, as Trumper walked out in the tense atmosphere, a great cheer went up. Trumper would succeed where the others had failed!

Armstrong drove Foster for three and then faced Barnes. Immediate exit! He snicked his first ball and Smith caught him behind.

Four Australian wickets were gone for eight, and of that very modest figure only a single run had been scored from Barnes. He had taken four wickets for one run! Test cricket had not seen the like of this before.

Ransford, on his home ground, now joined Trumper, and the latter brought a relieved cheer, like a clap of thunder, as he brilliantly back-cut Foster. The ball went like a streak, incidentally hitting Douglas on the shins, and the batsmen ran two. Rain began to fall now and the players came off after 45 minutes of play.

They were back again 15 minutes later. Barnes bowled a maiden to Ransford, feverishly defensive. Then in the next over, from Foster, Trumper made two delicious late cuts to the rails. It looked like another maiden over from Barnes to Ransford, but the left-hander got Barnes away to leg for a single off the last ball. It had been an hour since the previous and only run had been taken from Barnes.

Barnes didn't seem himself in his next over. He bowled a full toss that went high over Ransford's head for four byes. At the end of the over he spoke to Douglas. Barnes had been ill during the preceding week and there was a doubt whether he would play. He told Douglas that he couldn't see the other end. Everything seemed to be going round and round.

So, to the great relief of the Melbourne crowd – and also of the batsmen at the wickets – Barnes left the field. He didn't return until after lunch.

The Australian players, on their way from the dressing-room to lunch in another pavilion, had to run the gauntlet of many an anxious inquiry from the spectators. What was wrong? Was something amiss with the wicket? To all inquiries the humbled Australians gave the one reply, 'Barnes!'

Foster knocked Trumper's stumps back after lunch, and then Barnes took the ball again. Australia: 5 for 33.

Minnett, a notable performer in the preceding Test at Sydney, came next and promptly snicked Barnes to third slip. He was dropped. But after scoring two, he skied Barnes to cover, where Jack Hobbs was waiting. Six down for 38, and Barnes had the remarkable bowling figures cited in the first paragraph of this chapter – 11 overs, 7 maidens, 6 runs, 5 wickets.

Barnes got no more wickets in that innings. He finished with 5–44 off 23 overs. Actually, he should have had another wicket when Hordern spooned one up in front, a catch that could have been taken by any one of five men but for the fact that each one left it to the other fellow. He might, too, have had the last man, Whitty. All the players, including Whitty, himself, thought he had been clean bowled. Indeed, the usual procession to the pavilion had begun when Umpire Crockett, who was at square leg, held that the ball had come back from the keeper's pads and called out 'No, no!' The other umpire then gave Whitty not out, and 35 more runs were added to the score.

Ransford was Australia's best batsman; he played coolly and intelligently for 43. Hordern, after his let-off, got 49 not out, Carter a cheeky 29, and Whitty and Cotter 14 each.

The day provided many other incidents. With the score 8–125 Barnes came on to relieve Hearne. Very carefully, Barnes motioned his fieldsmen this way and that, upon which a portion of the crowd in the outer began to hoot him for not 'getting on with it.'

Barnes resented the hooting. He threw down the ball and stood with his arms folded. While a few still hooted, members and others cheered. 'It was,' wrote a Sydney critic, 'a most unwarranted display against a man who had bowled magnificently. It evidenced, too, a most partisan spirit. It was confined to a hostile section in the shilling stand, and such unfair treatment undoubtedly interfered with Barnes's bowling. In his next over there was a similar outbreak by the hoodlums, but the occupant of the members' reserve cheered him and the noisy element was quickly quelled by the counter-demonstration.'

'During the tea interval,' the Sydney critic added, 'the demonstration against Barnes was universally condemned, and it was suggested that the Victorian authorities should at once follow the example of the New South Wales Association and announce that they would prosecute offenders for unruly or riotous behaviour. After the interval, when Barnes bowled again, the crowd was perfectly quiet, a couple of policemen being in the middle of the noisy section. But it was the worst demonstration of partisanship seen on the ground.'

Spectators cheered Barnes all the way to the pavilion when the innings ended. It was said of Barnes then that he was too reserved, too stern, to be popular with his fellows, but I imagine that he, like the latter-day O'Reilly, looked upon all batsmen as his natural enemies. Not for him frivolities on the field or the happy exchange of pleasantries. He meant business from the first ball, and never more than on that Melbourne morning of 30 December, 1911.

It was perhaps the most historic morning in Test history. England won finally by eight wickets, Hearne and Hobbs getting centuries and F. R. Foster 6–91 in the second innings. Some said the Foster–Barnes partnership was the greatest bowling one ever.

Now, in his eighties,* Barnes is courteous, gentle and gracious. He is as straight in figure as on that Melbourne morning, a splendid specimen of physical fitness, and his mind is alert and discerning. He pays tribute to the modern bowler, if not many modern bowling methods, and I like very much this expression of opinion, one which the world of officialdom must listen to some day: 'The lbw rule, as it is now, has done much harm to cricket. It has shut out the lovely off-side strokes. There is too much defensive bowling outside the leg stump to leg fields and too much playing by the batsmen off the back foot. If you are going to get wickets, you must attack the batsman. If you are going to get runs, you must attack the bowler. That is the game of cricket. One must attack the other, and every bowler should welcome it when a batsman shows a desire to step into him. It is then, if he uses his head, that a bowler has most chance. But that lbw rule – no! It has done too much harm already.'

* This was written in 1958. Barnes died on 26 December 1967, aged 94.

AUSTRALIA V. ENGLAND

At Melbourne, 30 December 1911; 1, 2 and 3 January 1912
England won by 8 wickets

Australia –

C. Kelleway lbw b Barnes	2 — c Gunn b Foster	13
W. Bardsley b Barnes	0 — run out	16
C. Hill (Capt.) b Barnes	4 — c Gunn b Barnes	0
W. W. Armstrong c Smith b Barnes	4 — b Foster	90
V. T. Trumper b Foster	13 — b Barnes	2
V. S. Ransford c Smith b Hitch	43 — c Smith b Foster	32
R. B. Minnett c Hobbs b Barnes	2 — b Foster	34
H. V. Hordern not out	49 — c Mead b Foster	31
A. Cotter run out	14 — c Hobbs b Foster	41
H. Carter c Smith b Douglas	29 — b Barnes	16
W. J. Whitty b Woolley	14 — not out	0
Byes 5, l-b 4, n-b 1	10 Byes 14, l-b 7, n-b 2, w 1	24

Total	184	Total	299

Fall: 0, 5, 8, 11, 33, 38, 80, 97,
    140, 184

Fall: 28, 34, 34, 38, 136, 168,
    232, 235, 298, 299

	O	M	R	W		O	M	R	W
Barnes	23	9	44	5		32.1	7	96	3
Foster	15	2	52	1		38	9	91	6
Hitch	7	0	37	1		5	0	21	0
Douglas	15	4	33	1		10	0	38	0
Hearne	6	0	8	0		1	0	5	0
Woolley	1	0	0	1		3	0	21	0
Rhodes	–	–	–	–		2	1	3	0

Hitch, 1 n-b.

Foster, 1 w.
Barnes, 1 n-b.
Hitch, 1 n-b.

England –
J. B. Hobbs c Carter   6 — not out   126
  b Cotter
W. Rhodes c Trumper b Cotter 61 — c Carter b Cotter   28
J. W. Hearne c Carter b Cotter 114 — not out   12
G. Gunn lbw b Armstrong   10 — c Carter b Whitty   43
C. P. Mead c Armstrong b Whitty 11
F. R. Foster c Hill b Cotter   9
J. W. H. T. Douglas (Capt.)
  b Hordern   9
F. E. Woolley c Ransford
  b Hordern   23
E. J. Smith b Hordern   5
S. F. Barnes lbw b Hordern   1
J. W. Hitch not out   0
  Byes 2, l-b 10, n-b 4 16   Byes 5, l-b 5   10

     Total   265   Two wickets for   219
Fall: 10, 137, 174, 213, 224, 258,   Fall: 57, 169
  260, 262, 265

	O	M	R	W		O	M	R	W
Cotter	21	?	73	4		14	5	45	1
Whitty	19	2	47	1		18	3	37	1
Hordern	23.1	1	66	4		17	0	66	0
Kelleway	15	7	27	0		7	0	15	0
Armstrong	15	4	20	1		12	1	22	0
Minnett	5	0	16	0		1.2	0	13	0
Ransford	–	–	–	–		1.1	0	11	0

    Cotter 3
    Minnett 1 n-b
     Umpires: R. W. Crockett and D. Elder

16. Clarrie Grimmett

Thomas Carlyle once declared that genius was an infinite capacity for taking pains. No cricketer I knew could better illustrate the truth underlying the dictum than Clarence Victor Grimmett. It does not deny that 'genius must be born and never can be taught,' as Dryden insisted. It breathes the absolute necessity for cultivation if high reward is sought.

Grimmett had immense cricketing talent and he had, moreover, which is imperative if a cricketer is to scale the heights, an innate love of and obsession with cricket. Without incessant and assiduous concentration, however, his mere devotion to the bowling art would never have earned him his lofty seat among the cricket mighty.

C. T. B. Turner, the 'Terror' of the nineties, who once spread-eagled and nonplussed 314 victims in an English season, ascribed much of his success to constant early practice with the object of gaining mastery of length and spin. He marked the spot on the country wicket of Bathurst where he used to practise before Sheffield Shield and Test honours came his way, and kept pegging away until he was satisfied with his control of the ball. It was said of the Victorian Albert Trott, who subsequently became a consistent all-rounder with Middlesex for a decade, that it was his early custom to place a fruit case in front of the stumps to develop a capacity to turn around it into the stumps.

Grimmett possessed a similar tenacity of purpose. Born in New Zealand, he says he played no game other than cricket until he was 22. He tinkered with baseball on migrating to Sydney, a migration brought about by a hankering for good cricket and opportunity, but Grimmett gloried in the fact that he lived almost exclusively for cricket. Even through winter, he practised assiduously.

Grimmett's practice was never aimless. It was always with a set purpose, and the fitting manner in which to greet this warm, smiling little man after a winter's hibernation was not to inquire after his health or his family, but to seek knowledge of what new bowling mystery the winter had yielded.

'You'll find out soon enough,' Grimmett would say, enigmatically.

Neville Cardus once told me of how, during Hitler's war, he met

Clarrie in Rundle St., Adelaide. The conversation, to two such lovers of cricket, was understandably lugubrious.

'This is a terrible thing, this war, Neville,' said Clarrie.

'It is, indeed,' readily agreed Neville, 'when we think of all the art and culture it has left in ruins throughout Europe. The lovely old historic buildings, the –.'

'Yes, yes,' hastily cut in Grimmett, 'I know all about that. I was thinking particularly of a new ball I had discovered. I'll never have the chance now to try it out against class batsmen.'

Grimmett lived to perfect something new in the bowling art. He was forever experimenting, his wrist, his body, at this and that angle at the moment of delivery, his shoulder at varying heights. The last particular delivery he produced took him some twelve years to perfect before he would bowl it in a big game. This was known as the 'flipper', because of the click of his fingers as he released the ball. He bowled it with a leg-break action and the ball, making pace from the pitch, would come in from the off (Pepper, Dooland and Benaud copied Grimmett's flipper). Batsmen in neighbouring states, alert to the little man's magic in the off season, would warn one another of the 'flipper'. 'You can't very well miss it. You'll hear it from Clarrie's flick of the fingers.'

Sometimes, you might feel sorry for this frail little chap, whose perpetual service at the bowling crease over the years had given him a rounded right shoulder. It seemed such a pity that so persevering a disciple should labour for twelve years to produce a 'mystery' and then have it betrayed by the flicking sound of his fingers. There was something unfair, too, about the quick passing of Grimmett's secrets from batsman to batsman. Poor old Clarrie!

Not for nothing, however, was my dear friend Clarrie known as the Sly Old Fox of Cricket. He knew well what batsmen said about him, that they thought they had unravelled his mysteries.

So, then, with his picturesque little hop and skip at the beginning of his run, he jogged his few yards to the crease to bowl against the knowing batsman. Grimmett's right arm took its little swing back; the ball went on its way with a low trajectory and on the air was the unmistakable sound of the fingers flicking.

From the pavilion, you could almost see the comfortable smirk on the face of the batsman as he went forward confidently to meet the ball. The flicker, indeed, he seemed to say! 'Just watch how I deal with this.'

The ball, however, has not turned from the off. It is an ordinary leg-break – if Grimmett ever did bowl an ordinary leg-break – and the batsman's legs are spreadeagled in a sorry mess. The ball beats the bat, Grimmett turns to the umpire with his appealing finger up, and the umpire agrees with him. Off trudges a disillusioned batsman to the pavilion. Who told him that Grimmett's flicker came from the off?

You were fortunate, in such circumstances, if you were on the fielding side and working close to the stumps. The little chap would trudge over, his right foot pigeon-toed in a distinctive manner, and across his face would spread an impish smile of huge delight. Then it would dawn on you.

'Why, you old fox. Grum,' you'd say. 'I do believe you bowled a leg-break then and flicked the fingers of your left hand.'

Grimmett would hug himself in convulsive delight, but would not admit anything. He loved bowling against batsmen who 'knew' all his tricks, 'knew' how to pick his flicker. It was their wits against his. He had been in this bowling business a long, long time and he had to learn the hard way. Bowling was like the game of life, hard.

Grimmett was a master of detail. He proceeded according to plan. A study of the traffic down King William St, Adelaide's main street, had taught him that it paid to wait ten seconds after the green light shone. Cars behind would toot impatiently. Grimmett could not be flurried. He waited ten seconds and then drove off at twenty miles an hour. By doing this, he caught all the green lights down the main street.

Such thoroughness typified Grimmett. It illustrated his outlook on cricket and bowling. Without perfect control, he avers, bowling ceases to interest him. To attain that control, he placed a piece of card about eighteen inches square on the pitch, used one stump only, and never tired of experimenting.

When you were on tour with Grimmett, he would never bowl to you in the nets. There were several reasons for this. He wanted to concentrate upon control of length and direction without distraction from other players and not against batsmen, as often happens in the nets, who chance their eye and play strokes they wouldn't attempt against him in a match. This practice had no appeal to Grimmett. Moreover, looking into the future, he was too long in the head to give practice to a Test fellow who, upon returning to Australia, would be an interstate opponent.

He was a migratory soul. He came to Sydney from New Zealand, left there for Melbourne and found his permanent residence in Adelaide. It was while he lived in Melbourne that he got a load of Merri Creek soil, with which the Melbourne Cricket Ground pitch is made, and built his own pitch in his back garden. He practised on his home-made pitch at every opportunity, his sole fieldsman a fox terrier.

Grimmett used a number of cricket balls and taught the dog to lie down until he wanted them back. On Sunday mornings, neighbours came for a regular practice and it was interesting that one who came to bat on Grimmett's pitch was Ponsford, then on the verge of breaking into big cricket.

Grimmett had one paramount idea at his self-imposed and self-conducted practices – the attainment of length and direction as the solid foundation of his bowling. He experimented with all types of spin. He often used a tennis or ping-pong ball, observed the results of spin and came to the conclusion that speed off the pitch was the ideal to strive for. With characteristic thoroughness, he decided to discard, except for demonstration purposes, those spin deliveries which did not fizz off the pitch.

He learned how a ball swerved according to the kind of spin imparted and how the arm movement also had its effect upon the flight of the ball. While he was experimenting, he was building according to his own solid specifications what he calls his 'stock ball'. His practices always ended with ten minutes of two deliveries and nothing else, a slight leg-break of perfect length and direction, and an ordinary straight through delivery with leg-break action. At any time, Grimmett could pick up a ball and pitch it where he wanted. A batsman with a few runs on the board and, therefore, settled to his job with confidence, welcomes the advent of a slow bowler because there is almost sure to be a few full tosses or long hops until the bowler feels his fingers and settles into his job. No such helpings came from Grimmett. It was incredible how his very first ball came down on a perfect length, causing the batsman's feet to twitter.

As a young boy, I was watching my first Test when Grimmett played his first Test against England in Sydney. He was an immediate sensation. Coming on after Mailey, who got only five overs (and none in the second innings), Grimmett, as he was often to do for Australia in the years ahead, took up almost permanent occupancy of one bowling end. He took 11 wickets off 30 overs at a cost of 82 in the two innings.

Hobbs, whose wicket Grimmett took in the second innings, completely under-estimated Grimmett's potential when, after this game, he predicted failure for him on English pitches. Mailey had been the slow spinner for Australia in the four preceding Tests but here began a long reign for Grimmett, which, had it not been for a fault in Bradman's judgment in 1938, might have been even longer. Reverting to Hobbs: great cricketers have never been the best judges of other's capacity. Ponsford, on first meeting Harold Larwood, wrote that he was 'not really a fast bowler'. He played to rue that judgment.

Arthur Mailey gave the ball plenty of air, plenty of time for the spin to twist the ball in the air and thus time, which is important, for a batsman to muddle his stroke. Cricket books are full of batting failures against slow spinners, the batsman, not the bowler, getting himself out. Grimmett was much faster through the air than Mailey and had a low trajectory. Perhaps the pom-pom effect of Grimmett after the high explosives of Mailey, against which the Englishmen had constructed their defences during previous clashes, contributed to the shock they experienced when they first met Grimmett in Sydney. I can still recall the drama of that Sydney afternoon as this little gnome-like man devoured the English batting. Little did I think then that I would later play many Test matches with him. I would not have slept that night if I had.

I can discover only one more sensational first Test appearance by a slow bowler, also in Sydney, and by Dr H. V. Hordern, who took 12–175 in 1911. He took 32 wickets in the series at 24.37 but, for a number of reasons, this was the only series against England in which he played. Hordern must have been a bowler very much like O'Reilly, rather fast through the air. Grimmett once travelled on the same ship as Hordern and they swapped the secrets of their bowling trade on the deck one day. Grimmett said Hordern sent down only an orthodox leg-break and a googly and 'did not indulge in any of the modern subtleties of the art'. Grimmett might have been a little critical – or the Doctor could not have performed his best on the deck – but Hordern got the wicket of Hobbs four times in that one series and also those of George Gunn, Wilfred Rhodes and others in an English side with a record in Australia hard to beat.

A. G. Moyes, excellent judge on cricket, once wrote that many who saw Hordern, Mailey and Grimmett, rated Hordern the highest.

Despite Hobbs's prophecy in Sydney, Grimmett was destined to prove much more of a menace on English than Australian pitches. The capture of all ten Yorkshire wickets in an innings on his first tour in 1926 was outstanding and possibly (some Yorkshireman can tell me of this some time) the best ever bowling feat by an overseas bowler against such a redoubtable batting side.

Grimmett thought a bowler could work with more energy in England. The ball, too, can be made to turn more on pitches more responsive to spin than Australian ones. As Grimmett thought himself to be a better bowler in England than elsewhere, it might be said that England also had a 'Grimmett' who got precious little Test recognition from his own country and that only abroad. He was A. P. (Tich) Freeman, of Kent. He came to the game a few years earlier than Grimmett, but he bore a resemblance in many ways to Australia's wizard of spin. Like Grimmett, he bowled with a cap on; he was under medium height and he didn't give the ball much air. And he took a tremendous number of wickets.

Freeman first tilted with an Australian team in England in 1921 when he got 'stick' from Armstrong's powerful side. He bowled 29 overs for Kent and took 0–138. This was when Armstrong's team made 676, Kent 237, and Armstrong, much to the ire of the Canterbury crowd, batted again. Nip Pellew in Adelaide in 1971 told a story of that match which illustrated Armstrong's dogged approach to everything.

When Armstrong said he would bat again, Nip went to the big fellow, who was lounging in front of the pavilion in a deck-chair. 'Warwick,' said Nip, 'our opening batsmen will get the slow clap and the "bird" properly for us batting again. Don't you think we should make Kent follow on?'

'No, I don't,' said Armstrong, 'and as you have said our opening batsmen will get the "bird", you put on the pads and open up.'

Freeman came to Australia with Johnnie Douglas's side in 1924–25 and played in two Tests. He took eight wickets, averaging 57 (he also made a score of 50 not out). Freeman never played against Australia in England. He wasn't chosen in 1926 and he took 304 wickets, the biggest number in history, in 1928. He wasn't chosen in 1930, when he took 275 wickets for Kent. When Kent played Australia, Freeman took five wickets for 78 (Grimmett took 4–80 in the same game) and Freeman's victims were Bradman, Ponsford, Jackson, Fairfax and Woodfull. Freeman's non-selection in a Test team in England against Australia must remain one of the big mysteries of English selection.

R. S. Whitington, a near-Test batsman himself, who writes exceedingly well with the valuable knowledge of having been in the middle, has written a splendid book on O'Reilly and in it he writes, also, at length of Grimmett, with whom he played innumerable games for South Australia. Whitington makes a good point about England denying chances to its spin bowlers. He criticizes strongly Sir Donald Bradman for Grimmett being dropped from the 1938 Australian team to England. It is a criticism I support and so also will every other cricketer who played against Grimmett and Ward that year.

By not choosing Grimmett for England that year – and Ward's preference over Grimmett in the South Australian team that summer showed which way Bradman was inclining – Australia separated the best Test bowling spin combination of all time in O'Reilly and Grimmett. They came together in Adelaide in 1931 against South Africa. Grimmett played in three bodyline Tests before being dropped, but he triumphed again in England in 1934 and in South Africa in 1935–36.

Grimmett, in fact, took 44 of the 98 South African Test wickets that fell against Vic Richardson's side. O'Reilly took 27. The poor South Africans never knew relief from tormenting Australian spin. I fielded close up in the Test series and it was uncomfortable to see the worried looks on the faces of the Springboks as they would face, first, O'Reilly and then Grimmett. Whenever either wanted a breather, which was seldom, on would come another spinning ogre in Fleetwood-Smith. Yet, after taking the amazing number of 44 Test wickets against South Africa, Grimmett was dropped immediately from the Australian team. He never returned, although he would have been invaluable again in England in 1938, and in harness with O'Reilly, who never hesitated to say what he thought of the 'knifing' of his spinning comrade.

Grimmett was 44 years old when he was dropped, but he was still as good a bowler as ever. Several years later, when Bradman had restored him over Ward as South Australia's main spinner again, the great little man took a record number of 73 wickets in the summer. Quite obviously, Bradman erred in thinking Grimmett was over the hill in 1938. It was something Grimmett never forgave. The smile leaves his face even now when the subject recurs, because Grimmett lived only for cricket and his non-selection for England – it would have been his fourth successive trip to England – cut him deeply.

Grimmett could get through an Australian eight-ball over, assuming it was a maiden, in under two minutes. There was no time-wasting with the little man. He moved smartly, he wheeled quickly and over would go his cunning right arm, a devious mind behind everything he did.

Sitting in the Adelaide pavilion, keeping a watchful eye on his old partner, W. J. O'Reilly, to know should he decide that the time has come for a 'refresher' away from his newspaper work, Grimmett recalls the past with wonderful memories and laughs. Sometimes I will join them, although I have always to put up a mock fight. 'I don't know that we want any batsmen with us. I never liked batsmen.

Did you, Tige?' he would impishly ask the Big Fellow, who even, in after years, would consign all batsmen to some hot region.

'The cheek of you two,' I would say. 'All the catches I took for both of you and the runs I saved for you. Bowlers haven't any heart. That's the trouble.'

That ten-minute intermission, taken at a time when we could be on our own or have Len Darling with us, was wonderful fun. Clarrie loves to be reminded of his artful victories. He goes into ecstasies still when he tells of Philip Mead, the grand old English batsman, who had possibly more pronounced mannerisms at the wicket than any other cricketer. These mannerisms were ritual. First grounding his bat to take strike, Mead would shuffle up to it left, right, left, right, left, right with always the six short steps. Then, at the very last, he would look to the umpire at square-leg and touch his cap.

These remarkable antics performed, Mead would then be ready to receive the bowler. Grimmett's particular delight when bowling against Mead was to time his delivery so as to catch Mead in the middle of his shuffle or his cap-touching. It was a great battle, Mead often having to hurry his performance to be ready for Grimmett.

Grimmett possessed a quiet, pronounced sense of humour. He loves to tell of the time when he appealed for lbw against a prominent New South Wales batsman. The appeal was refused. The batsman called out 'Clarrie', and with index finger drew an imaginary straight line up and down the pitch, suggesting that Grimmett's appeal was a bad one.

There wasn't a flicker of a smile from the Fox. He wheeled again into the next delivery. Again the ball hit the pad.

'How's that?' said Grimmett, turning to the umpire.

This time the finger went up. As the crestfallen batsman left for the pavilion, Clarrie called out to him, 'Excuse me.' The batsman turned and saw Grimmett's index finger suggesting a straight line up and down the pitch.

With infinite relish, Clarrie told O'Reilly and me about his last club match in Adelaide.

'As I walked on to the ground,' said Grimmett, 'I was surprised to see the umpire come back to me. He held out his hand. I shook it with feeling. "Mr Grimmett," he said, "this is the greatest honour I have had in cricket – standing umpire to your bowling".'

'I made sure I bowled at his end,' continued Grimmett. 'I told him I would show him every ball I could bowl. So I went through them – leg-break, googly, flipper and so on, naming them to him before I bowled. I said "I will bowl two faster leg-breaks on the off-stump, going away, and then I will bowl my flipper the third ball and get him leg before". I did just that. As I turned to appeal, the umpire had his arm in the air, shouting "How's that?" '

A wonderful cricketer was my old friend, Clarrie Grimmett. I count it as great an honour to have played in the same Test side as Grimmett as anybody else I played with or against. Happy is the cricket-lover who retains the vision of a little round-shouldered bowler pegging away, pegging away for over after over. At such a time, and particularly if you were the batsman, you saw cricket subtlety, cunning, ability and great-heartedness at their richest best. Cricket never looked a more noble game than when Grimmett was bowling.

Grimmett played cricket as a science, a game of infinite skill and a means of adding to one's knowledge of his fellow man. He was, in his earlier playing days, one who used to dress quickly and get away from the dressing-room at the day's end. In his later days, he realized what he was missing from the convivial side of the game, the human side. He then grew to love the atmosphere of his cobbers over a drink, chewing over the day's happenings.

When the time came at last to go, possibly Vic Richardson, for whom Grimmett would have gone through fire in his underpants, would say: 'Come on, Clarrie. We can't possibly go until we have heard you sing the song that made you famous.'

After a little – not very much – cajoling, Grimmett would put his head back and warble, with the happiest smile imaginable on everybody's face:

> *She was a sweet little dickie bird,*
> *Tweet, tweet, tweet, she went.*
> *She used to sing all day*
> *Till my money was spent.*
>
> *She was always sighing,*
> *I thought she was going to die,*
> *But she was one of the early birds,*
> *And I was one of the worms.*

The uproarious applause from his fellows, which always greeted this, brought as much cheer to the heart of Clarrie Grimmett as when he took all ten Yorkshire wickets. Grimmett took 216 Test wickets for Australia against England, South Africa and the West Indies. He never played Test cricket against the other countries. A lovable little cricketer and gentleman – the Peter Pan of the game or else, as he secretly loved to be called, Sly Old Fox!

17. The Fast Men:
Larwood, Lindwall, Miller

It is not always easy to gauge the potential of a bowler unless you have batted against him. Then, too, some batsmen have more difficulty than others against particular bowlers. Whenever a new fast bowler appears, there is argument whether he is as good or as fast as those before him. Frank (Typhoon) Tyson was very fast on his first trip to Australia yet, in technique, I did not think he was on the same plane as Larwood, Lindwall and Miller. Tyson bowled hard, very hard.

Wes Hall, at his best (and it was sad to see him on his last visit to Australia when he had gone considerably down hill, although his heart was as big as ever), wasn't far behind the Terrible Trio. Charlie Griffith, as I saw him in the West Indies in 1965, was also of fearsome speed. Much was written about the dubious action of Charlie, yet it was remarkable that he bowled as perfect a 'yorker' as Lindwall and I would think such a precise ball is beyond the compass of anybody with a dubious delivery.

Another bowler of exceptional speed was Eddie Gilbert, of Queensland, the aborigine cricketer. I think his speed at the Woolloongabba cricket ground one murky Brisbane evening was as fast as anything I have seen. The ground is not big behind the stumps, but the slips were almost three-quarters way to the fence. Bradman was missed from his bowling before scoring and was still out for nothing. Alan Kippax, after withstanding Gilbert's withering speed, mis-timed a hook from another fast bowler, Pud Thurlow, and went off to hospital in a serious condition with a smashed skull. Understandably, Kippax, one of the most beautiful batsmen of all time, was never afterwards comfortable against bouncers.

I was down the other end once during that hectic late-afternoon, with Stan McCabe taking strike, and I remarked to Gilbert: 'You are pretty fast today, Eddie?' Gilbert, a slim little man of possibly no more than eight stone, looked shyly at me and said: 'I bowl a plurry lot faster if they let me take my boots off.' Gilbert didn't run. He walked in five paces and then slung, which was the best way to describe it, with a boomerang-throwing action. He was never as fast down south where, eventually, he was no-balled for his suspect action. I wasn't surprised.

Of the three, Larwood, Lindwall and Miller, possibly Larwood had the most perfect action. His run in was flowing and symmetrical, his speed increasing and the length of his stride widening as he moved in. The first time I was in runs against Larwood, as I was beginning to lead off, I thought he had fallen flat on his face. It was the scrape of his right foot. His final stride on the side of it in delivery had his entire weight skidding along the ground for a yard or more. Thus he got every ounce of his body, perfectly balanced, into the delivery. He had broad, strong shoulders (to meet the meek Larwood after his cricket was to be amazed that he was ever a fast bowler) and he got this strength from his early days in the coal pit. As did, also, Bill Voce and Freddie Trueman.

Larwood's right hand came down from as high as possible, straight up from his head. After migrating to Australia in 1951, Larwood made his first trip back to England in 1968 and I derived much pleasure from having a drink with him at the members' bar in the Trent Bridge pavilion – directly under the most perfect action picture of him in the moment of delivery.

Larwood had no family cricket background. Joe Hardstaff, senior, lived in a nearby village to Larwood's and induced him to come to Trent Bridge for a trial. It was a noble carriage of cricketers that used to go to Trent Bridge each day, Larwood himself first having to walk for three-quarters of an hour before he caught the train. Then they would walk from the Nottingham station to the ground, 'bowl our guts out all day' as Larwood put it, and then go through the same walk, train and walk process again. 'Modern fast bowlers never walk. It's always the car,' says Larwood. Bike-riding gave Alec Bedser his toned muscles. Others who travelled in the same train were Whysall, the two Staples, Voce and the two Hardstaffs. That was 1924. Two years after coming from the village of Nuncargate, Larwood was in England's Test team at the Oval, winning the Ashes.

The first time Larwood had ever been out of Nottingham was when he went to Sheffield to play against Yorkshire. Larwood worked out his own run of 12 long paces, then adding two hops at the end as his measure. He scoffs at those bowlers who think they must run 30 yards to get up steam.

Jim Iremonger was the county coach at Trent Bridge when Larwood arrived. All Larwood did then was bowl straight and hard. That was good enough to knock them over in Nuncargate and surrounding villages but Larwood found he couldn't get past the bat in the Trent Bridge nets. 'You'll have to learn to do something with the ball,' Iremonger told him.

So Larwood experimented with his body and angle of delivery. At Trent Bridge in 1925, he brought one back from the off with a body-break and knocked Jack Hobbs' stumps out of the ground. Hobbs was big cricket news. The Press rushed to know how an unknown had come to clean-bowl him. 'Oh, a fluke I guess,' said Hobbs. So Larwood knocked Hobbs' stumps back again in the second innings. Larwood thought because of that Hobbs, who, with Wilfred Rhodes was an English selector, advanced his Test cause.

With Hobbs and Rhodes, Larwood was a member of the English side that won the Ashes back from Collins' team in 1926. In 1927, with a Test trial at Bristol fizzled out, with no interest left in the last hour of play, that keen disciplinarian, Douglas Jardine, kept Larwood bowling. He put his foot in one of Maurice Tate's pot-holes and damaged the cartilage of his left knee. An operation followed and Larwood possibly wasn't at his best when he came to Australia in 1928–29.

Jack Gregory should have caught and bowled him in the first Test at Brisbane. In trying to make the catch, Gregory damaged a knee and retired from cricket. Larwood got the photograph from a Brisbane newspaper and framed it. Jack Gregory was his boyhood hero.

Larwood, himself, thinks he was at his peak in Australia in 1932–33 when Jardine used him as his main bodyline foil. He carried too many guns for the liking of the Australians. His control of the short-pitched ball in line with the body was as amazing in its control as the ire it raised on all sides. Larwood became Australia's public enemy number one.

With the new ball, Larwood could move it late in the air from the leg. The best ball he thinks he ever bowled was at the Oval in 1926 when he brought back a body-break of nearly a foot to knock over the stumps of Tommy Andrews, who had shouldered his bat.

I was in my early twenties when I played against Larwood in that bodyline series. Opening with Woodfull, I set out to bait Larwood in the first innings of the Melbourne Test. I knew that his most fearsome ball was that late swinger from the leg-side so when he bowled one a little short, I walked well down the pitch, much further down than where the ball pitched, and patted the pitch. Larwood glowered. He tried harder than ever then to hit me and it was a case of dodging. In his anxiety to 'pink' me, Larwood busted his boots. The ball also busted in that first hour. It was rather an eventful hour.

I heard later that some of my team-mates watching from the dressing-room didn't think much of my tactics. 'Larwood's bad enough without baiting him like this,' they grumbled. But it suited me. Larwood wasted the new ball against me. As I said – I was very young.

Larwood busted himself in the final Test at Sydney. He had got over 30 wickets and had a chance of beating Maurice Tate's record number of wickets in a series in Australia. 'I think I tried too hard when the Little Wonder came in,' said Larwood, referring to Bradman. 'I put too much pressure on to my left foot as it hit the ground and I broke a bone in the foot. While Bradman was at the wickets, Jardine wouldn't let me leave the field. Bradman and I left the field together, in silence. "All right, Lol, you can go now," Jardine called across to me, when Bradman got out. I never walked on to a Test field again.'

Larwood, who drove the ball splendidly, came in early as stop-gap batsman in that Test and got 98, a most brilliant innings. 'Maurice Leyland called me up the pitch and said "Look at the board, Lol, you're 98." "Well," I said, "that's 98 more than I thought I would get". I suppose I could have got a century by looking for two singles but I had just hit Lee for two fours and thought I could hit him for another. "Dainty" Ironmonger caught me out. I suppose I was unlucky in that, but I was happy.'

Larwood's pace was terrific. It was best seen as the ball hurtled through to the keeper. If one got runs against Larwood, the muscle between the thumb and the index finger of the bottom hand would ache for some days from the jolting concussion of ball against bat.

Larwood left English cricket a disgruntled man. He was a proud man, an honest man, and his concept of life in his generation was to do as his superior ordered. He was a professional cricketer. All amateurs were 'Mister' to him. Jardine was his superior as skipper and he did precisely what Jardine asked him to do. The reaction of the Australian press and barracker to him only determined him all the more to do his job. It baffled and distressed him that MCC should later ask him to apologise. 'For what? I only did as Mr Jardine asked me to do,' said Larwood. So he went out of cricket, embittered, but loyal to himself and Jardine. He wouldn't apologise.

I sat next to Larwood when Frank Woolley was given a dinner by the *Sydney Herald* newspaper and Kent supporters in Sydney in 1971. It was a glorious night of good food, wine and memories – Sir Robert Menzies and Frank Woolley making delicious cricket speeches of knowledge and humour – and we had with us Bill

Whitty, Australia's oldest surviving Test player, Nip Pellew, Bertie Oldfield, Johnnie Taylor (who died soon afterwards), Jack Gregory, Bill O'Reilly, the *Herald's* lucid and most knowledgeable cricket writer, Clarrie Grimmett, Colin Cowdrey, Derek Underwood, Denis Compton, Hunter Hendry and Jack Brabham, a champion in another sphere. Larwood has become a very good friend of mine. I was privileged to sit next to him for two reasons. He was the best fast bowler I knew. And he didn't eat Sydney oysters!

Ray Lindwall was a boy on the Sydney Hill during the bodyline series. Larwood impressed him so much that he decided to copy his run up. Lindwall was a good all-round athlete at school – cricket, rugby and athletics – and there was a suggestion of the long jumper also in his run-up, which was fluid and graceful and gathering, as it should, in momentum as he went. He, too, most perfectly got his whole body into his delivery. His arm, possibly, was not as high in delivery as Larwood's. Sir Pelham Warner thought Lindwall, in England in 1948, was the best fast bowler he had seen, and 'Plum' saw them all.

Bill O'Reilly had much to do with Lindwall's early days. Bill remembers that Ray and his brother Jack and several other youngsters were always playing in Hudson street in Hurstville as Bill came home from his teaching work. No doubt they were out to impress the great Bill and were hoping he'd take a bowling hand with them. Bill gave them a genial 'G'day' and passed on into his home. But even at that he noticed Ray, a slim, blonde-headed youngster who bowled hard and straight.

When O'Reilly returned from the South African tour of 1935-36, the young Lindwall was up at the St George nets. O'Reilly remembered him. Then he came into the St George side under O'Reilly's captaincy. 'I was hard on him but I think it did him some good,' says O'Reilly. 'He bowled with the wind, so did I, I told him: "I'm expected to get these bastards out. You will get three overs and then I'll come on. Now, give those three overs all you've got because you mightn't get any more." He was slim and skinny. He hardly ever uttered. Even if I wanted to, I couldn't bowl the guts out of him. So he gave those three overs all he had and I think this taught him how to go flat out.'

O'Reilly, as New South Wales captain, next caught up with Lindwall in the New South Wales team after the Second World War. Lindwall was very keen to learn. On the way from Adelaide to Melbourne, O'Reilly told Lindwall: 'I might have a few words to say to you when we get out on the field.' Tamblyn was opening for Victoria, and in the Woodfull manner he was a heavy scorer for his state. O'Reilly told Lindwall: 'I want you to bowl the first ball at Tamblyn's shoulders. He might do something silly.'

Lindwall, amazed: 'What, the first ball?'

O'Reilly: 'Yes, the very first ball.'

Lindwall's eyes opened up but he did as he was told and we got Tamblyn out early, O'Reilly reported. 'Lindwall said to me "He doesn't like a bouncer, does he?"'

O'Reilly relates how a long time after this Lindwall gave an injured Weekes, of the West Indies, a barrage of bouncers at Sydney. 'I saw Lindwall that same afternoon and I told him that I thought his tactics bloody shocking. That he had made himself look cheap and that I had written so for next morning's *Herald*.'

'Do you know who taught me to bowl the bouncer?' asked Lindwall.

'Yes, I did, but I will always be against it as you bowled it today and you can draw whatever analogy you like,' O'Reilly told Lindwall.

I was with O'Reilly that same evening when we ran into John Goddard, the West Indian captain, who had Weekes with him. Goddard complained bitterly of how Weekes had been subjected to so many bouncers. 'We thought we were coming to Australia to play cricket,' said Goddard. We both told him whom to speak to, not us.

After this, preceded by Bradman's side in England in 1948, I never shed even crocodile tears for Australian batsmen who got bouncers from Charlie Griffith in the West Indies in 1965 and John Snow in Australia in 1970–71. As a country sows, so it will reap, even years afterwards. Australia must never 'bleat' when other countries play it hard against us. At Old Trafford, in 1948, in the dying last ten minutes of the game with no likely result and with John Ikin in the nineties, Bradman took the new ball, handed it to Lindwall and Ikin was out. Even the scoring of centuries against that Australian side evidently meant something in the records!

I don't think Lindwall's bouncer was quite as venomous as Larwood's because of his slightly round-arm action, whereas Larwood's delivery was from high up. Learie Constantine, also a great fast bowler on his day, was another who delivered from high overhead. Strangely, I noticed this most when Learie came to Canberra in the late fifties as a delegate to the Parliamentary Commonwealth conference. Some of the House staff induced Learie to come to the rose garden on the Senate side of Parliament House and have a hit and a bowl, on a seldom-used pitch. I noticed that as Learie delivered, he looked up at his right hand. Why? 'My father taught me to do this,' said Learie. 'He didn't want me to be a chucker. He told me always to make sure that my right arm was fully extended. So I got into the habit of watching it to make sure.'

Lindwall was a glorious fast bowler, a man of guile and infinite variation. He, too, could move the new ball in the air and his usage of the width of the delivery mark enabled him to move the ball into the batsman. Pictures taken of him during the immediate post-war series in Australia showed that he had a considerable drag and, indeed, was often well over the line when he delivered. There were almost as many newspaper photographers as spectators when he bowled first at Worcester in 1948, but he overcame trouble by coming to an arrangement with umpires as to where they wanted him to put his back foot before delivery.

It was mainly because of Lindwall that the rule ultimately was changed to the front foot, a ruling that Australians don't like and have tried to change. As to the back foot – a camera shot of any bowler of any period would show that his back foot was up and over the line at the precise time of delivery. It is impossible to deliver a ball with the back foot on the ground, or so I think. Unlike Larwood and Miller, Lindwall I thought stayed on too long in Test cricket. He had some record in mind and laboured to get it.

On his day, Keith Miller reached the dizziest heights as a fast bowler. He was a natural bowler. I don't think he ever gave the slightest thought to technique nor much on how to diddle out a particular batsman. His usual run was twelve yards, but it was not uncommon to see Miller wheel around after walking back some six or eight yards and let fly the fastest ball. When he had his dander up, I often felt it was much safer to be watching rather than playing him. He had a perfect delivery, high overhead, although he would vary this at times, such was his temperament, with a round-armer or even a slow leg-break.

It was easy to tell when Miller's dander was up. He would clap his hands impatiently for the ball to be thrown to him and would toss his thick black mane as he strode back swiftly to his mark. At such a time, nobody liked facing Miller. He perpetrated the most undiplomatic gaffe of all cricketing time at Sydney one afternoon when he unleashed two successive bouncers, the first a rather harmless one, the next a most vicious one, at the august head of Don Bradman, chairman of selectors, in what was, I think, Bradman's last first-class match.

Bradman superbly pulled the first one for four. Before the ball, almost, crashed into the pickets, Miller was striding back, clapping for the ball. As he neared his mark, he looked up to the press-box and made a signal as much as to say 'Get an eyeful of this one'. It was as ferocious a bouncer as ever he had bowled. When the Australian team for South Africa was released after this game, Miller, undisputedly, I thought, the world's best all-rounder, was among the unnamed rest.

Miller cut rather an inept figure, himself, against a bouncer. He didn't like them. Otherwise, when he put his mind to it, he was a thrilling batsman. He drove powerfully. He didn't use footwork much but covered ground with his long reach and he hit some of the biggest sixes seen in first-class cricket. Those who saw it, still talk of the huge one he hit into the Lord's Pavilion when playing with the Australian Services team.

Miller, too, took some of the most sensational catches at slip seen in Test cricket. He had safe hands and quick reactions. With the ball, with the bat and at slip, Miller gave me many of my most pleasurable moments in cricket. He was, too, a most successful and inspiring New South Wales captain. It was said that he was too unreliable to be a Test captain but that was poppycock. Miller could rise to any situation or responsibility. He never led an Australian team, although he was several times its vice. Ian Johnson, after touring England in 1948, was not chosen in 1953 and I thought it most unjust to Miller that Johnson should have been chosen tour leader above him for 1956. Miller just shrugged his broad shoulders at that. He bowed his head often in the perspiration of endeavour – he never bowed his knee to cricket officialdom.

Trueman was another exceedingly good Test fast bowler, always attacking and chockful of stamina. He didn't seem to me to be of quite the calibre of the other three on a good pitch and against the best batsmen. Another Test opener who gave me much pleasure was Alan Davidson. He was a glorious mover of the new ball and I never once sat behind him, watching the ball do its late manoeuvres in the air, without thinking what a wonderful experience it would have been to have opened the innings against him. He, too, took some staggering catches; and his hard-hitting batting was a thrilling delight. I should recall, too, that Lindwall was a batsman well above the average of the lower order and once made a capital century against England in a Test.

The mind looks back over the years and the eye recaptures all these wonderful bowlers in their distinctive actions, their flowing styles I can see them all again, Larwood gliding in, Lindwall doing his calisthenics as he warms up, Miller clapping his hands and tossing his mane. These are the three I put on a pedestal, with Larwood of 1932–33, and considering the batting strength against him, possibly just a shade ahead. If I try, I think I can almost hear again the angry thunder of the Hill.

Part Four

CRAFT, CHARACTER AND CONTROVERSY

━━━━━

Gary Sobers and Graeme Pollock are two of the greatest batsmen of all time. For his Special Jubilee Issue of *The Cricketer*, E. W. Swanton asked W. J. O'Reilly, Leslie Ames, G. O. Allen and myself to choose what we thought were the outstanding twenty cricketers from 1921–71. All of us chose Sobers. I, alone, which surprised me, chose Pollock. Another I chose who didn't make the final twenty (decided by vote among the four of us with E. W. Swanton having the casting vote) was Neil Harvey. Otherwise, I had 18 of the twenty, Allen and O'Reilly 16, and Ames 14.

It will be of interest to name the 20: Bradman, Compton, Hammond, Headley, Hobbs, Hutton, Lindwall, Sobers, Tate, Bedser, Grimmett, Larwood, McCabe, O'Reilly (the only vote he missed was his own!), Ponsford, Evans, Macartney, May, Miller and Worrell. I missed out on May and Worrell.

Perhaps I had seen Pollock play more grand innings than some of the others. At all events, I am pleased to write about him and Sobers at length in some sort of a hazy theory I have that left-handers could have a batting advantage over right-handers. At the least, I think it is an interesting thought.

Included in this Chapter are a number of articles I wrote for the London *Sunday Times*. After seeing a few 'slips' in Australia in 1970–71, especially when Fletcher did a slide and Edrich was run out at Perth, I might be inclined to modify a few thoughts in 'A Big Boot Hoot'. But I think it stands up even if sprigs, rather than ripple-soles, might stand up better in one or two circumstances. I doubt that John Benaud, Richie's younger brother, has yet been forgiven for this brush with officialdom. John is a dogged character, who speaks his piece. Quite a few would like to have seen him walk out for Australia in the final Test in Sydney in 1971 when Illingworth's splendid length and crafty bowling tied the Australians down and won victory for England.

I tilted with E. W. Swanton, with good feelings on both sides, over the respective outlooks of various English and Australian skippers. I recalled a piece about bodyline, which occupied so much of my first book, *Cricket Crisis*. I was pleased, too, to pay homage to the brilliance of South Africa's Barry Richards and to draw, from him, comparisons on how many modern Australian batsmen don't give as much thought to batting technique. I thought several New Zealanders, especially Dowling, showed splendid technique when I saw them almost beat England at Auckland in 1971. Technique is all-important in batting. Interestingly, too, O'Reilly chose Richards in his best twenty. A few more years and I think Richards would have been a unanimous choice.

A chapter on wicket-keepers, 'Pepper and Salt', enabled me to do some justice, I hope, to a noble band of wicket-keepers, the Aunt Sallies of the game but never the Rich Uncles. I love them all, even our latest, Rodney Marsh, who has the spirit and the application – and very much so as a batsman – to overcome an indifferent beginning and rise to the top. Marsh, unknown and untried, was given this important post for Australia and kept his place, sometimes wobbly, for a whole series of six Tests. He even, in Melbourne, might have got a century had Bill Lawry not closed his innings.

In 1961, on my way home from England, I was walking down the Via Veneto and had words with a magnificently tall and good looking Roman policeman, with white helmet and long white gloves. He was waiting to go on traffic duty. I managed to explain that I wanted to buy a hat and he directed me where to go.

A long time later, I was walking back and there was my big friend, standing on a dais, waving his arms, lustily blowing his whistle and keeping the dense traffic moving. I gave him a whistle and when he looked, pointed to my hat. He left the traffic to itself, strolled over, took my hat off and admired it and said: 'So, el Roma capella.' He thought it a good buy. The traffic got very mixed up.

Ten years later, I placed that hat, of which I am very fond though it is not now as resplendent as it was, on the hat rack of a plane coming back from the Brisbane Test. Master Marsh, whom I didn't know, walked in and planked a string of suits on a hanger on top of my 'Roma capella'. When I protested, Marsh assured me most pleasantly that it 'would do the hat the world of good'. When Marsh tightens up his technique, he will do Australian cricket the world of good. I wish him well!

18. The Brilliance of Left-Handers

Is it an advantage to be a left-handed batsman? Apart from Richards, of South Africa, it is impossible to refute the argument that the most brilliant batting in recent years has come from the left-handed Sobers, Pollock, and the West Indian, Lloyd. Considering their smallness in numbers, it is remarkable that left-handers have been so prominent down the years. In other days, there was the great Frank Woolley, of Kent and England, and Ransford and Hill of Australia. Bardsley, also of Australia, and Mead, of England, were heavy-scorers but they weren't in the same brilliant class as the three named above. Percy Chapman and Jack Gregory were exciting, swashbuckling left-handers and in recent years have been the exuberant Donnelly, New Zealand, and Harvey and Morris of Australia. Left-handers, all of them!

When Sir Donald Bradman saw Graeme Pollock for the first time in Perth, in October 1963, he said Pollock could well make in all ways the success of the Springbok tour. Pollock had just hit a century (18 fours) in 88 minutes. Sir Donald doesn't lightly enthuse. His patronage, like that of royalty, is not widely distributed and he proved prophetic about Pollock. He hit at Sydney and Adelaide two of the most scintillating Test centuries seen in Australia.

Those with memories mellowed in cricket said Pollock was Frank Woolley all over again when they saw Pollock hit 122 in Sydney. Many recalled how the tall man of Kent – Pollock is also over six feet – flowed forward to the kangaroo-bounding fast bowling of Jack Gregory and clobbered the ball through the off against the picket fence. Old men are apt to say, in deference to their own generation, that they will never see the like of so-and-so again; but before Pollock in Australia we had seen Sobers, who scaled even higher heights than Woolley.

Nobody in cricket has given me more sheer delight than Sobers. His brilliance has been breath-taking. For the West Indies and South Australia, for which state he played for a number of Australian summers, he has played many of his greatest innings in Australia and the classical ease of his stroke-making recur readily to memory. One day in Sydney, on his first tour of Australia, he moved forward to play Meckiff off the front foot. Of a sudden, he went into reverse and off the back foot, with a cross bat, he hit Meckiff wide of mid-on for a huge six. This stroke was unsurpassed in its brilliancy of conception and execution. Meckiff was no slouch in pace and only a genius could so quickly and completely change the whole nature of his stroke.

In his last innings in Sydney, for an MCC side, I saw Woolley hit a double century, but he never hit with more power on the off than Pollock did in his Sydney Test century. One cover-drive off O'Neill was unforgettable. It travelled, one thought, almost with the speed of light to the boundary. In this innings of 122 – and Pollock was then only 19 years of age – he hit one mighty six to leg, square, and with 30 yards to spare over the fence. He scorched 19 fours, most of them on the off. He interspersed his off boundaries with some hefty sweeps to leg yet one thought the leg-side was not his strength. Benaud fished for him often in this innings, with several near nibbles, but there wasn't a chance to hand until he reached 104. His 122 was exactly half his side's total when he was dismissed and he retired to an acclaim seldom heard on a cricket field.

Pollock's second 50 was hit in 57 minutes and this rich glut of strokes was shown on a pitch which, only some seven months before, was denounced by both English and Australian Test batsmen as an impossible one on which to play strokes!

Several weeks later in Adelaide, Pollock sent 22,000 spectators into rhapsodies as he played an even more brilliant innings. The Australians had struggled over 450 minutes for 345 runs. It wasn't thrilling to watch, and Pollock's first 50 in 86 minutes was like a sea-breeze in a heat-wave. His second 50 almost took the breath away. It took him only 40 minutes! Sitting in the pavilion, Gary Sobers was one of the spectators who rose to their feet to applaud Pollock back.

Once again, as in Sydney, Pollock specialized in off-driving, in a lazy, languorous manner that sent the ball whizzing away. But he also pulverized Benaud and Simpson with his smiting to leg. Pollock differed from Sobers significantly in his footwork. Sobers rarely danced down the pitch, as I remember him, but this day Pollock went yards down the pitch to both Simpson and Benaud. He hit Benaud far and wide over mid-wicket for six; he went even better against Simpson, hitting him for two sixes off successive balls. Several years before, Les Favell had hit Alf Valentine, of the West Indies, for two successive sixes in Brisbane's unforgettable Test.

All Pollock's sixes were hit towards Adelaide's Cathedral, just outside the ground. 'Murder in the Cathedral,' murmured Bill

O'Reilly. Pollock also hit two successive balls from Simpson for four so that he hit 22 runs off four successive balls. No wonder the crowd roared! I saw old-timers in Nip Pellew, Stan McCabe and Clarrie Grimmett stand with the thousands to acclaim Pollock that day. His century was chanceless, carving the Australian attack into small pieces. It is given a few to inject such enthusiasm and enjoyment into a crowd.

In writing at the time that Pollock was Frank Woolley all over again, I had an analytical look at Pollock and wrote this: 'As soon as one looks at Graeme Pollock at the crease, one begins to think of how he could be improved. His stance is an ugly one. He holds his short-handle bat at the bottom of the handle. As he stands well over six feet, he has to pop his posterior in the air to fit in everything and he forms an ugly, elongated, upside-down figure of S as he stands awaiting the ball. In such a stance his head is far away from his feet. He cramps himself, one feels, on the leg-side and, indeed, he is cramped on that side and, if he has a weakness, it is just behind square-leg. But suddenly his stance is immaterial as he blazes forth with ferocious, fiery off-drives that surge across the turf.'

Pollock was only 19 when I wrote this. He proved in Adelaide that he was almost as strong on the leg as on the off, and in subsequent innings against Australia in South Africa Pollock has shown that it is merely a toss-up which is the better batsman when Sobers and Pollock are both at their top.

I have never tired of singing the praises of Gary Sobers. So many times to me he has been absolute batting perfection. Nor is that all. He has been an amazing fieldsman, taking wonderful catches in the slips and throwing the stumps down from the field, and he is the best all-round bowler the game has known. I once described his bowling as being like a packet of mixed dried vegetables – something of everything – and, indeed, there has not been a type of left-hand bowl that Sobers has not used. In 1968, in Australia, he was worried by a piece of floating bone in his right shoulder. It hurt him, oddly, to bowl his over-the-wrist spinners. After three overs of fast bowling in the Brisbane Test, Sobers turned to slow, orthodox spin, breaking from the right-hander's legs, and took 6–73 off 37 overs.

Sobers said this was his best bowling in a Test and he thought it interesting that he should have gained such figures by reverting to the type of bowling he first used in cricket.

Some have used statistics to embellish their point that this one or that is the greatest cricketer the world has known, but figures – the statistical ones, that is – leave me cold.

In discussing great all-rounders once, some critics omitted to mention Jack Gregory and Charlie Macartney and in ability, glamour and cricketing character, they rank with the leaders of all time. Then, too, players of other eras didn't have their Test playing days, like the moderns, filled to satiety.

Armstrong got only 87 Test wickets but 74 of these were against England at a time of notable batting strength. In my book, O'Reilly's 102 English wickets in four series takes a lot of beating, considering the opposition.

I like, too, to savour Alec Bedser's Test figures against Australia of 104 wickets at 27.49 each and with Bradman, Morris, Barnes, Hassett, Harvey and Miller playing against him, Bedser got few 'rabbits'. It was a measure of his calibre that Bedser turned Morris, one of the very best left-handers of all time, into a broken reed towards the end of his career. Could Bedser have done the same to Sobers? Who can say, but he certainly seemed to have the answer to Morris, swinging late across his legs and cutting away towards the slips.

Statistics, not definitive, can be most misleading. The point is that a great cricketer would be great under any circumstances and in any era. That is the test of greatness and one arrives at an estimation of capacity, not by the number of runs made against possibly indifferent bowling, but by analysing technique and studying stroke-play.

I have seen Sobers play immortal innings and strokes not reminiscent of any other batsman. So, too, with Bradman, McCabe, Compton and Hammond. They displayed an individual flair in playing strokes that one could recognize immediately in one peep after rounding a pavilion corner. I have watched Sobers many times and thought he had only one chink in his armour – he doesn't always pick the bosie, which is strange for a man who bowls a perfect one himself.

I saw Sincock turn him inside out one day at Port of Spain with a bosie and the hysterical motions of a man who thought the ball was going the other way were a strange suggestion of clay. Nor did he pick Gleeson in Sydney one day in 1968, a snick going to slip. This incident was notable in two ways: first, the mistaken judgment of Sobers; and, secondly, the incredible whooping war-dance that Lawry did on the pitch at Sobers's downfall.

Strangely, as I wrote earlier, Sobers was not extravagant in his foot-work. When Barry Richards faced up to Gleeson in South Africa, he waltzed down the pitch before Gleeson had bowled and hit him for four fours in one over. This showed a blatant disdain for

Gleeson's ability to turn the ball, but Sobers always played Gleeson from the crease in Australia, and with suspicion. His footwork, then, was confined; but it was impeccable in the crease and his batting was helped by a long reach.

Davidson (and here was another mighty left-handed smiter of the ball!) was a better user of the new ball than Sobers. Davidson was the best left-handed user of a new-ball I have seen. Voce bowled a more dangerous bouncer than Davidson or Sobers and I think Fleetwood-Smith was a better over-the-wrist spinner than Sobers. Fleetwood was faster through the air and also spun the ball more. Bradman often mauled Fleetwood and, had they been pitted, would have done the same to Sobers. Spin didn't worry the Great Man and his footwork would have quelled Sobers's spin at the outset.

But you don't measure Sobers's bowling against a Bradman. There has never been another bowler like Sobers. The Australian, Bill Johnston, one of the most delightful characters ever to tread a cricket field, was another splendid left-hand bowler with the new ball but neither Davidson, Voce nor Johnston could bowl spinners. I once advocated the thought in the London *Sunday Times* that Sobers was not only the greatest all-round cricketer of all time, but there was nobody else even to approach him. Sir Donald Bradman later also expressed the same opinion.

There is an abiding memory of the centuries I have seen Sobers hit. In retrospect, there never seemed a period in them when he didn't look like hitting a century. Some centurions struggle, go slow and fast in patches, have their lucky streaks, possibly bog down in the nineties and emerge, at last, gasping at the three figure mark. There was nothing like this about Sobers. He just flowed on and on, his technique and stroke-play on a pedestal.

His best shots were the two most spectacular and most productive – the drive and the pull. In the drive, he had a full flow of the bat and like Pollock, he possessed an intuitive genius that enabled him to cleave the fieldsmen on the off side. There was no stroke he could not play. He could cut – Martin Donnelly says later that few left-handers cut – and square-cut and force majestically off his toes. This requires the very epitome of timing. I have written in another place of his very own inspirational stroke when he stood tip-toe, as if in defence, only at the very last fraction of time to swivel his body and send the ball screaming past square-leg. This stroke was pure genius.

Sobers was a complex study when he came to Australia in 1968, coming from a heavy county season with Nottinghamshire. His cricket appetite was clearly jaded. He made to[...] playing for his own country in the opening game at him, during that match, at the Australia Open g[...] there was no mistaking where his sporting interests l[...]

He played in the second game, making a superlati[...] he omitted himself from the third game, in which the[...] were beaten by a combined team. The team manage[...] was a hearty concurrence. He concurred with Sobers whep[...] he said, because it was wrong for the West Indians to rely[...] much upon Sobers. My own thought was that the place[...] skipper at the beginning of a tour is on the field, to be[...] spirit and confidence.

Sobers played at Adelaide, against South Australia. [...] Indians put up such a woeful display that Sobers summoned[...] behind closed doors and tongue-lashed them. Mr Gaskin con[...] curred. The things that Sobers had said, commented Mr[...] needed to be said. It might have been thought that somebody[...] to say a few direct things to the skipper, pointing out that his[...] progress for the tour was not all it might be. Although one who[...] been through the mill could recognize the signs with Sobers. He[...] gone stale with too much cricket in England. It was no longer a game[...] to him: it was hard work, and he had to drive himself.

It was not surprising, therefore, that Sobers should have turn[...] often to the golf course for relaxation. He played golf at every oppor[...] tunity and several times on the eve of a Test, when he surely should have been at the nets with his fellows, even if only watching his team lifted itself against Victoria and New South Wales but then Sobers went back on his tracks. Instead of going to Brisbane for the last first-class match before the Test, he returned south to Melbourne 'on business'. This, too, met with Mr Gaskin's approval.

The West Indies hit rock bottom against Queensland, but their splendid win over Australia in the First Test saved Sobers and the team management much criticism. They took too much for granted in that victory. In no time, they sloughed again and, finally, were no match for Australia, losing the series 1–3.

I don't think Sobers likes the responsibility of being captain. Unlike Frank Worrell, altogether a different personality who was always with his 'boys', Sobers is a loner. Some of his men grumbled that he left them too much to themselves. Manager Gaskin said Sobers didn't attend the nets before the Third Test in Sydney because he was having treatment for his corns. Those corns didn't stop Sobers from having 18 holes of golf that same afternoon!

I often saw Sobers on the cricket field going through the motions of a little wedge golf shot. Obviously, he found on the golf course the mental relaxation denied him on a cricket field. He continually wore a frown on the field (one saw it through binoculars) and when taxed with not bowling himself enough in Adelaide, replied wearily: 'I am not a cricket machine.'

For all his frowns, for all his worries, for all his apparent cricket staleness, Sobers still managed to hit two peerless Test centuries in Australia in 1968. One was in Adelaide, 110 in 132 minutes with two sixes and 15 fours; the other in Sydney, 113 in just over two hours, with 20 fours. In Adelaide he batted in his now-customary position of number six and ran out of partners. He fell in trying to keep the strike. It took a lot to budge him from that number six position.

Sobers cast a spell over the Australian attack in each innings but in each case his century was too late to give full value to his side. He came to bat at Adelaide at 4–107; at 3–30 in Sydney. A century innings from him in either city at number three or four would have had much more effect upon his side's innings.

Sobers has now hit 25 centuries in 86 Tests (I can't accept those matches in England in 1970, hastily arranged when the South African tour fell through, as Test matches, which, surely, are between one country and another). Bradman leads with 29 Test centuries. Hammond has 22, Harvey and Sobers each 25, Sobers passing Barrington in Sydney. Sobers again hit his peerless form in England in 1970 but retention of keenness will be a big factor if he is to pass Bradman's 29. The cricket yoke is beginning to tell on Sobers.

I like to recall Sobers in that thrilling over at Swansea in 1968 when he hit Malcolm Nash for 6, 6, 6, 6, 6, 6 – over long-on, long-on, long-off, mid-wicket to the on, long-on, mid-wicket to the on. Two hits went right out of the ground. This was a world's record for an over in a first-class match. Nash was philosophical about it. 'I suppose I can gain some satisfaction from the fact that my name will be permanently in the records book,' he said. He wanted to have the ball mounted – but it never came back the last time Sobers hit it out of the ground.

And so I return to the original theme of this chapter – is it an advantage to be a left-handed batsman? Is driving easier for them than a right-hander? Or, and this is a point which gave me much thought, are some left-hand batsmen really stronger in the right hand and does this give them an advantage in driving in that their top hand, the main driving one, is the right hand? Golfers, right-handed ones, know how important is the left arm and hand in the drive and how abortive the stroke becomes if there is too much right hand, and too soon, in the shot.

Pondering on this, I wrote to Graeme Pollock, Gary Sobers and Frank Woolley in England, asking them pertinent questions. Pollock and Woolley were good enough to answer immediately and with most interesting information. I spoke at length with Arthur Morris and Neil Harvey in Sydney and, after speaking with Martin Donnelly, he was good enough to put his magnificent thoughts on paper. Gary, not surprisingly, didn't get around to answering!

Pollock agreed with me that left-handers excel in the drive and, in his own case, says he has an advantage in that his top (right) hand is the stronger one. He plays every single-handed game right-handed. He writes right, throws right, plays tennis right but as soon as the two hands are required, such as in cricket and golf, he goes left-handed. But Sobers, Pollock writes:

> is left-handed in everything he does. This is probably the reason for his strong on-side play off the back foot, where his left hand dominates.
>
> Left-handers are probably fortunate because most bowlers tend to move the ball away from us. This gives you lots of room in which to play your shot, whereas with the ball coming into the body you are inclined to become cramped. It is said that left-handers are weak outside the off-stump, but this is only natural because of the terrific concentration of bowling directed at this side of the wicket.
>
> The same can be said for right-hand batsmen when facing a left-arm quick bowler from over the wicket. How many right-handers are suspect outside their off-stump to this type of bowler? Left-hand batsmen have to contend with this angle of attack for 90% of their batting time. The biggest bugbear for left-handers is the rough outside the off-stump from the third day onwards of a Test. Off-driving then has to be treated very carefully. Only when the ball is right up can the shot be played with any confidence. This is the reason why all left-handers like to bat first because this eliminates for a while the problem of rough outside their off-stump.

Graeme Pollock's views are most interesting and I am indebted to him for so lucidly explaining them – even though brother Peter is the journalist!

Neil Harvey writes right-handed, bowled right, kicks with his right foot and plays tennis right-handed. This suggests he is a more natural right-hander than a left one. When it comes to two-handed action (including wood chopping, he said with a wide grin), he goes left. His right did the work in the drive but his left in the cut, square-cut and the pull and he was most proficient in all these strokes.

I asked him which eye was stronger. Martin Donnelly had put to me the interesting and intricate theory that the left hand side of the brain dominated the right eye, which seemed to give the left-hander another advantage, but Harvey, now bespectacled, staggered me by saying he was weak in both eyes. 'Ever since I was 14,' he said, 'I have seen strange shapes. I could never read the scores on the board. Our Australian team in South Africa once had their eyes tested and only Drennan had worse sight than mine. The specialist said to me, "Who leads you out to bat?" '.

Harvey had one thing in common with Sobers. He, too, had difficulty at times in picking a bosie. Bill O'Reilly told me the tale of how Fred Johnston, the New South Wales slow bowler, once had Harvey completely at sea with his bosie when Harvey was playing for Victoria. 'Hutton told me,' said O'Reilly, 'that Johnston was the best slow bowler never chosen by Australia for England. And many not as good were chosen. He said he would have got over a hundred wickets there every time he toured.'

I am glad that story came from O'Reilly because I was responsible for Johnston going from Canberra into big cricket in Sydney. I asked O'Reilly whether he would mind if I used this story. 'Do what you like with it,' said the affable O'Reilly. 'I would remind you of the story of the judge who received an anonymous letter one morning while his case was part-heard. As the court assembled, the judge fixed its members with a stern eye and told them he had received an anonymous letter that morning. "It ill-behoves me," said the judge, "sitting where I am now, to say what I did with that letter, sitting where I was then." '

Frank Woolley wrote me as follows:

I don't think left-handers are fortunate in being left-handers. My experience was that more right-hand bowlers can make the ball move in the air into a right-hander and away from a left-hander, which is the most difficult ball to play. Also, a left-hand batsman has to cope with the bowler's rough and particularly in my time on a 'sticky' wicket. These, with covers being used, are no longer known in the game.

Because of the bowler's rough, a cover-drive was always diffi-cult for a left-hander, or so I found it. My left hand was always the

main force in my batting. My right hand, for me, was only a
steadying hand, just with my thumb and first finger, which allowed
the bat to go straight through. But I am not left-handed in all
things. I write right-handed, eat right-handed, play billiards
right-handed and pick up most things with my right hand.

At eighty-three, Frank apologized for what he described as his
scribble. He said his right hand was full of arthritis. I thought his
writing magnificent!

Martin Donnelly, as rich a character as he was an all-round
sportsman, wrote me an enthralling letter on the subject. He is a
left-hander in all things – writing, eating, playing tennis, throwing,
shooting and kicking.

> You ask which was my 'motive or power hand'. I am not certain
> that these are the same. I would regard my left hand as the power
> hand because this is the one that puts most power into shots,
> whether off or on-driving, slashing behind point (I almost said
> 'cutting', but few left-handers I saw really played the cut shot
> properly) or in hooking or pulling. However, the top hand, in
> my view, must always be the control hand and the guiding hand.
> You might even call it the motivating hand – in all shots. It must
> be primarily responsible for the arc through which the bat moves
> up and down and in so doing must harness and direct the power
> hand (i.e. the bottom hand), which is the hand that dictates speed
> and power. This is the hand with which the bat is moved in
> executing any stroke.
>
> To my mind, the golden rule in batting is that the top hand
> should have at *all times* not only a firm but a tight grip on the bat
> and this grip should never be changed or relaxed in the playing of
> any stroke (either defensive or offensive). Clearly, the hands work
> together, but basically, as I see it, the top hand must be the control
> hand, the bottom one the power hand.
>
> On the eye question, I checked with an eminent ophthalmic
> surgeon who said there was no basic rule about eye dominance and
> certainly gave no support whatever to my hopeful, but embryonic
> theory about the right eye being dominant in left-handers and the
> left eye dominant in right-handers. However, we did establish that
> M.P.D. is left-eye dominant. Incidentally, the simple test on this
> one is to point your index finger at a focused object on a wall and
> then to close each eye in turn. The eye that sees the finger in line
> with the object is the dominant eye as opposed to the one which
> throws the finger off to the left or right.

I hope not too many right-handers find, as I did when I tried this test, that their right eye is the stronger one. If a right-hand bats-man's shoulders are not allowed to come round too far to the bowler, thus giving him what is known as a two-eyed stance, the left eye does much more work in batting for the right-hander than the right one!

Martin Donnelly was also a magnificent footballer, capped for Oxford and England. Only the war and his later studies at Oxford prevented him being an All Black. Stewart Harris, the Australian representative of the London *Times*, who has an office next to mine in Parliament House, Canberra, remembers Donnelly with awe playing against Harris's Cambridge side. Harris said Donnelly was the most brilliant handler of a football at five-eighth he remembers. Modestly, Donnelly says his Oxford half-back, Ossie Newton-Thompson, threw a perfect dive-pass, which, says Donnelly, enabled him to get moving quickly and play well away from the forwards. He observed that when he played for England against Ireland, Ireland, 22–3, had their greatest victory to that date over England!

Donnelly and I once figured in an unfortunate incident in a club game in England. He bowled little – he says he bowled a ball that spins at the bowler's end and goes with the arm at the other end – and we both detected a sniff on the face of the batsman when Donnelly was given the ball. The batsman was E. W. Swanton and, as I recall it, he was plumb lbw to Donnelly's first ball, which was as straight as a barrel. As umpire, I didn't hesitate. EWS gave one of his most noted stares down the wicket – but he had to go! Both Donnelly and I were members of the Arab Club, of which EWS was founder. We are both still members!

Arthur Morris is left-handed in everything, and left-footed also. He says his left hand was definitely stronger – and his left eye also stronger. 'I don't use my top hand very much in batting,' Morris told me. 'I think I drove mostly with my shoulders and wrists, but I didn't drive in any pronounced fashion, neither to the off nor on. I think I was more a square-player and forcing them off my toes.' And, I might add, an exceptionally good player, too.

There is the case for left-handers, as I see it, although it is to be noted that some of the famous left-handers don't agree on all points. What can be agreed upon, however, and especially when remembering their meagre numbers, is that left-handers have been far more out-standing in brilliancy in recent years than their right-handed fellows.

Pondering that, I wondered whether left-handers might not profit from having the right hand the top one on the bat when I reflected that many golfers consider the top left hand to be the dominant one in a right-hand golfer. Golf can teach batsmen a great deal in driving. So many batsmen are bottom-hand conscious and I can think of no better illustration than Bobby Simpson. Simpson played golf off scratch and he possesses a glorious golf swing, fluid and full. Yet, when he came to batting, his bottom hand was the dominant one and he never drove as freely as nature equipped him to do. I think, in the main, this was brought about by the period in which Simpson played. He, with others, saw a vacancy in the Australian Test team for an opener and, in making himself into an opening batsman, Simpson concentrated upon defence and so used his bottom hand more than the top one.

Yet, if there is anything in my theory, why are there so few prominent left-hand golfers? I asked Gary Player this once and he said he could recall only one, Bob Charles. Arnold Palmer said Charles was not the only left-hander in tournaments, only the best known, but he could not name any others. Palmer said it was a matter of statistics, that a smaller number of left-hand players were willing to dedicate themselves to the game, but he looked a little blank when it was pointed out to him that there were a large number of champion left-handed tennis players, Laver and Roche, to name two. Many would contend that Laver has been the greatest tennis player of all time.

Palmer says definitely that golf is a right-hander's game and that courses are made exclusively for right-handers. I wonder would the mighty Jack Nicklaus have hit them even further had he turned about and got even more punch out of his right hand as the top one? The prospect is mind-boggling!

Several of us had dinner one night with Gary Player in Canberra and he advanced the theory that golf was the most difficult of all games to play. I couldn't agree with him. Golf is a forward game, with every shot played the same way with obvious variations in power and technique yet with the back-swing invariably the same, differing only for an intentional slice or pull and that only in a slight degree. The ball is never played backwards – and the cut and the glance are two of the most telling strokes in cricket – and the cover drive, one of the most brilliant strokes in cricket, would correspond to the golfer's nightmare – the socket or shank!

Yet, in the drive and the use of the top hand, golf, I repeat, has an important message for all batsmen because the drive is the very foundation of good batsmanship. It is the safest of all shots because the bat comes to the ball full face, minimizing risks; it pays the richest dividends in runs scored and, finally and most importantly, it has a demoralizing effect upon bowlers. No bowler, and particularly a fast bowler, likes to be driven. A bowler is encouraged when he sees a batsman cutting or deflecting, taking risks, but no bowler likes to be consistently driven. It is then that he tends to drop the ball short so that the drive, as I see it, is the dominant stroke in batting. It paves the way for the other strokes.

It is their ability to drive that makes Sobers and Pollock two such brilliant batsmen. Whether nature has given them an advantage over right-handers is something to be pondered. All that remains for me is to express my thanks to so many brilliant left-handers for telling me so much about themselves.

19. Test Openers are Gloomy Fellows

As one who has been booed (and with considerable justification, I might add) from Brisbane to Birmingham, via South Africa, I approach diffidently the subject of Test opening batsmen and their apparent shortage in England at the moment. Not, be it noted, that there mightn't be just as many opening gaps in the ranks of teams of other countries if they were suddenly confronted with Hall and Griffith!

Test openers are an interesting study, a race of their own. In all innocence, they retain their sense of humour as they pass quietly in their blooding through the various stratas of team strength. They have pleasant relations with their families, nod in a friendly style to tradesmen – who, at this stage of the opener's career, are pleased to nod back – and they number a reasonable number of friends until that fateful day when they find the cap of their country on their head and emerge, in trepidation, to take the first ball of a Test at, say, Melbourne or Lord's. This is the moment of emergence in all ways. There is no turning back. For worse – I'm afraid there is no better – the opener has put his cricketing head on the chopping block.

Look at it from the opener's viewpoint. As he walks out with his partner, he sees the opposing fast bowlers running, skipping, jumping, stretching as they limber up. They have, undoubtedly, had a hearty breakfast of steak and eggs. The fieldsmen are wide awake (one or two might snooze off a little later and be caught napping instead of doing the catching) and eager to get on with the job. The umpire, too, is avid to impress his presence.

The critic, sharpening his pencil, checks again on how to spell 'nibble', and most critics I have known are never at their most charitable before lunch. The new ball is rosy-red as it is tossed by the umpire to the bowler and its stitches stand out in raised array, ready to veer this way or that in the air. The first over could produce the unplayable ball (it never comes when the ball is old) that is the nightmare of all openers. No wonder Test openers are gloomy fellows, broody, introspective, ready for impending disaster. The members look at them with suspicion (unless they happen to be Hobbs and Sutcliffe) as they walk out. They turn their backs on them in icy frigidity if they return early, and with bored intolerance if they stay long. The openers quickly become the butt of buffoons who, no doubt, would make an interesting study facing up to a Larwood and the first ball of a Test.

As I suggest, we are a sad and melancholy sackful. A few weeks ago, in Johannesburg, I met again one of the brotherhood, Bruce Mitchell, his face lined with the worries of many a new ball in a Test. We looked at each other, shook hands warmly – and sighed. Even years afterwards, we are never ones to make light of our burdens and toss in the casual remark of how easy it is for lower down batsmen – the ball old, the bowlers jaded, the pitch with its fire lost.

It is morbidly pleasant for me, therefore, to come to England and find people bemoaning the lack of capable opening batsmen.

For many reasons, one being that he was utterly unselfish and another being that we trusted each other implicitly in our run calling, I have a deep feeling of affection for W. A. Brown. Many a time we walked out together for New South Wales and Australia, but there came the time when Brown packed his traps and left our native Sydney for Brisbane. The New South Wales captain, Stan McCabe, startled me by announcing one day that, in future, he would open the New South Wales innings with me. And, moreover, being the skipper, he would take strike!

I thought exceedingly ill of the notion. McCabe was of that rare and illustrious type that in fifteen minutes could not only take the opposing bowlers to pieces but could also destroy all those carefully nourished hardships of opening an innings.

We walked out together at Sydney against the New Zealanders, on their way home from England, and McCabe went to the striker's end, something which I had always done with Brown.

Jack Cowie was the bowler and, sure enough, McCabe got in that very first over that unplayable ball which I have already mentioned. It was of perfect length, swung late from outside the off-stump, seemed to make pace from the pitch and sent McCabe's leg-stump flying. From my safe haven at the other end, I tendered thanks that McCabe had taken strike.

Understandably, no doubt, McCabe was inclined to stress the virtues of that particular ball when we came together later in the dressing-room. I shook my head. 'No, no,' I told him. 'It must be your eyes. It was just a straight ball.'

Undeterred, McCabe took strike again in the second innings and again Cowie gave him the perfect, unplayable ball. This time, however, it did the opposite of everything the first had done. It swung late from the leg and toppled McCabe's off-stump.

I got the propaganda in early in the dressing-room this time. 'Now don't tell me,' I said to McCabe, 'that that ball was anything else but a straight up-and-downer.' It was probably the only time the brilliant McCabe had ever bagged a first-class 'pair'. He never again opened with me for New South Wales.

C. F. Walters and C. J. Barnett were two swashbuckling and successful types of openers for England. The two knights, Jack Hobbs and Len Hutton, had all the strokes, but each felt his way circumspectly through the opening overs. Two other ideal openers were Herbert Sutcliffe and Bob Wyatt. They still talk in Australia of how Hobbs and Sutcliffe stole their singles, with perfect understanding and no need of calling.

One day in Melbourne, Hobbs and Sutcliffe batted all day in a Test against Australia. It was one of the few occasions that ardent lover of cricket, Sir Robert Menzies, induced his wife to come to cricket. She didn't think much of watching the two same batsmen all day. Dame Pattie, as I have suggested, was not one of the world's avid cricket-watchers but her husband took her along to Lord's on a visit to England and, sure enough, Hobbs and Sutcliffe were batting. 'Goodness gracious, Bob,' said Dame Pattie, 'don't tell me we haven't got those two out yet?'

There must be something radically amiss for England to have had so many opening batsmen since the forties. They have been in and out like French governments before de Gaulle. Basically, it could be that they – the batsmen, not the French governments – are not technically correct. An opening batsman cannot afford to have flaws in his defensive technique.

Recently in South Africa I also spoke with Herbie Taylor, one of the greatest batsmen of all time. He was a perfectionist in style and a vigorous advocate of the side-on theory in batting. He maintains that a batsman should even be side-on when playing back defensively.

It might not be necessary to go all the way in this with Taylor, but I do know that a batsman who allows his back shoulder to turn towards the bowler in his stance puts himself immediately into a tenuous position. His back-lift must be towards third-man – it is physically impossible for it to go straight back on the line towards the stumps – and so there is the initial error of a batsman playing across the line of flight of the ball. When that happens against a swinging new ball, there are batting shoals ahead.

Bob Wyatt, an extremely sound judge of the game, has been pointing this out in England for a long time and thinks the present lbw rule has made English bowlers concentrate upon in-dippers and off-breaks, working the ball in towards the batsman for lbw.

Many batsmen prepare themselves for this type of attack – and such a stance is an aid in playing to the on – by deliberately standing full-chested to it, thus bringing around their back shoulder. They are not side-on, as Taylor advocates, and it is when they are pitted against a fast bowler like Griffith, who can bowl a perfect late-swinging yorker, that they are in dire difficulties. This is the hardest ball of all for a full-chested batsman to play. There seems, too, in England to be a tendency to look askance at a batsman who has a shortened back-lift, yet I think such a lift is essential to an opening batsman at the beginning of an innings. It gives him maximum control against a ball swinging late. Don Bradman, who really became an opening batsman when he came in early at first wicket down, denied his back-lift altogether when he wished to defend. His bat, under such circumstances, never left the perpendicular.

England will get good openers again. It has had the best of all time in Jack Hobbs – Len Hutton not far behind – but I don't think they will come until the technique is perfected. As C. B. Fry did, they should check their back-lift in a mirror. To choose somebody with technical defects, is only to compromise. I hear very good reports of Boycott* and another Hutton is said to be following in Dad's footsteps.

Len Hutton, I am sure, will agree with me that a reliable opener must have a nose for the job and he must get it down on the pitch, so to speak, to set the stage for those to follow. He has got to take the sting out of the bowlers, subjugating himself meanwhile. It is a job with few compensations, yet its value is appreciated by those who know their cricket.

It breeds, too, a man well-versed in the subtleties of the game. Like the one I knew in other days when there was no limit to the number of light-appeals. This worthy had been turned down several times by the umpires. Of a sudden, his partner called: 'Come on, Fred.' The canny Fred called back: 'No, no, Bill. I can hear you. I recognise your voice – but *where* are you?' They got the next light appeal! There must be a footnote to this. There is now a super-abundance of opening batsmen in England, whose selectors are hard pressed to find reliable lower-down batsmen. This is put down to the many one-day matches, now so popular with spectators in England, in

---

* I loved the quip against Boycott at Old Trafford in 1968. He was No. 1 on the scoreboard and his run-getting had bogged down very badly. A fed-up spectator roared out at him: 'Come in, Number one. Your time is up.' The ground rocked.

which the openers get the best of things. Batsmen who follow them have generally got to move into the attack immediately and thus, it is argued, have little chance to settle in and develop their innings along orthodox lines. A batsman of the calibre of Denis Compton, for instance, would revolutionize English cricket at the moment. Another aspect to be considered, with so many internationals engaged from other countries, is that English county cricket has taken on the flavour of country cricket and many young English batsmen, accordingly, are denied the chances that other generations knew. One-day games, obviously, are a poor nursery for Test matches.

Boycott's figures are phenomenal. He is an extremely sound opener, lacking, at times, in his judgment of a run. Otherwise, he is the perfect professional cricketer.

The lbw rule has now been altered and it remains to be seen what effect it has upon in-swing and off-break bowlers. And batting technique.

It is the Australian batsmen who now are deficient in technique, and especially when set up against the peerless technique of the South African, Barry Richards. John Snow, following the tactics of Peter Pollock and Mike Procter, who confused Lawry's Australians in South Africa in 1970, played upon the weakness of the average Australian in 1970–71 when playing against a short ball. Keith Stackpole is one of the best pullers of a short ball that I have seen, but the lesson he so splendidly gives every time he bats seems to be lost upon some of his fellows. Stackpole's back foot goes across the pitch for a pull, thus opening his shoulders. Others go back towards the stumps, thus locking their shoulders and making them unable to pull. In such circumstances, all they can do is duck, which is ungainly for the batsman and encouraging for the bowler.

20. When Cricket turned to Near-Murder

The 'Mods', I am afraid, often find my generation boring when we dip into the past, but you can't always ignore history when it has to do with the present.

At Lord's, recently, the International Cricket Conference issued some nebulous stuff asking all countries to ponder the curse of pad-play. At the same time, I was chatting with Harold Larwood at Trent Bridge and I couldn't help thinking that without Larwood there would not have been this prevalent pad-play.

Of necessity, it sends me back to 1932–33, a turbulent period that burst upon me as a youngster in his first Test series against England. And as one connects Larwood with pad-play, so it must be added that had there been no Bradman, there would have been no Larwood bodyline. It was, in itself, a tribute to Bradman's greatness.

Bradman had made Test scores in England in 1930 of 131, 254, 334 and 232. He not only cut all bowlers to shreds. He was the greatest cricket challenge England had known and a dour, remorseless Scot named Douglas Jardine was given the job of bringing Bradman to heel and, of all places, in Australia. Jardine was 130 years after his time. He should have gone to Australia in charge of a convict-hulk.

So many of that English team have told me subsequently in England that they abhorred bodyline and wanted nothing to do with it. But it was a deep plot that obviously had its genesis before the English team was chosen for Australia. When the side was chosen, it included four fast bowlers – Larwood, Voce, Bowes and Allen – and Bowes just previously had bowled bodyline against the great Jack Hobbs on his home ground, the Oval.

Nobody criticized Bowes's tactics more than Sir Pelham Warner. He wrote sternly that it prostituted the art of cricket and that if it were continued, it would ruin the game. Warner demanded that Bowes stop it immediately.

Soon after that, 'Plum' Warner was made manager of Jardine's team to Australia. There must have been many nights when he didn't sleep a wink.

In simple terms, bodyline bowling was aimed more at the man than the stumps. To be true, the stumps were often hit but it was first impressed upon the batsman that he had to look to his physical safety. It was conceived for Bradman and, with Larwood the perfect executing agent, it cut Bradman down to comparative size. But, as Warner said, it wasn't cricket. The batsman's first thought, against the thunderbolts of Larwood and Voce at his ribs and at his head, with a close-packed leg-side field, was of self-preservation.

I still recall the whistle of a bouncer from Larwood past my temple. I almost moved into it. Some Australians certainly showed up poorly against bodyline. Several weren't keen on playing; one, indeed, asked the selectors to drop him. We were widely accused by the English of being 'squealers' and one or two might have come within that category, although none of us relished playing against bodyline. The mutterings were intense. Some Englishmen at first tried to assist a hit Australian but as the intent was so obvious, these gestures were later forsaken. As the series wore on, no Australian passed the time of day with an Englishman.

Riding the storm — and crowd riots were often imminent with mounted police on call during the Adelaide Test – was the imperious, unflappable Jardine. He saw his job, and he did it, impervious to all, including Warner, who remained publicly mute during the whole tour.

But Warner was more worried even than the Australians. I saw a letter which he subsequently wrote to a distinguished Englishman stationed in Australia and in which he wrote, in a *cri de coeur*: 'I could do nothing with Jardine. I pleaded with him to stop it, at least to ease it. He coldly ignored me. I am not sure I would trust him again. He is a queer fellow. When he sees a cricket field with an Australian on it, he goes mad!'

G. O. (Gubby) Allen alone stood up to his skipper. Jardine told Allen before the second Test that he wanted him to bowl bodyline. Allen, who was a very good fast bowler, refused. 'Then,' said Jardine, 'you won't play.' Fifteen minutes before the game began in Melbourne, Allen was still in his street clothes. 'Why aren't you dressed, Gubby?' asked Jardine. It was Jardine's way of admitting that he had lost the argument with Allen. But it was the only point Jardine lost on the tour. Allen could afford to go against Jardine. He was an amateur; Larwood, Voce and Bowes were professionals, accustomed to do as they were told.

Pataudi, the Indian, who had hit a century in Sydney in his first Test, lost his place after Adelaide. When Woodfull was hit a sickening blow over the heart, Jardine, with incredible disregard for Woodfull and the crowd, immediately strengthened the leg-side field. He motioned Pataudi across. Pataudi refused. 'Ah,' said Jardine, of the Indian Prince, 'I see his Highness is a conscientious objector. You come across, then, Hedley.'

There was the day in Adelaide when Warner and his assistant manager, Palairet, also an old school-tie man, came into our dressing-room to commiserate with the stricken Woodfull, who, under medical attention, was stretched out on a massage table.

Woodfull was terse to the two Englishmen. 'I don't want to discuss it,' he said. 'There are two sides out there. One is playing cricket. The other isn't.'

Warner and Palairet left the room in acute distress. Warner never recovered from the snub Woodfull gave him. The words cut him deeply.

Writing of the incident later in a book, Warner commented: 'Unfortunately, there was a member of the Australian team who was a journalist and next day the story was blazoned all over the front page of their newspapers.'

That was a direct dig at me. I was the only journalist in the two teams and I knew inside stories of that tour that would have made a pressman's pen drip with ink. But, being new to all of it, I had the sense to keep my own counsel. Claude Corbett, of the Sydney *Sun*, was given the story that evening by a member of the Australian team, who made a rendezvous with Claude in a car on the Adelaide North Terrace. Claude himself later told me this, and the player who had given him the story. He thought it too hot to have on his own and he shared it with some others.

Like Jardine, Warner later became a good friend of mine. We corresponded and I wrote many articles for his *Cricketer*. When he knew the true story, he was good enough to apologize to me. But it was naive of him to expect that such a story could be kept quiet. It's immaterial, now, who the Australian was who gave the story out, but it is interesting that Woodfull also blamed me as the culprit. When I told him, years later, who it was he said: 'A pity. That cost you a trip to England.' I have had plenty since.

But Warner, at the time, was so incensed with me and upset about the publicity, that he went to Larwood and said: 'I will give you a pound, Larwood, if you can get Fingleton out for nothing in the second innings.' Harold got his quid from Warner!

The whole tour was a distressing business. Bodyline was immoral in its conception against Bradman but Jardine's mistake was in using bodyline unrelentingly by Larwood and Voce against all the Australians. Bowes did not have the fire of the others, although he got Bradman for a blob in Melbourne.

It took years for the bad feeling to subside and some of the bruises never healed. Bradman and Jardine never made it up, although all the rest of us did with both Jardine and Larwood. I sat in front of Jardine and Bradman in the press-box at Leeds in 1953. Somebody with an odd sense of humour had sat them side by side. 'Good morning, Mr Bradman,' Jardine would say on arrival. 'Good morning, Mr Jardine,' Bradman would reply; and that was it for the day.

No Australian deep down blamed Larwood, who was a wonderful bowler. As I talked with him at Trent Bridge the other day, it was beneath a graphic picture of him delivering the ball. It all came back to me again – the classical upright pose of the body, everything in balance, with every muscle and sinew coming into the delivery. It is one of the immortal pictures of cricket.

It was odd that he should have settled in Australia. In 1948, George Duckworth asked me if I would come with him and visit Larwood in his little shop, in a back street in Liverpool, in which he sold sweets and cigarettes. Larwood was too proud to have his name over the door. Thinking I was after a story, Larwood greeted me suspiciously. His wife told us that he rarely went out. George and he chaffed each other over a row at Old Trafford, after the Australian tour, when Larwood broke a rib of George's and Lancashire decided it didn't want to play against Nottinghamshire unless bodyline was banned.

On this day at Liverpool, we induced Larwood to come with us for 'a sup of ale' and from this flowed a warm friendship between Larwood and myself that led to him emigrating to Australia with his family.

One Saturday in 1950 in Canberra, I received a cable from Larwood. It ran: 'Leaving tomorrow with wife five daughters and eldest daughters fiance stop can you find jobs and accommodation.'

It was, at a time of housing shortage in Australia, a tall order and it was an Australian Prime Minister, Ben Chifley, who helped Larwood most to settle. 'I think,' said Chifley, when I sought his aid, 'that Larwood was too good for you chaps. He was the greatest fast bowler I saw.' And, at his peak in 1932, probably the greatest that anybody else saw, either. 'That,' Larwood once told me, 'was when I hit my top.'

Mr Chifley combined with Mr Tom Watson, of Sydney brewery

fame, and Mr Hooker, real estate, to settle the Larwoods down comfortably in Sydney. But Larwood refused attractive offers to be helped in business.

I told Larwood when he arrived that he should come to Canberra and thank Mr Chifley. He was delighted to do so. I took him in to Mr Chifley and Larwood, in his Midlands accent, thanked Mr Chifley. Chif., as he was known, looked at Larwood and then at me, in some amazement. 'What did he say, Jack?' he asked. I interpreted. Then Mr Chifley, in his broad, nasal voice, said some nice things to Larwood, who looked wonderingly at me. 'What did he say?' asked Larwood. Again I interpreted.

Larwood had been invited back to England in 1968 by his old county club and somebody asked him at Trent Bridge whether he would like to return for good. 'No bloody fear,' said Lol, 'I'm a bloody Australian now.' Formerly a very shy person, he says Australia, where he now has seven grand-children, has made him lose his shyness and inferiority.

A much-mellowed Jardine, who maintained his contacts with Oxford, would have me to dinner when the Australians played there. He had a wonderful, wry sense of humour. He had doubts about how he would be received if he returned to Australia and he came with some diffidence in the fifties. He was received with warmth. Australians don't harbour grudges. While he was there, Jardine was thrilled to be asked to speak over the national broadcasting system as a 'Guest of the Nation'.

Jardine once told me of the remark he enjoyed most during the bodyline tour – there were many he didn't enjoy. It was at Brisbane where Jardine walked out to bat against the aboriginal, Eddie Gilbert. 'Get stuck into this —— Pommy, Gilbert,' roared a barracker. 'It was his —— mob that took all that land from your —— mob.' The Jardines were early investors in Queensland.

As I said earlier, it is easy for an old-timer to become boring. I really set out to draw a parallel between Larwood's return to his homeland and MCC's edict on pad-play. I am inclined to think that if there hadn't been a Larwood, there would not have been bodyline nor, after bodyline, a revision of the lbw rule allowing a decision to a ball pitched outside the off-stump.

This was a sop, suggested by Australia, to draw attention away from bodyline and distract bowlers from attacking the leg-stump. It led to a flood of off-spin and seam bowlers and this, over the years, has led to the batsmen negating these theories by prodding the front pad at the ball, and not offering a stroke.

Larwood was a shy man, a modest man, a wonderful bowler – but standing quietly with him in the Trent Bridge pavilion it was interesting to reflect what a tremendous effect he has had on cricket – even to the present day. Maybe, soon, to cure the ills of pad-play, cricket will revert to the old lbw rule. It would be the final and fitting tribute to Larwood.

(And cricket *has* reverted to the old rule. The ball now must pitch in a line between the stumps for a batsman to be lbw. If the ball pitches outside the off stump and would, in the opinion of the umpire, have hit the stumps, the batsman shall be out if he offers no stroke at the ball and pads it away.)

21. The Big Boot Hoot

It was an evening in 1961 as the Australian cricketers ate at London's Euston Station, trans-training on the way from Hove to the first Test at Birmingham. As Mr. Frank Hole, then general manager of British Transport Hotels, is a close friend, I don't suggest the railway 'bangers' were responsible, but the Australians generally were cranky.

There were hot words. Syd Webb, Queen's Counsel, was the manager. Richie Benaud, OBE, was the skipper. O'Neill had been injured at Hove and Webb said O'Neill wouldn't play at Birmingham. So they swopped woulds and wouldn'ts, and with the co-selectors siding with Benaud, it looked as if Webb would have a strike on his hands.

Striking and drinking beer are two of Australia's favourite pastimes but it was Webb who struck his colours. O'Neill played and made a handsome 82. But Benaud's attitude displeased Webb, who later officially banned Benaud from giving press interviews. As Benaud was a pressman, that would be the equivalent of *ordering* Michael Parkinson to write something adulatory about MCC and Lord's.

Webb and the Benaud clan clashed again the other day in Sydney when Webb, as chairman of the august New South Wales executive – not a Test cricketer on it – read an edict banning John Benaud from playing for flouting authority by wearing rippled-heeled boots. It was almost as if Mr Webb had put on the black cap of the death penalty, although the drama was spoilt a little when he called Benaud a naughty boy and would insist upon calling him Richie.

It mattered not that young John had just led New South Wales to its third successive victory after several years of drought. He had defied authority and there being no dialogue between the two generations, John got the axe. Stupidly.

As one generation views another, as they think and feel about each other, so they will communicate. Or not communicate. There was no awareness or flexibility in the happening. Benaud said he would conform to the official boots when he got used to them, which was reasonable enough. He had just made 56 and 42 in the banned boots but for some matches the New South Wales selectors, upset by dropped catches, had been entering black marks in little books and they came down against rippled soled heels in boots. John, oddly, hadn't dropped a catch. He had a captaincy flair like his brother. Crowds were coming back to the Sydney ground. But, no matter, he had flouted the Colonel Blimps.

The New South Wales selectors don't make statements to the press but as they were going into committee on John Benaud, before Webb delivered sentence, one who must remain unnamed – I musn't imperil my life membership of the New South Wales association – was heard to remark darkly: 'We'll see who comes out on top in this boots business in the end.'

Moreover, although possibly infringing the Official Secrets Act, I can definitely deny that the selectors' meeting began with the chairman quoting Kipling: 'Oh-my-God-keep-me from going lunatic! (Boots-boots-boots-movin' up an' down again!)'

Bob Wyatt was the first I knew to wear rubber-soled boots and from the springy lilt in his gait, a leprechaun, the Irish fairy who makes shoes, could well have had something to do with their making. Denis Compton wore them and so did, and do, Gary Sobers and Graeme Pollock. Thinking back on all the runs the four made and which two of them continue to make against Australia, I rather wish they had been shod otherwise. Nobody would wear rubbers when the field is wet, as witness the tennis players who change to sprigs (spikes) on wet courts.

There was once a very famous captain of Australian Test teams who moved, as so many have done since, from the cricket field to the press-box. Despite his genius on the field, the great man found intense difficulty, if not in interpreting, in putting into words what was happening on the field below but he had, so to speak, an eye for boots. Let anybody make so much as a suggestion of a slip on the field and the flood-gates of words would open on the necessity of being well shod and sprigged, the importance of it in moments of crisis, reminiscences connected with it and so on. On such occasions, as they said in the press-box, he was always good for at least half a column with very little effort although, understandably, with much repetition.

'Boots' was the humblest person in a hotel when hotels cleaned boots. The House of Lords used to call the junior Bishop, whose job it was to read prayers, 'Boots' and called him so because he came to the Lords in the boots of a bishop who had died and left the vacancy. There was also a medieval form of torture called 'boots' in which a leg was encased and wedges inserted until the victim either confessed or fainted. So perhaps young John was lucky in getting only the order of the boot.

What's behind it all? Well, let me illustrate with a story about my very dear friend, Sir Arthur Fadden, a noted and down-to-earth political humorist in Australia. He was addressing a meeting once and a heckler, apropos an alleged scandal at the local meatworks, called out: 'Eeh, Fadden, what's behind the Brisbane abattoirs?' And Artie, as he was widely known, shot back: 'Animal manure' – which wasn't exactly the term he used. But that's what is behind this footling nonsense.

Years ago they banned Harry Hopman from playing in Sydney because he dared to wear shorts. Earlier this summer, New South Welshmen were ordered to stop wearing Edwardian-type flannels because, allegedly, they couldn't bend in them. Well, even baggy breeches give, as witness the time in the mid-fifties at The Oval when Langley's split handsomely and Keith Miller amazingly and fortuitously had a big safety pin in his pocket to make Langley chaste.

Kenneberg has been told to erase his facial fungus, for all that he once, and historically, made double figures this summer; others have been told to have a haircut and Steele, the new New South Wales skipper, has been ordered – ordered, mark you! – to use a long-handle bat in future. No thought here of the damage the longer handle might do to the remnants of his umbilical cord or any other physical appendage. Steele, by the way, has just hit two glorious centuries in Sydney with a short-handle bat.

What it really amounts to is just another generation clash, one that could easily have been averted over a quiet and unofficial beer. No sportsman would allow himself to enter a field poorly shod and in this instance, I am staunchly on the side of the youngsters. And so is Barry Knight, England's cricketer here, who is agent for the boots and is shipping them to England by the dozen.

Already the New Zealanders, who will soon play Australia's Second XI, have them. Most of Bill Lawry's side in South Africa which will return soon, with the greatest profits booty in history, wear the banned boots and will continue to wear them. Knight couldn't buy the publicity his boots have got.

I telephoned Tom Graveney in Brisbane this week. He has had execrable luck there, being dismissed in his first innings for none and then suffering a broken arm in his next game before he had scored. Tom told me that when he rang his wife with the news that he had broken his arm, she responded in a wifely manner by saying: 'Well,

I told you you were too old to play cricket.' It might be that one or two of our officials are too old, also.

(Six months later, the boot was made official. In the interim, Richie Benaud resigned his life-membership of the New South Wales Cricket Association.)

22. A Classic Example

Batting technique is absorbingly interesting, yet often neglected. It is freely discussed in the highest circles but here, I think, the emphasis is more on abstruse theory than on basic principles. It is easy to confound the pupil with woolly talk and infinite regard for things which too often are secondary. The important things in batting are basic: correct stance; correct initial positioning of the feet and shoulders; correct back-swing and follow-through and correct foot-work.

When we were about fifteen, Frank Conway, with whom I grew up in the cricket world of Waverley, procured from his library a book by C. B. Fry on the art of cricket. It both impressed and confounded us because we had, first, to work out the intricacies of C.B.'s technical language. This wasn't at all simple, but it made us think for ourselves and discuss.

The world of golf is different to that of cricket. When a person wins the British or American Open, immediately his hints on the game are published for all to read, marvel at, and wonder if some given little wrinkle on technique is all that's needed to put the duffer into single figures. Golfers analyse and think infinitely more about their game than cricketers. They also practise more. If a particular shot hasn't satisfied Gary Player (even though he may have shot a 68), he will hie himself from the last green to the practice fairway and hit a hundred balls to iron out his fault.

A cricketer can hardly do that. If the pull shot has let him down, he could go to the nets and ask a bowler to give him short balls so that he can try and rectify his fault; but he can't set the shot up as a golfer can. In one game, the ball moves; in the other, it sits there waiting to be moved.

Gary Player came to the Sydney Cricket Ground in late 1970 to watch play between MCC and New South Wales. He had only a few hours to spare, having dropped in from Japan, before catching a plane to South Africa. He came and chatted in the press-box. Just previously, I had had dinner with him in Canberra with Phil Tresidder, of the Sydney press, and Wally Gale and Darrel Welch, two popular and efficient Sydney professional golfers, and it was absorbing to hear them discuss technique. I have known Player for years. When he first came to Australia in the mid-fifties he confessed that he hadn't a bob to bless himself with and he was delighted when I told him that I wanted to write about him for the South African press.

Player, then, had just arrived from South Africa, where he had been giving lessons at fifty cents a time. Business wasn't good. To attract custom, Player offered to give the fifty cents back if he couldn't rectify his client's fault. 'One very sad chap came to me one day,' said Player, 'and I asked him what was his fault. "Well," he said, deliberately, "I am hooking my shank." I gave him his fifty cents back to go right away from me!'

Player got to the top by sheer hard work, and he has never forgotten his lowly beginnings. He works just as hard now to stay at the top. Some, not so successful, begrudge him his success but this is life. Player lives a spartan existence – no alcohol, no smoking, arduous physical jerks every day of his life. He doesn't flirt with his gifts, yet he has an impish sense of humour and is always ready – though he has been let down badly at times in Australia – to help the press get their stories.

In Melbourne, in 1970, he accepted a challenge against a prominent Australian Rules footballer and they went to a football field, Player to hit a golf ball through the uprights against the footballer to kick goals – and accurate kicking is the feature of this particular football game. Player selected a five-iron and promptly put six shots plumb between the uprights from 150 yards out.

He never missed once. The footballer had six kicks from 50 yards out, drop kicks and drop-punt kicks, and got five out of six. To cap his performance, Player gave an exhibition – which was some sort of sacrilege on such a football ground – of Rugby dive-passing. The next day he played his first round of the Australian Open, which he won for the sixth and record time.

Player had to hurry to the airport from the Sydney Cricket Ground and I thus had no chance of getting some opinions from him on the batting techniques he saw. This was a pity. Player, a master of swing technique, would have had plenty of opinions and they would have been worth hearing.

Jim Mills, the professional at Kooyonga, Adelaide, once told me a story of Player which demonstrated his incredible stroke capacity. Player was winding up a clinic at Mills' club and towards the end of it began hooking his drive. He called Mills out in front of the crowd. 'What am I doing wrong, Jim?' he asked. Mills suggested a change in the grip. Next time Player's drive was not so hooked. Mills suggested another slight change. This time the drive sailed without deviation. 'Ladies and gentlemen,' said Player to the gallery, and he had, of course, played a very clever part in the deception, 'this goes to show that when a fault creeps in, the man to see is your professional. Thank you, Jim.'

It is interesting that the most technically correct modern batsman is another South African, Barry Richards. During Sydney's first Test of the 1970–71 series, three enthusiasts, Warren Saunders, Peter Philpott and Doug Ford, carried out to perfection a most ambitious inaugural dinner of all living players who had represented New South Wales. It was an outstanding success. They came, so to speak, out of hollow logs and down from gum-trees, players who hadn't met one another for two or even three decades, and the spirit of the evening was cricket at its best. Johnnie Taylor stood up and received an ovation. Sir Robert Menzies, of Victoria, who was given the 'privilege' of being a New South Welshman for the evening, spoke as special guest and made a memorable speech. So, also, did Sir Donald Bradman in responding.

Sir Donald that evening referred to Barry Richards as possibly the best batsman in the world today (Sydney had not then seen him) and those of us who had watched him bat in England, South Africa and Australia, heartily concurred. Sir Donald spoke of a letter he had just received from Richards's mother after her son had made 356 in Perth in November, 1970, against West Australia; 325 in a single day. The mother told of how her son had been given Sir Donald's book 'How to Play Cricket' when he was seven years of age and of how he used to bat against a ball swinging from a rafter and tied in one of his mother's stockings.

I see no resemblance in the batting of Bradman and Richards, apart from footwork. Each is, or was, a genius in his own way. What every batsman must do is study his gifts and make the most of them. Emulation can be carried to excess, becoming unnatural. Inspiration is another matter.

I sat and yarned with Richards in the Adelaide grandstand one day in late 1970. I had interviewed him once before, at Lord's in 1968, and I had sensed then how too much cricket was wearing thin his enthusiasm for the game. It was so, also, in Adelaide, although his scores didn't suggest it. He lived in a perpetual whirl of cricket, playing, talking, coaching and even travelling into Victorian country districts to give talks.

'The offer of a dollar a run to Richards will be the making of him,' said Illingworth sagely in Adelaide after the South African had made 223 against MCC when he first met them. 'It will make him a second Don Bradman'. Illingworth had a Yorkshire appreciation of 'brass' and it would be true that this dollar offer made Richards concentrate more.

Richards told me in Adelaide that Sir Donald's book had sparked his interest in cricket but he soon realized – to his credit – that Bradman was Bradman. He had copied Don's stance, the bat resting on the ground between his two feet, and his grip on the bat handle with the top hand further around to the right. This was the grip that enabled Sir Donald to turn his left hand so quickly and effectively over the bat in the pull shot that the ball went quickly to earth. I can never remember Sir Donald being caught on the pull in a big game. He was a master of the stroke.

Early in his career, then, Richards changed from the Bradman stance and grip. He became essentially Richards, which was sound, clear thinking.

Coincidentally, it was on Adelaide Oval, in the early thirties, when I was 12th man for Australia, that I had a batting talk given me by another magnificent South African player, Herbie Taylor. Taylor was then in the sunset of his career. He will always be noted in the Hall of Fame as the batsman who played so superbly against the fearsome bowling of Syd Barnes on matting wickets in South Africa before the first world war.

Taylor was a stylist, a perfectionist, but unfortunately he was past his best when he came to Australia with Jock Cameron's side. He was adamant that batting was always side-on, but he destroyed some of my belief in his theories this day by maintaining that Don Bradman played back wrongly. Taylor maintained that Bradman was in error in playing back defensively full face to the bowler, not side on. As Bradman had made 135, 226, 219, 112, 167 and 299 not out against the South Africans on this tour, I remember thinking that it was perhaps just as well for the Springboks that The Don *did* have a fault in his batting!

Years afterwards, I acknowledge Taylor's sound thinking, though I still haven't been convinced that it is necessary to play a defensive stroke side on. I never saw anything wrong with Bradman's defence.

Richards turns full-face in back defence but that is the only time, apart, naturally, from pull shots or forcing strokes to the leg. Richards is beautifully positioned side on for all other strokes and he plays all the strokes. He differs vastly to most Englishmen in his defence against fast bowlers. I think it was Sir Leonard Hutton – and

I defer to none in my appreciation of his ability – who made defensive batting against fast bowlers, particularly, such an involved affair. Most Englishmen believe it is best to play forward to fast bowlers and most, now, also trail the back foot across the pitch to intercept any snicks.

Geoff Boycott has closely followed Sir Leonard Hutton in the forward defensive ploy. His defence is so impregnable that it seems impossible for a ball to get past it yet, in prodding forward, Boycott suffered a broken left forearm in Sydney in 1971, against McKenzie in a one-day game, that put him out of the final Test when he needed only 19 runs to break Wally Hammond's record tour aggregate for Australia of 1554. Boycott could well have escaped that broken arm had he played back. He would have had more time, for instance, to see the ball rear and so avoid it. One other point about Boycott's defence is that it is so concentrated that often the poor ball gets him out. This happened several times in Australia in 1970–71, Boycott failing to unwind himself properly for attack.

Richards firmly believes that against a fast bowler on a length, the batsman's back foot moves *back* and *across* the pitch, the body turning to bring the face two eyes to the ball. I believe in it implicitly. A batsman who misses the ball in such a position deserves to get out!

This is not to claim that a fast bowler should be played like this all the time. The important point with Richards, as it should be with every batsman, is that he has a clear mind *before* the ball is bowled. He has no preconceived notion of how he will play a ball before it is bowled. He treats every ball on its presented merits, but he defends against a good length ball from a fast bowler by going back and across the pitch.

If a batsman decides before he goes in that a particular bowler must be played forward, that batsman denies himself of a stroke to a ball just short of a good length. To such a ball Richards shows his supreme art. He draws back and, with a full sweep of the bat, he forces the shortish ball wide of mid-on. The batsman who has gone initially forward deprives himself of this stroke.

So many essentials are necessary to make a class batsman. Imagination is one; courage another; timing is another; correctness of technique is essential and, as I have stressed, footwork. A batsman must practise his footwork, even in a bedroom, until it is subconsciously perfect. The mere sight of the ball, which dictates the stroke, should bring the feet into immediate position. And footwork, which moves the body-weight into the stroke, should always be on the balls of the feet. Running the figure '8' on the balls of the feet is a handy aid for nimble footwork.

The stroke Richards likes to play most is the cover-drive. It is close to being, I agree, the apogee of class batsmanship although Richards doesn't think the stroke often presents itself to right-handers. In view of what I have written of Pollock and Sobers, the two left-handers, I was most interested to hear Richards say that he thinks left-handers are favoured in the cover-drive. 'Their bodies seem to be freer for this shot than a right-hander,' he says, 'and, with the ball moving away from them, allowing them to go into the stroke, they get many more opportunities for the cover-drive than right-handers.'

Richards is neither a top-hand nor a bottom-hand player. He believes, and rightly, that each hand in the job individually plays its important part, for guidance or for power, and there are times when they must work in unison.

Richards changes the length of the ball by the distance he goes back, thus giving himself more time to watch the ball and, if it swings or lifts, of not playing at it. The English contention, as I have heard it put, is that the swing is minimized by playing forward. I have yet to be convinced.

The most admirable facet about Richards's batting is his footwork. It is superlative. His feet are never pinned. They adjust to the length of the ball, forward or back, thus finally dictating the length of the ball. I have never tired, in the big innings I have seen Richards play, of watching his footwork. He is the Rudolf Nureyev of the batting stage.

Denis Compton was also magnificent in his footwork down the pitch, although I think he was the last Englishman I knew to ignore the safety of the batting crease. Most modern Englishmen now hug the crease tenaciously with their back foot.

Richards plays to perfection the running on-drive, several yards down the pitch, to an off-break bowler. Assuming that he goes three yards down the pitch, as he often does, these are the foot movements he must make: his body sways back to take the weight off the left foot to release it to go forward; his left foot goes forward a yard, finishing side on with the weight on the ball of the foot; his right foot, thus released, comes up and goes behind and half in front of the left foot, side on, and with the weight on the ball of that foot; the right foot, relieved again of weight, goes forward and this exercise is repeated again to bring the body, with perfect timing and judgment, into the proper side on position for the stroke.

This footwork reads much more involved than it is in practice and it produces a most glorious stroke, wide of mid-on. In its back swing,

23, 24 and 25. AUSTRALIANS IN EXCELSIS: (*top*) Victor Trumper, announcing aggressive intent; (*bottom left*) Billy Ponsford, revealing what the left elbow was made for; (*bottom right*) Don Bradman doing what he liked with the bowling, as usual.

26 and 27. RUNS GALORE:
Unarguably the dominant
figures of the decade before
World War II: (*left*)
England's Walter Hammond; (*below*) Australia's
Don Bradman.

28. CHARACTERISTIC DEVASTATION: The pull was Don Bradman's most prolific stroke. He learned it on concrete pitches. Critics told him it wouldn't work on turf. Bradman made an extra few thousand runs to prove them wrong.   29. CHARACTERISTIC DEFENCE: Barry Richards, South Africa, plays back, across, and two-eyed. 30. CHARACTERISTIC OFF-DRIVE: The Nawab of Pataudi plays forward, straight and, remarkably, one-eyed. He lost his right eye in a motoring accident.

31, 32, 33 and 34. MASTERS OVER 40 YEARS: contrasting in style, character, and temperament, they had the common ability to fill cricket grounds and drain the critics dry of adjectives: (*top left*) Jack Hobbs; (*top right*) Stan McCabe; (*bottom left*) Len Hutton; (*bottom right*) Denis Compton.

35. INCOMPARABLE TWINS: In the English summer of '47 they were as inseparable as Roland and Oliver. Between them they scored 7,355 runs in that single season. Bill Edrich (*left*) scored 3,539 (12 centuries), at an average of 80.43. Denis Compton made 3,816 (18 centuries), and averaged 90.85.

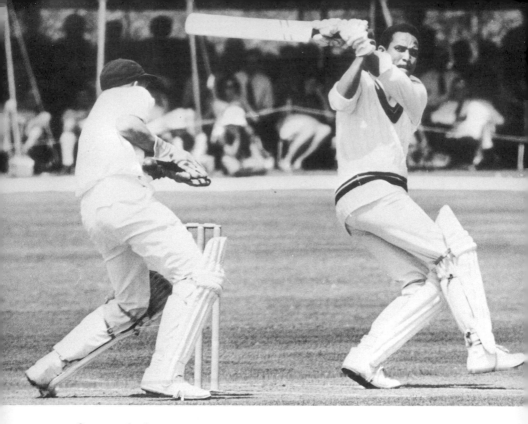

36, 37 and 38. CONTROVERSIAL UNDERTONES: (*above*) Gary Sobers lashes out during his much-criticized visit to Rhodesia; (*bottom left*) Doug Walters takes off during Australia's disastrous tour to South Africa; (*bottom right*) Geoffrey Boycott throws off his hat to acknowledge his century in Perth. Later he was to throw his bat in Adelaide.

39. PICTURE FOR POLITICIANS: Gary Sobers meets Mrs Ian Smith as Rhodesia's Prime Minister smiles defiantly at those who said it could never happen. Their meeting was to cause a political storm in the West Indies.

40. PICTURE FOR POLITICIANS: In this setting the Springbok Rugby Tests in Australia in 1971 were a travesty of sport and good behaviour.

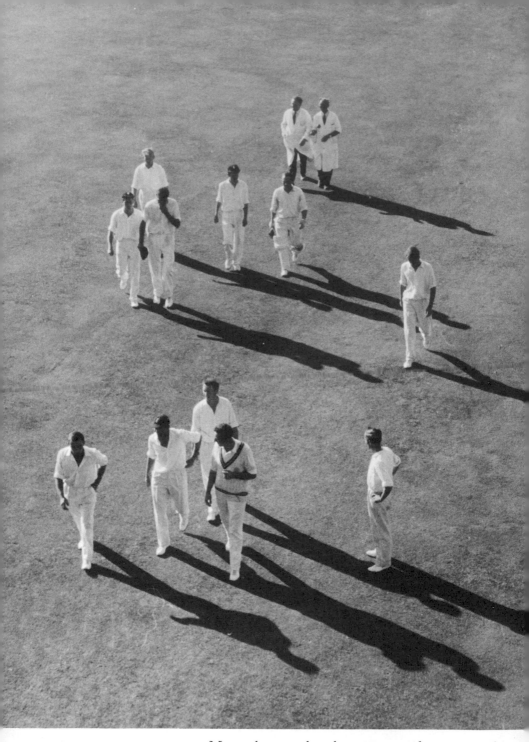

41. CLOSE OF PLAY: Many photographers have attempted to capture the mood of this moment. Cyril Jackson, of Australia, achieved it at the Oval, London, as Surrey leave the field, dwarfed by their own evening shadows.

the bat must go back towards third man and swing through wide of mid-on, to evade him. All essentials must meet in perfect unison at exactly the right moment of timing – judgment of the stroke, foot-work, back swing and follow-through. To see Richards play this stroke, along the carpet and with his wrists giving the ball tremendous impetus, is to see batting genius at work. To watch Richards's feet alone is a text-book in batting.

I have become, I'm afraid, somewhat fanatical about footwork in batting. It distresses me nowadays to watch Doug Walters batting and to see the tangles he gets himself into by an initial wrong movement of the front foot. *Before* the ball is bowled, Walters takes a step across the pitch with his front foot. And he doesn't know that he does it! An old-timer is always chary of advancing his opinions to the moderns but Walters is a cheery, likeable person and one day, when I met him on a golf course, I asked him whether he knew he was moving his front foot before the ball was bowled. It was news to him!

Neither foot should move before the ball is bowled and not until the batsman decides his stroke. This is fundamental yet Walters, with his pre-delivery move, commits himself and tangles his body, particularly to a short ball in line with his body. The wonder of it is that he has scored so well despite such a handicap; the tragedy of it is that one, like Bradman, who brought such tremendous batting genius from the bush to the city, should so saddle himself with such a horrible fault. He picked it up, I think, against the bouncers the Springboks gave him in 1970, subconsciously moving out of the way.

Stackpole, Australia's best batsman against the short ball although he several times hooked his wicket away in the series of 1970–71, being caught on the shot, has his weight back and his stance slightly open. He is thus immediately set for shots off the back foot but is at a disadvantage when brought forward. John Inverarity, of Perth, has much inherent ability but handicaps himself, as the ball is being delivered, by making a big back-swing towards his middle stump. He can play soundly on the on-side, but has to check and realign his swing to play a cover drive.

An abundance of talent wasn't fully tapped in Norman O'Neill because somewhere in his early career he allowed his back-swing to fly out initially towards third man and it was never corrected. He was thus, invariably, playing across the line of flight of the ball and was worried much more than he should have been by in-swingers and off-breaks. Lawry is another who allowed an early fault to develop. He moves forward, initially, to every ball. Trueman, a hard head, recognized this and could shut Lawry up almost completely by bowling around the stumps and moving the ball across Lawry's legs with two men close up on the leg-side.

Shrewd captains and wily bowlers will recognize a batting fault immediately and direct their tactics accordingly. A batsman with hands apart on the handle, for instance, will be vulnerable to a catch on the drive, one hand working against the other. A batsman, too, will often give himself away before the ball is bowled. If his feet twitter, it means that he isn't mentally composed. Several Australians against Snow showed agitation in the expectation of a bouncer by shuffling their feet as Snow approached delivery.

Peter Burge, of Queensland, whose 160 at Leeds in 1964 is one of the very best Test innings played since the war, is the most correct batsman Australia has produced in modern times. Bobby Simpson would have rated high in my list of accomplished batsmen had he not made himself into an opening batsman and, concentrating upon defence, so necessary in an opener, turned himself into a bottom-hand instead of a two-hand batsman. This was doubly a pity because Simpson is a par golfer, like Ted Dexter, with a gloriously long and free drive. Dexter used this swing to the glory of cricket fields – I can remember no better driving batsman – but Simpson rarely drove in cricket, giving his bottom hand, low on the handle, most of the work. The top hand is the important one in the drive and the drive is still, and always will be, the best paying stroke in cricket. The bat meets the ball full face, minimizing risk, and no bowler likes to be met with a full, flashing blade. The higher the hands on the bat handle, the freer is the swing because of the bigger swing arc. So many moderns get finger hits because of their low grip.

Burge not only drove powerfully, he was a big man, but he was a glorious puller of the short ball, like Stan McCabe. Here again, footwork is all-important in the pull stroke. Wally Hammond did not pull, nor did Hutton, and I cannot recall that Peter May, gifted batsman as he was, ever played the pull to a pronounced degree. Denis Compton, on the other hand, was a thrilling puller of the short ball.

Hammond possessed, as no other batsman in my time did, that tremendously powerful hit off the back foot through the covers to a short ball. This, too, is the 'pullable' ball, but Hammond got himself into the position for the hit through the covers by taking his right foot back towards the stumps, his bat perpendicular. This position, however, locks the shoulders for a pull and makes the shot impossible. For a pull, the back foot must go across the pitch, opening the shoulders and taking the head outside the line of flight of the ball.

Hammond so instinctively got into the habit of his right foot going back towards the stumps for his hit through the covers that he couldn't assume the proper pulling position. Those who were privileged to see Compton most courageously pull the furious short balls of Lindwall and Miller at Trent Bridge and Old Trafford in 1948 – and Stan McCabe in his miraculous innings at Sydney in 1932 and Trent Bridge in 1938 – will appreciate the point I make that the back foot must get into the correct position for the pull. McCabe, Compton and Burge flowed readily and smoothly into the proper position. Walters, who played the shot perfectly when he first came into Test cricket, can play it no longer because of that wandering front foot. Stackpole, I think, is the best modern puller of the ball. Two of the best strokes of the 1970–71 series were the pulls Stackpole played off Snow's first over in Adelaide. Stackpole hit 15 from the over. It was Snow's roughest treatment in Australia.

Footwork in batting is neither intricate nor involved, even though it may sound so. The more simple it is the better, but it must be correct. McCabe was not lavish in the number of steps he took but his feet always moved correctly and, particularly, in the pull shot. Two of the best stroke-making innings played by an Australian in recent years were by Paul Sheahan at Hove and at Swansea in 1968. In each instance, Sheahan was left only with the tail for support and he was prodded into playing his strokes . . . yet Sheahan, a good free driver of the ball, struggles against the short, fast ball. Strangely for one so gifted, he has never learned the basic footwork for the pull. This makes him so vulnerable, as the South Africans proved, to a bouncer.

I hope I have not been over-technical in all this. There has been nothing worse in what we could term post-war cricket than the tendency to make batting more technical than it should be . . . the 'professor' trying to make his science so very abstruse to the ordinary cricketer while impressing him how deep a thinker the 'professor' is! Deep thought and practice must be given to the art and science of batsmanship, but not to the point of stultification.

In Sydney, at the moment, is Kerry O'Keeffe, a tall boy who has a future as a slow bowler but who has a tiny fault that robs him of much natural batting ability. When O'Keeffe plays a forward stroke, he allows his front foot to point down the pitch. It should be side on. By pointing his toe down the pitch, O'Keeffe brings his right shoulder around and so he plays the ball full face. He can't, thus, swing back through his body, so that his drive is nullified. When Richards plays down the pitch, his front foot, and so his body, are side on.

Basic batting principles cannot be ignored. If they are, men of capacity are hobbled by a silly and simple little error that should have been rectified early in their careers. Casting my mind back, I am sure that a practical discussion along these lines would have been of great assistance to me in my formative days. For all that New South Wales has been the richest state in batting traditions – Trumper, Duff, the Gregorys, Macartney, Kippax, Andrews, Taylor, Jackson, McCabe, Brown – nobody thought it worthwhile to get the generations together until this cricket dinner of 1970. Legislators over the years, and most of them have been a sadly uneducated lot in the art of cricket, have liked to spread the gospel among the moderns that the 'old timers' are a crusty lot, apt to spread dissension.

Some of the older generation do talk too much, do live in the past too much and they tend to be too captious in their criticisms at times, but they still have much to do to carry on the culture of the game. Cricket's culture must be nurtured, understood and passed on. Once it dies, it's gone for ever. Alan Davidson is now President of the New South Wales Cricket Association and, through his inspiring drive, I hope to see the mother state reach a pinnacle again in Australian cricket. New South Wales has been down too long. When New South Wales cricket is strong, so, too, is Australian cricket.

I felt at the end of the 1970–71 series against England that a discerning committee of the older generation could well prune the television films and then conduct a week's clinic of viewing and discussion with the present generation on what the camera revealed. There would be plenty to discuss because in technique and approach, in the little but important things of the game, Australia have lost much ground in recent times in addition to losing convincingly against South Africa and England, and a Test to India.

The most correct Australian batsman at the moment is Greg Chappell, although, in his liking for the on-side, he is apt to leave his leg stump wide open. Playing in the same South Australian side as Barry Richards has done much for the younger Chappell. I think it has also inspired Woodcock and Ian Chappell, who paced it in scoring with Richards the first time South Australia faced MCC.

I am sure that when I see Gary Player again he will have some pretty sound ideas on batting technique. So much in golf can be applied to batting, especially the importance of the top hand in a free swing. And playing strokes, as Barry Richards does, side on!

23. Pepper and Salt

Wicket-keepers are the pepper and salt of the cricket field. They rarely complain, they suffer in silence the chips and breaks of bones and finish in old age with gnarled knuckles that must give them tremendous arthritic pain. They never want to discuss the 'one that got away' and they are lavish in their praise of the great deeds that have gone on in front of them, for which they have a dress-circle squat. Every now and then – and they are entitled to this – they are apt to grumble about a 'terrible' decision some umpire gave against them thirty years before. They have long memories and, generally, they live long lives.

They are a race often maligned, sometimes slandered. As a very small boy I used to walk a long distance each Saturday to Centennial Park to watch my father and an uncle play junior cricket and I used to gaze in awe at a huge African wicket-keeper whose name, I think, was Mills. He had the reputation of being a 'fiddler'. It was said that he stood very close to the stumps and his trick was to rise up as a ball just cleared the stumps, say 'a beauty', and dislodge the bails meanwhile with the top ribbing of his pads. Looking back, I don't believe it. In all types of cricket, I have known just one or two dubious types who stood vulture-like behind the stumps yet if a proposition about their honesty was put to them, they would probably say that sometimes their enthusiasm got the better of them; that often the difference between a snick and a miss is infinitesimal and it is best to let the umpire decide. At least, that is their story.

Ted Dexter told me the first time he batted in front of Wally Grout he was dumbfounded when Grout gave a tremendous appeal for a catch behind. It was disallowed. Dexter turned to Grout and said: 'You don't really think I hit that, do you?' 'Oh, no,' said Grout, in his most affable manner, 'I was just clearing my throat.'

At Trent Bridge, once, Grout instinctively made one of the most sporting gestures I have seen in cricket. Titmus, chosen by Dexter to open when Edrich withdrew at the last moment, collided with the bowler Hawke when running for a quick single. Hawke came out of the crash best and threw the ball to Grout, who merely caught the ball and as quickly returned it to Hawke. Titmus made his ground.

The beauty of the incident was that Grout never hesitated a moment. He took the ball over the stumps and threw it back.

I began cricketing life as a wicket-keeper and rather fancied myself at it until one day, on a concrete pitch, I lost 'sight' of a ball on the leg-side and stopped it midway between my nose and eyes. I lost enthusiasm for the position immediately. I forsook wicket-keeping until one day in Sydney when Bertie Oldfield, who seldom left his post, went off the field when New South Wales were playing Jardine's MCC team. I offered my services and stumped Les Ames off the slow bowling of Hughie Chilvers, who was an exceptionally good leg-break bowler. Ames had his toe on the line. To make sure, I took the three stumps as well as the bails.

Fortunately, or I might go on with a boring recapitulation of such feats, I afterwards kept wickets only twice in a first-class match and each time as a fill-in for Charlie Walker, who left the field injured. At Essex, on a bad pitch, in which we narrowly averted defeat, I didn't enjoy it. But, on this same 1938 tour of England, I loved it at Oxford. I stumped two batsmen and it should have finished at two. The last man in was running well out of his crease when a perfect return from Bradman came to me over the top of the stumps. I caught the ball – and threw it back to the bowler, Fleetwood-Smith.

Bradman wasn't pleased. In strong words, he demanded to know what was going on. 'Don't worry,' I told him (and I'm afraid I was carried away by this time), 'I'm going to stump him any minute.'

Strange to relate, I did stump him. I never fail, when I am in England, to pass the time of day with Desmond Eager, secretary of Hampshire. W. Murray-Wood and R. E. Whetherly were my other friends.

My first skipper in the Waverley first grade side, which also included that prince of batsmen, Alan Kippax, was Hanson (Sammy) Carter, a really great wicket-keeper. No 16-year-old could have been more fortunate in his captain. Carter was a vibrant, humorous man, over-flowing with cricket knowledge, and a kindly, generous helper of the young. He was one of the Big Six who fell out with the Board of Control in 1912 and ever afterwards was regarded suspiciously by high cricket officials. He was Mr Carter to me for years, as he should have been. He was helpful to the young in his advice, particularly as to how they should dress if chosen to represent their state or country. Always a coat at meals, always a tie, and never the representative blazer worn in public, only in the dressing-room and its precincts. I am glad he was spared the modern casual trend of tourists leaving their motel in thongs, shorts . . . wearing their international blazer – and inspecting a Test pitch in such attire!

Australia has been well served for the most part by wicket-keepers down the years. The chosen have mostly held the post for many years. Blackham was the first of the accepted line, then Jarvis, J. J. Kelly and Carter, often called 'Sep' because that is what he restricted his appeal to. Carter played his first Test in 1907 and at 43 years of age replaced Oldfield for the fourth Test in Melbourne and stumped three and caught three. He allowed five byes in 599 runs. The next Test, in Sydney, he caught three and stumped two and allowed six byes in 484 runs. Those were the days!

Carter went to England again in 1921 and kept in four Tests, Oldfield taking the gloves for the final Test. Oldfield kept them on, then, until 1937 in a truly remarkable career.

In the Melbourne Test of 1921, Carter took one of his greatest catches. Off Ted McDonald, whom Sir Neville Cardus claims as the greatest fast bowler of all time, Carter, standing back, caught Jack Hobbs low to the ground in front of second slip. He covered an enormous amount of ground and that at forty-three!

Jack Hobbs must have had recurring nightmares about Australian wicket-keepers. This is his remarkable list of dismissals by Australians behind the stumps in Tests:

> c Carter b Saunders 26 (Adelaide, 1908)
> c Carter b Laver 19 (Lord's, 1909)
> c Carter b Cotter 22 (Sydney, 1911)
> c Carter b Cotter 6 (Melbourne, 1911)
> c Carter b Hordern 178 (Melbourne, 1912)
> c Carkeek b Macartney 66 (The Oval, 1912)
> c Carter b McDonald 27 (Melbourne, 1921)
> st Oldfield b Ryder 66 (Melbourne, 1925)
> c Oldfield b Gregory 0 (Sydney, 1925)
> st Oldfield b Grimmett 13 (Sydney, 1925)
> c Oldfield b Grimmett 40 (Sydney, 1928)
> c Oldfield b a'Beckett 20 (Melbourne, 1929)
> c Oldfield b Hendry 1 (Adelaide, 1929)
> st Oldfield b Grimmett 74 (Trent Bridge, 1930)
> c Oldfield b Fairfax 1 (Lord's, 1930)
> c Oldfield b Wall 31 (Old Trafford, 1930)

Even in the late 1920s, when he was over fifty years of age and keeping in a faded Australian cap, Carter was a consummate stumper on the leg-side. His innumerable bent fingers bore testimony to the many breaks he got when standing up to the stumps to fast-medium bowlers. He shrugged his shoulders at wicket-keepers who stood back to other than express bowlers and didn't think they had a right to belong to the wicket-keepers union. Neither do I.

Carter was an absolute riot as a batsman. He leaned with his weight back and concentrated upon the late cut, and a roisterous yoick over his shoulder to fine leg to a good length ball on his stumps (at Waverley we called this the 'shovel-shot'). It was apt, because Carter was the local undertaker (when Tommy Andrews played Test cricket for Australia at the same time as Carter, Australia played two undertakers). At Waverley, once, before I was in the team, he gave Jack Scott, a round-arm fast bowler, later a Test umpire and not a very good-tempered man, the greatest lacing of his career. Carter hit an incredible century in under an hour. When the great Syd Barnes was at his best in Australia in 1911–12 it was said Carter played him as well as anybody.

It was an old wives' tale about Carter that he would try and talk a batsman out from behind the stumps, urging him to use his feet, for instance, against a slow bowler. This was absolute drivel. In all the club games I played with Carter, I never heard him utter to a batsman apart from a generous 'good shot' or a warning 'Keep off the pitch, please' if the batsman ran down the pitch. I never batted or fielded to any keeper who tried to talk a batsman out. Carter was meticulously fair, in all ways, and his appeals were all founded on fact, not fancy or hope.

A wicket-keeper has enough to do to maintain his own concentration and I played against none who began a conversation with me. They would speak when spoken to, not before. I once heard Jack Ellis, of Victoria, say some cutting things to Don Bradman's back in a match in Sydney – it was my first Sheffield Shield match – but this was as Don was nearing his 340 not out and Ellis, a red-faced, volatile person, had very much run out of patience in his interminable squatting behind Bradman. Ellis's remarks had to do with whether Bradman's run appetite hadn't been appeased . . . Ellis was a member of the Victorian side, by the way, that made 1107 against New South Wales . . . but his colourful remarks didn't worry Bradman.

Carter stumped like a flash of lightning. I was playing with him once in a club game on the Sydney Cricket Ground when he stumped George Williams, a Sydney legal man, who was yards down the pitch. Williams threw his bat towards the pavilion and, walking after it, kicked it on its way, quite a performance. George reckoned it a disgrace to be stumped.

Waverley was a strong baseball district and most of us had pretty strong arms which we liked to display garishly when opportunity offered and often when it didn't. Roy Levy, a brilliant baseballer, used to hammer returns back at Carter from the close in-field, but

Carter never demurred. He took them high, he took them low, he took them on the half-volley, but he never deserted his stumps. That is a true test of a keeper – how he takes bad returns from the field without leaving his stumps.

Carter knew the rules backwards. He was the bane of Sydney grade umpires, who were chary of his intense knowledge. Once at Old Trafford, he told Armstrong that Lord Tennyson was in ignorance of the rules in making a closure in a game cut short by rain. Armstrong relied implicitly upon Carter's knowledge. 'You sure, Sammy?' he asked. 'Certain,' said Carter. 'Right,' said Armstrong and ambled off the field to tell Tennyson that he couldn't close his innings. The crowd roasted Armstrong and Tennyson then had to circle the field, explaining that Armstrong was right.

Big Armstrong then ambled back and bowled an over and as he had bowled the one preceding the turmoil, he became the only bowler in Test history to bowl two successive overs. Armstrong knew what he was doing. He was that type of personality.

Oldfield took over from Carter – he had kept in three Tests in 1920–21 – and he kept unceasingly and unchallenged until 1937. He was a glorious wicket-keeper, full of poetic grace in his movements. He kept to many of the greatest Australian bowlers – Gregory, McDonald, Mailey, Grimmett, O'Reilly. He was unobtrusive in his work, never clamant. Cardus said he stumped a batsman with the ball in one hand and an apology in the other. Sir Robert Menzies, whose possessions of these adornments should have made him an outstanding wicket-keeper himself, said Oldfield appealed with a slight interrogation of his eyebrows. As a youth, on the Paddington Hill, I saw Oldfield brilliantly catch Jack Hobbs on the leg-side off Jack Gregory from a well-executed leg-glance.

Strange to relate, in a digressing manner, Jack Gregory just scrambled into that A.I.F. side. He got the last position. There were twenty nets in action at Kennington Oval to help choose the A.I.F. team and the selectors had decided upon thirteen players. There was one to go. A tall chap was heaving arms and legs in all directions as he bowled and the selectors called him up. Had he played cricket before? Yes, for North Sydney Thirds. Nobody thought to ask the big bloke his name and when it was put down for the final position, nobody associated him with still the most famous family name in Australian cricket. He was put on the boundary in the first game and was so awkward that he stepped on his own hand. He came up with it bleeding. So they put him in slips and he became the most spectacular slip-field known to cricket.

Herbie Collins, a wonderful character, once told me the story of how Oldfield was found for the A.I.F. side, the team of Service cricketers that established such a high reputation in England after the European war.

Gregory had something to do with Oldfield's discovery because the fast bowler slipped a ball through wicket-keeper Long's gloves and split his face. The A.I.F. team didn't have another keeper. They searched through various units and at headquarters, in Horseferry Road, somebody told the questing and worried Collins that in the neighbourhood was a young chap who had done some keeping somewhere. His name wasn't known but Collins was taken to a nearby dingy apartment where he found a smallish, quietly-spoken chap in khaki, writing letters home.

'I believe you keep wickets?' said Collins.

'Yes, I have a little, back home in Australia.'

'How would you like to keep for the A.I.F. team?' asked Collins.

'Oh, no, I'm not in that class,' said the other.

'Well,' said Collins, 'we have to go to Oxford tonight on the 9.30 train. Be at Paddington at nine. Got any flannels?'

'Not even a shirt.'

They rummaged up some cricket togs. Collins remembered how the new chap sat in a corner of the compartment, a few cricketing odds and ends tied in a bundle, and barely uttered a word during the whole of the run to Oxford.

In the very first over of the match the new-comer caused whistles of excitement among his team-fellows. By the end of the morning, a new star had risen in the cricket firmament. He was W. A. Oldfield, whom Collins dubbed the best keeper he ever saw.

When the players came in for lunch, a disconsolate Long mooched up to Collins. 'Well, Herbie,' he said. 'I guess you won't be wanting me any more now. I can catch the next ship home.'

Long, however, stayed on as second wicket-keeper. I was in my first year's cadetship at the Sydney *Guardian* when Long came to join us to do expert commentary upon the Australian tour of England in 1926.

I would have thought Oldfield's catch of Hobbs on the leg-side off Gregory that day in Sydney would have been the highlight of Oldfield's career but in all modesty – and Oldfield was inherently modest – he thought perhaps (and he uttered the word 'perhaps' with a tone of humility) his stumping of Hobbs off Ryder the preceding Test was the dismissal he liked to savour most. Ryder, fast medium, much faster, for instance than 'Slasher' Mackay, was bowling downhill. Hobbs shaped for a leg-glance but, the ball rising high, he missed it. He had wandered out of his crease in executing the shot and Oldfield had to bring the ball down and on to the stumps.

'Perhaps that was out, Bob?' Oldfield appealed to umpire Crockett. Crockett agreed. Hobbs was out for 66, when batting remarkably well. In that same innings Oldfield also stumped Woolley, Chapman, and Whysall, the latter off the fast-medium bowling of Kelleway. Four stumpings in an innings! He also caught one and conceded only six byes in 548. In the 1954–55 series in Australia against England, neither side had a stumping in the whole series!

Would Oldfield, had he his time over again, have preferred to be a great batsman or bowler, rather than a wicket-keeper? 'Oh dear, no,' he says in horror. Nothing could equal the infinite joy he knew when a batsman, not picking the bosie, would play to the off against Mailey, and Oldfield, in position on the leg-side, would stump him. I have a recurring vision of Oldfield, sitting in the dressing-room during the innings of his own side, and working his gloves for some hours into a pliable state after applying eucalyptus oil. Knott, on the other hand, once told me that he never uses any application on his gloves.

Oldfield was a gentlemanly appealer. Indeed, the fact that he had appealed was generally known only to those in close proximity to him. Bill O'Reilly should have got his first Test wicket earlier than he did. Playing against South Africa in Adelaide, O'Reilly was convinced that Oldfield had caught a batsman out. But as Oldfield didn't appeal, O'Reilly, the new chum, decided upon discretion and didn't utter. Soon afterwards, drinks came out and Oldfield said to O'Reilly: 'Do you know, Bill, I think that was a catch behind.' The umpire, hearing the conversation, said he would certainly have given the batsman out. On the basis of that experience, O'Reilly never afterwards was hesitant in appealing!

Oldfield was a delectable sight on the cricket field, as neat in his clothing as in his technique. Warren Bardsley, then a public servant as Oldfield was when he was young, was a fanatic on fitness and would walk several miles to work, across Sydney's Pyrmont Bridge. Oldfield, who did not know Bardsley personally then, dotingly walked some twenty yards behind him, all the way to work.

In his store in Pitt Street, Sydney, Oldfield has large photographs of his two 'classics' against Hobbs. The staff noted a small, oldish man who came frequently to look at Oldfield's catch of Hobbs in Sydney. One of the staff said to the man one day: 'You must be very interested in cricket, to come so often to look at this photograph?'

'Well, I do like cricket,' said the old man, 'but I come here when business is bad to look at that crowd on the Hill. Do you know that every one of them is wearing a hat? I'd be a millionaire today if hats were still the fashion.' He owned a hat store just up the road from Oldfield's.

Australia's two wicket-keepers in England in 1938, Barnett and Walker, were not quite outstanding. Barnett missed Hutton behind in the forties off Fleetwood-Smith at the Oval as Hutton was on his way to his record 364. Oldfield and Tallon were undisputably Australia's two best keepers of the period but neither was chosen (Grimmett, also, mistakenly got the axe for that tour). Tallon was a glorious wicket-keeper, like a flash in his leg-side stumping. Godfrey Evans claims that Tallon in Australia in 1946–47 was the greatest wicket-keeper he saw.

Gil Langley, rather rotund, took over from Tallon; Grout from Langley and Jarman from Grout. All three were capable men behind the stumps. Langley's shirt-tails were often fluttering and Miller, from slip, was his constant valet, no more so than once at the Oval where Langley's trousers split capaciously and Miller, who, to this day, doesn't know how the pin came to be in his pocket, produced a huge nappy pin and fixed Langley's trousers on the spot. Langley is now the Government whip in the South Australian Parliament. He was always a good organizer on tour.

Langley, Grout and Jarman, unfortunately, I think, became disciples of the wicket-keeping cult Don Bradman introduced in 1938 of standing back to medium-pace bowlers. On one other occasion when Walker retired hurt, Bradman took over the stumps for South Australia. He stumped O'Reilly in the first innings; he took three catches standing back to Waite and Williams in the second innings and afterwards strongly advocated that a wicket-keeper was more use standing back than up to medium-pace bowlers. The old school have still to be convinced. When Sir Donald Bradman retired as Australian selector in 1971, Bill O'Reilly gave him a cabbage leaf in his retiring bouquet, blaming him for wicket-keeping deterioration in Australia. Certainly, Marsh has been the least prepossessing wicket-keeper I have seen in the post for Australia.

I thought there was some suggestion of diplomacy in Marsh's choice in 1970. Perth was having its first Test in history and it seemed to me that in choosing a veritable greenhorn in a most responsible position, the selectors were perhaps keen to encourage Perth's interest in the Test. Taber, it seemed, had fallen foul of Lawry in South Africa by criticizing his field behaviour but Jordan would certainly have been my choice to keep for Australia. A wicket-keeper must be quick, nimble and anticipatory. A fitting test for a wicket-keeper is to know, for instance, whether he could pick up catches at short-leg. I could not imagine Marsh, a big, solid man, doing this. He could improve. A West Australian sports writer asked me in Sydney what Marsh could do to improve himself. I told him he dropped the ball far too often, his positioning was bad for field returns, and that he should make a call for a talk on technique with Bertie Oldfield before leaving Sydney. I doubt that the suggestion was acted on. My writing friend seemed to think the eastern critics were too harsh on Marsh.

Standing back to medium-fast bowlers never appealed to me, bred as I was in the Carter tradition. The policy smacked too much of a first slip with gloves on and nobody in such circumstances should miss a catch, although I concede that Grout, particularly, and Langley and Jarman took some phenomenal ones. I like to think of Strudwick standing over the stumps to the fire-bolts of Maurice Tate; of Godfrey Evans standing guard over the stumps to Alec Bedser. I thought the poverty of what might be called the 'Bradman system' was never better exemplified than at Adelaide once when Ted Dexter stood two yards out of his crease to Mackay, who was never faster than medium. A batsman gets confidence from knowing that he won't be stumped.

Under the heading 'Quiet for the Admiral', Colin Cowdrey wrote an obituary on George Duckworth that I would dearly have loved under my name.

George came frequently to Australia, several tours as a keeper, then as a writer and finally as a scorer-general assistant. The later teams knew George as the 'Admiral' and Cowdrey wrote of how when he came into the dressing-room after the day's play there would be a general call 'Quiet for the Admiral' and Duckworth would give a critical analysis of the day's efforts. George was a colourful Lancastrian, never lacking in opinions or colourful words to express them. Cowdrey magnificently captured his colourful personality and character.

Duckworth was one of my best cricketing friends. He gave me a Lancashire player's tie almost the last time I saw him and I have fond thoughts of him whenever I wear it. Perhaps he was the most colourful wicket-keeper to stand in Tests within memory. He was rotund, he wore wide pads so that he seemed to waddle along the pitch. He wore, in Australia, a big, white sun hat. He had an English complexion of peaches and cream and he wore a white kerchief knotted about his throat. He had a loud whining, piercing appeal that reverberated around the grandstands and it would not surprise me that air-raid sirens were modelled on George's appeal.

George was a cartoonist's bread and butter, and more especially when it transpired once that he used a sliver of raw steak under his gloves to soften the velocity with which Larwood and Tate cannoned the ball into his hands. If one had to choose an international team on character alone, George would be the first man chosen and would be skipper as well. With his lovely rich Lancashire accent – and no county boasted a fonder son where county loyalty was concerned – George was as rich a companion off the field as on.

I think Oldfield did well to oil his gloves and get them soft and pliable because I imagine there's a fair amount of luck in catches taken up near the wicket. There's no time to misjudge. A snick either stays put or pops out and soft, yielding hands are a necessity. I saw Ted Dexter drop a 'sitter' in the outfield at Leeds in 1968. Ted had been recalled from retirement and his responses understandably weren't conditioned for a catch which took a long time to come to him. Ted tried too hard, his fingers too rigid, and the catch was dropped. Some Englishmen used to refer to one Australian wicket-keeper as 'Iron Gloves' and others the 'Ancient Mariner' and the terms were apt. A wicket-keeper must have soft prehensile fingers that yield just enough to make a catch acceptable. There must never be any grabbing or clutching at the ball.

A wicket-keeper can never relax in concentration and his energy must be as vital in the last over of the day as in the first. A good keeper can lift his bowlers and his fieldsmen and in Godfrey Evans and Alan Knott, England have had two whose efforts never flagged on the longest, hottest day. Evans was a man of incredible vitality, some of his diving catches being almost unbelievable. He bustled in everything he did, saving bowlers and fieldsmen in dashes to a close-hit ball.

On his first trip to Australia – although he had played a season as coach in Tasmania – Knott left an imperishable memory. He, too, was full of colour, twisting and turning and flexing his muscles. He told me once that he was stiff-jointed by nature and he had to keep constantly moving to keep mobile. Bill O'Reilly gave him the accolade at the end of the 1970–71 series by saying that he was the best he had ever seen wear the gloves for England, which is exceptionally high praise from such a critic. I don't know, however, that I could quite rate Knott in that category. He was a tremendous asset, but one has to assess a wicket-keeper's capacity against the bowlers he has to take.

I cannot forget Evans standing over the stumps to Bedser and, in that position and to that grand bowler, catching Neil Harvey twice, in Brisbane and the following Test in Melbourne, high up on his right shoulder on the leg-side. Those were catches that can't be forgotten.

Knott, I think he will agree, did not have very difficult bowlers to take on his tour of Australia. This is not to minimize his infinite capacity but, in addition to Bedser, Evans also had to take Douglas Wright, no easy man to take with his sharp break at a sharp pace.

I saw Knott, at Auckland, come within six runs of making a century in each innings of a Test, something never achieved by any keeper. No Australian keeper, incidentally, has made a Test century against England, Don Tallon's 92 in Melbourne in 1947 and Rodney Marsh's 92 not out, also in Melbourne and in 1970, being the closest. Lawry closed his innings on Marsh, not at all a popular closure over in Perth, at least.

I saw Knott play his first game for Kent in 1964, against Cambridge. He is a small, puckish young man with the odd superstition of giving a bail a twirl in its groove as he passes it when wicketkeeping or batting. His father was a wicket-keeper but not like father like son. Evans had these words to say of Knott's success in Australia: 'In a couple of years, Knott will be ready to take his place among the great wicket-keepers of modern times. At the moment, I put Tallon, Oldfield and Ames in this category. Knott's feats in Australia show he is skilful enough to join them now but I would prefer to wait until he has had two more top-class series. Don Tallon, who was magnificent in Australia in 1946–47, is the best Test wicket-keeper I have seen.'

A generous tribute, that, from a great keeper. Evans never saw himself keep wickets. I did!

24. The No-Balling of Ian Meckiff

I have not known a more dramatic or more jarring cricket incident than the no-balling of Ian Meckiff at Brisbane on Saturday afternoon, 7 December 1963. Previous to this, Meckiff had played for Australia against the West Indies in Australia in 1960 and then, somewhat unceremoniously, was bundled out into the cold.

He wasn't chosen for England in 1961 – though after all the fuss over his bowling against May's side in Australia in 1958–59, all cricketing England was anxious to have a look at Meckiff and make up its own mind about his action. He was ignored by the Australian selectors when Dexter's team toured Australia in 1962–63 (during which season two umpires no-balled him for throwing in two different Shield games); and he was ignored again when the national selectors chose An Australian Eleven to play the South Africans on Meckiff's home ground of Melbourne.

The ranting over Meckiff did cricket much harm in Melbourne. It is a city of intense loyalty and as Meckiff had never been no-balled there, it was understandable that his own folk should have thought he was being victimized. They regarded him as a martyr. Crowds dwindled alarmingly at Melbourne and many who still went, and mostly the youngsters, cheered everything that Meckiff did and hooted many other people. The game went through an unpleasant period in Melbourne and all because, one sensed, of Meckiff.

I was one who could not pass Meckiff's action against May's side in 1958–59, although he was not the only Australian with a dubious action. Burke wasn't bowled much in Tests but whenever he did, with the worst action I have seen in cricket, I felt like putting my head under a bench. I wrote a book on that series, which Australia won, entitled *Four Chukkas to Australia*. I often thought in that series that Australian officials were still nettled over the Old Trafford and Leeds Test pitches that had been given the Australians in England in 1956 . . . they were there for the bowling advantage of both sides, incidentally . . . and I had the further impression that May's Englishmen got very much the rough end of the stick in Australia in 1958–59. So often does some niggling in a series continue on to the next!

The bowling controversy assumed high dimensions after 1958–59 and Sir Donald Bradman and Mr W. J. Dowling flew to England for a special conference on the malady. Sometime afterwards, Meckiff was shown a film of his bowling in Australia and told that he would have to alter his style if he wished to be considered for England in 1961. Meckiff did, in fact, change his style and he became an innocuous bowler. He wasn't chosen for England and in 1961, obviously in an embittered mood, a book under his name was published entitled *Thrown Out* by Ian Meckiff and between his Christian and his surname appeared the word 'Chucker'. By Ian 'Chucker' Meckiff! It was understandably acidulous.

When Meckiff did not go to England, he reverted to his old bowling style and in 1961–62 he took most wickets for an Australian. But, it will be noticed, he still didn't get selection against Dexter's English team in 1962–63.

When Meckiff was brought back from the wilderness to be chosen in Australia's First Test team against the South Africans in late 1963, it staggered most. Bill O'Reilly wrote that it represented the most fantastic somersault in cricket politics in his time. Lindsay Hassett, who extended his horizons a little far, I thought, said Meckiff's selection had surprised but delighted practically all followers of the game in Australia. Then he added, which seemed to be pretty revealing and inconsistent, that he detected only two balls from Meckiff in his last game in Melbourne that could have been called. The position was that there should not have been a single ball that could have been called.

Every now and then, we get a few startling opinions in Australia on cricket. One worthy wrote: 'Meckiff will not be called in Brisbane unless he blatantly chucks.' Anything less than blatant, seemingly, would have been in order with this critic!

I could see Meckiff's selection meant that, once again, we were to go round and round the Meckiff bush. We were reverting to the *status quo* of 1958–59 when Test umpires would not call Meckiff, or anybody else, it seemed, because they came to the Tests with the *imprimatur* of selectors Bradman, Ryder and Seddon upon them. After that unpleasant series, I had appeared on television with one of the Test umpires and he told me that he had given Meckiff the benefit of the doubt. In this, he was wrong. If there is any doubt, it should go against the bowler.

The new Chairman of the Board, Mr E. G. Macmillan, denied after Meckiff was chosen for Brisbane that there had been a rift in the Board over his selection. Mr Macmillan was being loyal and diplomatic. I heard at least one Board member express himself strongly against bringing Meckiff back.

Under Sir Donald Bradman's chairmanship of the Board, Australia had sailed through some pretty troubled throwing waters, yet had emerged with credit. No bowler with any suggestion of doubt in his action had been chosen by Australia. Yet Sir Donald was now a member of a selection committee that not only negated its policy of the preceding few years but said, in effect, that policy was wrong. It was a muddled set-up.

Over in London, E. W. Swanton, with a well-reasoned and documented article in the *Daily Telegraph* tracing the throwing crisis, considered that Mr Ryder and Mr Seddon had out-voted Sir Donald Bradman on Meckiff's recall. 'Assuming this,' wrote Mr Swanton, who is a canny bird, 'one cannot but sympathize with Sir Donald's dilemma. Will he resign on the issue of principle? If he does, his influence on immediate events ceases. It looks as though he may have decided at least to await events at Brisbane.'

Nobody had to wait long for 'events' in Brisbane. Colin Egar, thirty-four years old, who wears spectacles, who dry-cleans in Adelaide for a living and whose sporting interests – he has never played cricket of any consequence – are confined to whistling Australian Rules footballers as an umpire in winter and putting his finger up against cricketers in the summer, knew a 'Chucker' immediately even if the Australian selectors didn't.

Meckiff opened the innings against the South Africans. Egar was at square-leg and Meckiff's first ball passed scrutiny. But the second, third, fifth and ninth were all no-balled by Egar, even though all twelve balls in this sensational over were delivered with the same action by Meckiff.

Benaud did not ask Meckiff to bowl again. It was thought that the Australian skipper might have tried him for at least another over at the other end to give umpire Lou Rowan, a Brisbane detective, a chance to finger-print him, so to speak, but Benaud accepted the verdict from Egar. I asked Benaud once whether he was surprised that Meckiff was 'called'. He said, after a pause, no, he wasn't, but I didn't pursue the subject further. Benaud might have had firm opinions of his own.

The Brisbane crowd didn't take kindly to Meckiff being dropped. They chanted 'we want Meckiff; we want Meckiff' through the long afternoon but Meckiff had been through his ordeal on the sacrificial altar. His cricketing throat had been cut for all time.

At the day's end, some of the crowd surged on to the field and carried a grinning Meckiff off shoulder-high. They put him down at the dressing-room gate and returned to hoot umpire Egar. It was a dramatic day in all ways but a day, one thought, that should have been spared Meckiff and Australian cricket.

Was this calling of Meckiff pre-determined? It had some odd aspects. Umpire Egar had stood to Meckiff in a Test against the West Indies and had not called him. In what respect had Meckiff's action changed from when Egar had also stood to him in Shield games and passed him? If his action had changed from legal to illegal, one would have thought that Egar would have taken more time to have summed up what must have been to him a surprising and staggering change in Meckiff's action.

But Egar had made his mind up by Meckiff's second ball. His terse answer to obvious questions at the day's end was: 'No comment.' Richie Benaud commented: 'I have always accepted the umpire's decision. Ian Meckiff will not bowl again in this match.'

So from ten past two to six o'clock at Brisbane on 7 December, 1963, this highly-likeable cornstalk Australian, uncapped and sunburned, whose bowling action should have been corrected early in his career, mooched with drooped shoulders from mid-on to mid-on, a picture of abject dejection. His fellows obviously felt deeply for their cobber.

It was in keeping that the Australian officials should have been tight-lipped about the whole affair. They were tight-lipped in Melbourne when Peter May's England side toppled for 87 in the second Test of 1958–59 and Meckiff took six cheap wickets, although one or two of our officials muttered that the set against Meckiff was a 'Fleet Street' plot, aided and abetted by several Australian 'fellow-travellers'!

We travelled to the end of the Meckiff road in Brisbane but the one I felt extremely sorry for was Meckiff himself. He could well have been spared that final and ignominious journey.

Trevor Goddard, the South African skipper and opening batsman, kept his head while Meckiff's was falling amid all the 'no ball' calls. One wondered what umpire Egar would have done had Goddard's wicket fallen to any of Meckiff's legal balls. Would there, I wonder, have been a revoked call of legality and yet another 'no ball' called belatedly? It would, otherwise, have been pretty hard on Goddard.

25. Barbadians Love the Tumult

Today is Sunday and it brings a welcome relief from the din and the tumult of the cricket ground. You will have heard the off-stage noises on the radio early in the Australian morning but one has to see and hear the scene, so to speak, to appreciate it fully. It doesn't desist for a single minute – shouts, jeers, cheers, claps, laughter, calypsoes – the whole gamut of the West Indian temperament and character.

Here, in Bridgetown, they have what they call the Schoolboys Stand near the press-box. It is almost impossible to hear one's typewriter in the din. They are wedged in like sardines long before the game begins and those in front bulge against the wire barrier that confines the stand, which is an essential precaution when one considers the turbulence that rages all day long.

In front of the wire-compound, as one might call it, stands a number of Barbadian police in their colourful garb of white helmets, white coats and black trousers piped with red. They are merely incidental to the scene. Their presence doesn't deter. The yells increase as the players come on to the field. There is an early disagreement and two schoolboys shape up. This is great fun. The whole stand rises and boys and girls stamp their feet in time and roar challenge and encouragement to the combatants: 'Fight, fight, fight.'

When Hendriks, who comes from Jamaica, let a ball through for four byes the 'Schools' arose and with one voice declaimed for five minutes for their own Barbadian wicket-keeper. 'We want Allan; we want Allan.'

But it is when a batsman enters the nineties that they really let themselves go. The whole stand, hands going in unison, start a one-one-one, two, three clap that rocks the stand and, no doubt, if he isn't innured to it all by this, rocks the batsman also as he wends his way through the nervous nineties. One can appreciate the relief with which the many school-masters deliver their charges into the compound early in the morning; and what lies behind the call over the loud-speaker in the late afternoon: 'Will the boys of . . . school now go outside the Challenor stand and meet their master, Mr Willie.' Poor Mr Willie!

Yet it is not only the schoolboys and schoolgirls who make a noise. All the West Indians are voluble all day. They never tire . . . deprecating, appreciating, advising, cajoling. A plump, dusky maiden walks in front of a stand and cricket is forgotten as the stand whistles, gurgles, 'ooh-s', and so on. Is the maiden abashed? Not at all. She loves it. She giggles and then wiggles and the stand erupts. Griffith, loosening up, puts his hands high overhead and then does a quick shimmy-shake with his posterior. That also brings down the house. A barracker once ran on the field here and gave Frank Worrell a live rooster when he made a Test century.

Unfortunately, it is not easy to catch all the humorous calls. The Barbadian speaks quickly and they have some sayings all their own. The double-negative is often used. In my rear and almost in my ear yesterday, was a stentorian Barbadian who had his fellows in gales of laughter with his sallies, many of them directed in digs at Richie Benaud, who has written critically of Charlie Griffith's action.

A policeman sidled up to the barracker and pointedly asked him: 'You stay here, man, or you go home, man?' 'You big man, man,' said the barracker, 'an' I stay here.' So he became silent, which, I thought, was a pity.

We pass the wharves going to the cricket, passing the water-police who are dressed as the sailors in Nelson's days were. A curvacious seller of mauby (a favourite drink made from the bark of a tree) walks slowly by the banana boats, selling her wares: 'Mauby coo-coo-cool.'

A lounging male calls to her: 'Hey, Sylvie, I en sih yuh fuh long and long enuf. Let muh sih how yuh stan.' Sylvie recognizes a compliment when she hears one. With a beaming smile, she turns about, presents the posterior view and does a wiggle.

The job of a doctor here is not easy. Barbadians have the strangest terms for their illnesses and it is not simple to keep the record straight, as this shows:

Doctor: What is your son's name?
Father: John.
Doctor: John who?
Father: I doan know. He either go in my name or mother name.
Doctor: What is the Mother's name?
Father: Estelle.
Doctor: Estelle what?
Father: I doan know.
Doctor: (becoming exasperated): How many children have you two?

Father : Five, but I doan know she last name cos I doan tek so much notice o' she.

They call me here 'Mistah Jack'. When I say something which they don't understand and they want it repeated they say : 'Hallo, Mistah Jack?' The local description of a headache is 'beating in de head'. It is pleasant to have a Sunday off and get away for a while from 'de beating in de head doan at de cricket, man'.

26. 'Tiger' Pataudi

It can be taken, I think, that the 1967–68 tour of Australia did the Indians an immeasureable amount of good. They shaded New Zealand completely – the best the West Indians could do after them was draw the series there – and it is obvious that Pataudi's men went from Australia with considerable confidence because of the showing they made here. They had excellent chances of wins at both Brisbane and Sydney – particularly Brisbane – and, in Melbourne Pataudi played the most brilliant innings of the whole series, leaving his famous cricketing name emblazoned there in memory.

This is the second Indian team we have had here and this one came under some pronounced difficulties. Most of the team had not long finished their short tour of England – a tour hampered by bad weather – and, compared with the preceding tour here by Amarnath's side in 1947–48, Pataudi's tour could also be termed a short one. These short tours have become an accepted fact because of the now-incessant tours, their heavy cost and the desire of most players not to be away from home for too long.

Of necessity, such tours have their disadvantages. There is little leisure time to become acclimatized to weather, new pitches and varying conditions. The tourists jump early into the serious business of the tour and, if they do not strike immediate form, players are more or less due for a poor tour. This happened with a number of Indians this time, although Jaisimha, a replacement, proved himself a freak by making a splendid Test century at Brisbane only a few hours after landing from a long flight from India. He came as a reinforcement.

Once again was the old adage proved to the hilt: to win matches, cricketers must hold their catches. This was the prime disadvantage the Indians suffered. The bowling, true, was light in quality and quantity. It is apparent that Indian pitches and conditions just do not produce speed bowlers but such bowlers, though important, are not an absolute necessity. Amarnath was only medium-pace yet in Brisbane, in 1947, he produced one of the best pieces of new-ball in-swing bowling it has been my pleasure to see.

It was unfortunate that Pataudi was so long in coming into the

Indian Test side. He hurt his leg in the first game of the tour at Perth and was never afterwards properly fit. At a time when he should have been moulding his Test side in games against the states, Pataudi was on the sidelines. Pataudi did not play until the Second Test at Melbourne and it was immediately apparent how much his batting skill and inspiration meant to his countrymen. He played several of the most attractive Test innings seen in this country and the wonder of it was that he was not only hampered by his leg injury but he now, since his car accident several years ago after a game in Sussex, possesses only one good eye. As was said here: 'What a wonder he would be if he had two good eyes and two good legs.'

Pataudi has had to improvise since losing that eye. He has to turn full-face to the bowler, to bring his good eye into full vision, but he has most sensibly kept his shoulders side-on so that his body is in a perfect batting position. Twice, in his brilliant innings in Melbourne, he almost hit McKenzie over long-off for six. He is a superb puller of the ball, the most exciting stroke in cricket.

Pataudi was an interesting study as a captain. I always sensed that he batted too low in the order, mostly at number six (as Sobers did in the following tour here), but he advanced the leg-injury as the reason for this. He reasoned that, being unable to run sharp singles, he would rob his best batsmen of runs if he batted higher but such was his skill, such was the authority which came into the innings when he came to the middle, that, on balance, I think he erred in not batting at least number four. Melbourne was a case in point. India made a woeful beginning – five down for 25 and later seven down for 72 – yet it was then that Pataudi played his gem of an innings for 75. He took the Australian bowling by the scruff, as he did again in the second innings when he made 85.

This Indian debacle – Australia winning by an innings and four runs – had much influence upon Pataudi's later captaincy. He had batted first in Melbourne and regretted it because of the early life in the pitch. He sent the Australians in at Brisbane and Sydney yet, in all three instances – had he fielded first in Melbourne – Pataudi did not have the new-ball bowlers to take advantage of anything there might have been in the pitch. In Sydney, possibly in an attempt to try and prove that he had made the right decision in sending Australia in, Pataudi persevered with his non-spinners for too long, I thought, whereas Prasanna, who got 25 wickets with his off-breaks in the four Tests – an outstanding feat in any series of five matches – was delayed his chances.

Even then, though, had the catches been held, the Indians must have won one Test and possibly two. Chappell was missed four times in Melbourne in making 151; Cowper, let off early because of an incredible catching mix-up between Jaisimha and Surti in Sydney, went on to make 165 out of 292, the match-winning score. Surti barged in on what was indubitably Jaisimha's catch and the chance went to earth.

I was once staggered to read something of the background of Indian cricket at home by Pearson Surita in the English *Cricketer*. He wrote: 'The selection of the team for England left much to be desired but that is hardly surprising if the picking of cricket teams is left in the hands of football administrators and the like.' What a woeful state of cricket affairs! Only the Indians can remedy this and something that also must be remedied, if Indian cricket is to advance, is the fielding.

No Test side can justify itself if the catches can't be held. An international must *make* not only *take* catches. A good fieldsman will take seemingly impossible catches. On the evidence, as I have seen them over the years, poor fielding is endemic in Indian cricket. In the same edition of the *Cricketer*, I read this on the Indian schoolboy cricket tour of India: 'That Jasbir Singh did not take more wickets was due entirely to ill-luck with dropped catches . . .'. Now, there is no ill-luck in dropped catches. It is purely bad cricket. Given ordinary athletic capacity, any cricketer can turn himself into a good, reliable fieldsman by hard work and application. The ability to field doesn't come uninvited, on a plate. Wadekar and Bedi were two good fielding examples in this team.

Engineer, who also had some good keeping days, played several splendid innings as did Abid Ali, Surti, Jaisimha, Borde (who often failed because of a strange lack of confidence in himself) and Prasanna and Nadkarni were useful at times. Abid Ali has it within himself to become a great batsman. Prasanna, a splendidly equipped off-breaker, carried the brunt of this work and I wish we had him in our Australian side. I regretted that Chandrasekar had an injury as he looked a good bowler to me, although he seemed to lose spirit on the plumb Melbourne pitch.

Seemingly, there are some good young Indians coming along in Laxman Singh and Jasbir Singh and the two young Amarnaths, sons of the former Indian Test skipper. I hope they make themselves into fielding specialists. Sir Donald Bradman warmly commended this side on its general behaviour. I second him. I was a guest at a team party one night and was fascinated by the fuss the Indians made of their guests. It was a very friendly side, well versed in the social graces. This is important – and sometimes overlooked by international touring sides. I thought it reflected credit upon the Indian manager, Ghulam Ahmed.

27. No Play at Lord's

'Rain at Lord's – no play.'

Which doesn't always mean that the day's activities are lost. Like last Saturday, for instance. Sir Neville Cardus, with his brolly, turned on his usual century before lunch, enlivening his stories with manifold digs at the ribs; Dr Finlay sat in the Warner Stand and one wondered, in his absence, how Dr Cameron and Janet were getting on in the surgery at Tannockbrae; Cowdrey, Jnr, chased autographs, like many other schoolboys.

I returned to our hotel, to write letters home. Lacking air-letters, I went down to the office to get some, leaving my door ajar meanwhile, and returned to find a gentleman in the room. Thinking I had entered the wrong room, I went out to check again on the number. It was mine and I entered again to find the visitor with his hand in my overcoat pocket.

'What,' I said, realizing it was a question that didn't need an answer, 'are you doing here?'

He dived past me through the door. I am not as fast as I was, but I made ground on him and tackled him, rather neatly, I thought, some ten yards down the corridor. I was always taught in a tackle to make the other man take the brunt of it. We rolled to and fro, him up, me up, while I yelled to Belinda, my daughter, who was in the next room to mine, to ring the porters. He fought free and I threw a punch which missed, which convinced me I wasn't as good as I was, if I ever was.

He sped away and scampered down the stair-well. Now, the stair-well at our hotel is a vast affair. It opens up on to a huge descending vista and at this moment varied Americans, French and British of both sexes were meandering up and down. My hero speeded down between them. I yelled: 'Stop that man in the overcoat. He's been stealing in my room.'

Possibly nobody understood my Australian accent. At all events, as people are apt to do in a crisis, they merely stood and gaped. My man, shrewdly, dropped his pace on the final flight and walked down sedately.

Belinda, who lacks nothing in alertness, had painted a graphic picture of the incident to the porter at the front-desk. The staff sprang to action stations. The assistant manager, the deputy assistant manager and several porters were hurriedly converging on the man as he reached the front swing doors. He might have won the race, though by the narrowest of margins, had not George, the Front Porter, with great awareness from the outside of something going wrong on the inside, barred the swing of the door with a well-planted big shoe.

Our man was in close custody, as they say, when the Australian party, Belinda and me, made the ground floor by the lift. Everybody was rather flushed and breathless. Now, in time, and summoned from the nearby Charing Cross railway station, came a fine example of the sturdy, admirable, unflappable British constabulary to ask questions, quietly probing at first and then undeniably aggressive.

'It was all a mistake,' said the man. 'I entered the wrong room. I was looking for a party being given by Mr Smith.'

The PC sniffed. 'I'm a bit long in the tooth for that one,' he said, 'and, moreover, at the moment, I'm without some teeth' (opening to show a considerable gap) 'This gentleman is a distinguished visitor to our country' (I tried to look my most distinguished). 'And, what's more, I was just beginning my tea in the station and now it will be cold.'

The Black Maria came and we walked in procession through the hotel corridor and through the swing-door. George, the front man, was there with his brolly to escort me to the rear of the Black Maria. He saluted smartly as I mounted the steps to sit in the rear with the PC and the man. We, the PC and I, talked of the soccer final as we went up the Strand to Bow Street.

A journalist who has covered the courts rather fancies himself in making a statement. 'My name is . . . I am a . . . at approximately . . . I said . . . he said . . . where I recognized the man in custody as the man who had been in my room.' I hoped the Detective Sergeant, who took the statement down, was impressed. At all events, he drove me back in one of the better Police cars to my hotel.

The hotel (and the fault was entirely mine for not locking my door) turned on reviving hospitality and we chatted of this and that. But something was on the mind of the Det.-Sgt. 'How exactly,' he asked, 'does Gleeson hold the ball for his flick spin?' I did my best to show him.

'I am an off-spinner myself,' said the Det.-Sgt., modestly, 'but last Sunday our police team was held up badly. The skipper put me on. I tried to bowl a flicker. It went past our keeper's ears. I tried another. It pitched on a length outside the off-stump and took the middle.'

I am, as the force's guest, to see the Bow Street Eleven in action soon. I hope the flicker works. I have a good excuse if I am asked to play – both knees skinned in that Rugby tackle along the hotel carpet. At Bow Street, on Monday, my man got three months. He had, as they say, a record.

This was my second experience of crime in London. The other was in 1961 but my comrade on that occasion, thoughtfully pointing out that he had to live in London after I had gone home, preferred the incident to be kept quiet. It was after a BBC dinner – and the BBC always give themselves splendid dinners. I had televised and broadcast for them during the summer and this dinner was to say farewell. My friend was driving me back to my hotel when a policeman, running hard and blowing his whistle, cut across our car. His action reminded me of the delightful words of that wonderful man and writer, 'Crusoe' Robertson-Glasgow, of Maurice Tate's action. 'After a short, galumphing run, like some policeman easing his conscience by a token pursuit of the uncatchable, Tate hurled into his delivery the harmonised strength of loins, back and fingers; a perfect engine.'

We proceeded on and I said to my friend: 'I think we had better go back. That policeman seemed to be in trouble.' So we turned about and the policeman was certainly in trouble. The escapee had doubled back over the fence of a parking-area. The PC had scrambled over the fence, also, but had lost his helmet in the process. He had also lost several hundred yards. But he was still valiantly blowing his whistle on the midnight air.

We took the PC aboard and ran down the wanted one. We nabbed him and put him in the back with the constable. The wanted one was a huge, strong man given to using strong language. It appeared, as he told the constable, that he didn't think much of the London Police.

We returned to the parking-area and while my friend went off to ring 999, Scotland Yard, the constable was hard pushed to hold his man. They rolled on the ground and twice I had to lift the man off and establish the constable on top again. A police car hurried in and out tumbled five alert men in blue. They were most solicitious about their comrade. 'Are you all right, Ted?' they asked anxiously. Ted, still helmetless, was blowing badly. The helmet was found, they all piled into the car and made off with the wanted one. My friend and I thought they might at least have said 'Thanks'!

28. Cricket Farewells

Twiddling the peak of his cap, as is his wont, Len Hutton walked from the Sydney ground and into the pavilion depths just as the workman on the balcony above hauled down the MCC colours for the last time.

Behind Hutton came the rollicking Compton, surrounded, as he invariably is in Australia when play ends, by a doting band of the visiting British merchant service who unfailingly convoy him from the field and then, after depositing him at the dressing-room door, just as unfailingly convoy themselves in the general surge to the Members' bar. And behind Compton came Evans, his red-faced gloves tucked under his right arm and his left consolingly about a pleading small boy who, like his ilk, thinks time and place of no autograph consequence.

In a short time the pavilion had swallowed them all up, the tour was finished, and the sad thought grew that possibly no Australian ground would ever again see Hutton, Compton and Evans.* In such a way did Grace, Trumper, Ranjitsinhji, the Gregorys and all the illustrious rest pass from cricketing sight. There is a moment in every cricketer's life when he is on view; another moment and he is no more, nor ever will be again.

Lord's could not comprehend in 1948 that it had seen Bradman for the last time. Thousands stood on the grass in front of the pavilion after the last Australian game and called for their hero. They found it hard to leave a sunlit scene where so often Bradman had made the hours immortal; they found it harder to credit that he had gone from their sight for ever. So also with Hobbs in Australia in 1929. On his last day in Sydney, he walked the full circuit of the boundary with Noble while the crowd rose to him, singing 'Auld Lang Syne', and the procession halted at the Hill while they presented him with a birthday fund.

Hutton and Compton won't of a surety be seen again in Australia. Evans could come again. Wicket-keepers go until their knuckles grow callous, and Strudwick and Duckworth became as familiar on the ship's run to Australia as the Galle Face at Colombo.

* Evans did come once again, in 1958–59.

Those who thrive on statistics will say that Hutton did this and
that on our various Australian grounds, that Compton once got two
Test centuries in an Adelaide game, and that Evans, always a bound-
ing bundle of bustle, knew peerless stumping days in addition to
batting often with pronounced success.

Others, however, will have even richer memories.

Of Hutton in Australia I will always remember the sheer brilliance
of the perfect innings he played in Sydney in 1946. It didn't pass 40
but it ran the whole gamut of the batting art. I can see him again in
his own elegant manner driving the fast bowlers straight and to the
off – glancing, and he knew no peer in glancing – and forcing Miller,
and all the time fiddling with his cap before he settled to his stance,
or cradling his bat as he ran. Those mannerisms were part of Hutton.
That classical innings, though small, was flawless. It gave Sydney
an imperishable memory of Hutton.

Compton, like the majestic Hammond before him, knew some of
his greatest and some of his poorest days in Australia. The latter are
soon forgotten. Those who know genius will always carry the mental
picture of Compton sweeping the ball fine to leg as only Compton
could; of the sheer beauty of his cover-drive and the devastation of
his pull; of his impish run down the pitch to a slow bowler before
the ball was bowled and, sometimes, his guilty scamper back like a
schoolboy caught helping himself to jam.

In Melbourne, once, when that weird bowler, 'Wrong Grip'
Jake Iverson (who flicked off-breaks from his second finger with a
leg-break action) was befuddling the Englishmen at their first
meeting, Sheppard, who had been playing Iverson best of all,
walked down the pitch and asked Compton, who was relieving Hutton as skipper for the match, whether he (Sheppard) shouldn't
change from defence to attack. 'Go on as you are, David,' said
Compton, who had been in the most abject bother. 'And leave the
antics to me.'

Evans, always tremendously vital, will be remembered most as the
man who stood over the stumps to Bedser – as Strudwick did before
him to Tate at his greatest.

These are rich cricketing characters, all of them, fading from the
scene, but their memories will remain. There is poignancy in thinking that we will see them no more, poignancy and regret. When the
last flag from the grandstand had long been furled, I looked up from
my press work and saw the saddest sight of all. In the gloaming I saw
a man in civilian clothes treading the pitch as if he were a pilgrim
in Mecca. He walked, at last, towards the pavilion and then turned

and 'took one long and lingering look, and took a last farewell' before he, too, went into the pavilion for the last time. It was Alec Bedser.

This has been a depressing tour for Bedser, one of the greatest bowlers of all time. Shingles put him aside early in the tour. Hutton, who surely must have had immense captaincy problems on his mind not to consider Bedser's feelings, said brusquely at the last minute before the Melbourne Test began: 'You won't be playing today.' And Bedser didn't play for England again.

How sad it was that Bedser should have finished his last tour of Australia in mufti, and not flannels. English cricket has never had a more faithful servant. He had suffered a horrible attack of shingles when he first arrived in Australia on this tour but it was Hutton's general policy, that cost Bedser his rightful Test position. Hutton, once, did tell Bedser that he got through an over too quickly and this was the beginning of an era of confining the batsmen with a slow over rate. It got tediously slow under Hutton, with his fast bowlers, Tyson, Statham and Bailey, and many field re-arrangements during an over. On the first day of play in Adelaide, over 300 minutes, only 58 overs were bowled by the Englishmen. Australia averaged 15 overs an hour throughout the match.

Like Hutton, G. O. Allen had three fast bowlers when he toured Australia in 1936–37, but his team averaged 15 overs an hour.

In a book published after his retirement, Sir Leonard Hutton wrote: 'I am convinced that a pair of quality fast bowlers make a far more potent weapon than one brilliant fast bowler supported by someone of much less pace. The absence of a second fast bowler affords a batsman some respite. Indeed, he can be shielded from the fast bowler's attack. If two fast bowlers of real quality had arisen earlier, the problems about Alec Bedser which arose in Australia in 1954–55 might have come to the fore earlier than they did.'

Tate was not a fast bowler. He was similar, in all ways, to Bedser. The only time the 'problems of Bedser' could have come to the fore earlier was in 1953 – when Bedser took a record number of 39 wickets against Australia, under Hutton's captaincy. The Australians would like to have been spared Bedser in 1953!

29. On Politics in Sport

Towards the end of the cricket season in 1970, a notice was put on the board of the Parliamentary Press Gallery in Canberra inviting members to add their names for a game against the National University. It was the time of the ripple-heeled dispute in Sydney and, light-heartedly, I put my name down as umpire – if allowed to wear ripple-heeled boots!

And I did umpire. In between the fall of wickets, for it was that type of game, I had a few strikes and from that, although my arteries told me I was being foolish, I was induced to play, playing from memory, in a subsequent match against a Parliamentary side which included the then Prime Minister, John Gorton, and several of his Ministers. As a game, it was not a tremendous success. Heavy rain over-night washed out any likelihood of play on the turf pitch and, with the Prime Minister baring his knees in shorts to a freezing wind off the Australian Alps, the game got under way on an odd kind of slippery malthoid pitch (the very deuce in its low bounce for stroke-making) on a nearby school ground. The Prime Minister, somewhat astray in bowling direction, had one wicket and a brilliant run out.

The Prime Minister and Ministers being on view, departmental heads saw that the ground had a speedy preparation. The game began with mowers still wheeling in the outfield and with school children wandering on the field. Yet the game produced much fun. One Minister, who shall be nameless, emulated the modern Test cricketers of his state by appealing vociferously for everything. His knowledge of the lbw rule was abysmal.

In a few short minutes, I pondered, a game of cricket will yield a good insight into behaviour and character. Many trite and sententious things have been written and spoken of cricket down the years; yet of one thing I am certain. No other game can compare with it in bringing together a wide assortment of people of different generations. At the most, only four can play a game of tennis. Golf, which I love, is a highly personalized and often selfish exercise, producing the most tedious sporting bores of all time. Football, hockey and baseball are impossible for men of advancing years. Cricket is the only game that can bring together a band of men of varying ages for the ultimate in a day's fun and friendship in the sun. The game is usually set in idyllic surroundings and its very movements and sounds are peaceful. No other game yields such a soothing or distinctive sound as that of leather on willow.

As I stood umpire in the first game, I reflected on two things: how incredible a colour is green with all its manifold tints; how vivid is the difference between a 'bush' game of cricket in Australia and a club or village game in England. Such a game in Australia revolves around the inevitable keg of beer, or once did until cans of beer came into noisy existence. These cans have often annoyed me beyond measure in Melbourne as I have sat working, after the finish of play, to the shrill cacophony of thousands of empty cans being swept by cleaners down the concrete corridors.

I blinked, as umpire, when some of the journalists brought their cans on to the field of play and put them in their fielding positions. As they finished them, they piled them behind the stumps. It would not have done for Lord's – nor would the attire of some have passed muster in most quarters. Several, who took pride in the game and themselves, were well turned out; but mostly the clothing was bizarre. Some wore no shirt, wallowing in the sun as so many spectators now do in the big Australian grounds. One, indeed, wore no footwear, inviting the disaster which often came to his shins and toes.

Yet all entered into the game with gusto and it was amusing to see the look of anxiety and nervousness on all as they shaped up to their first ball – and the happy reaction when they 'got off the mark'. Several, not noted for any long experience in the game, came to the bowling crease with decided views on how they wanted their field placed, although they had little idea of where the ball would pitch when they bowled. There was a laugh every minute and, at the day's end, in the cool twilight under the trees, the happenings were re-lived again and joked about as the remnants of the beer were finished.

Nor is the day monopolized by the men. The wives meet and chat as they prepare the picnic lunch and the children are never still. No other game, I emphasize, can bring so many people of so many shades so quickly together in such a tranquil setting and with all participating in full bore. To participate is the main thing, the breeze filtering through the open shirt, the sun warm on the back.

Years before, when I first went to Canberra, these games brought Parliament and the Press into close contact. In one such game, Speaker Sol Rosevear had his days shortened when he received a nasty hit on the head when standing up as wicket-keeper. There is always a danger in such games for one moving on in years and un-accustomed to quick movement. Another who played in those games of other years, before they lapsed, was a member named Joe Gullett. Joe went to Greece in the early sixties as Australian Ambassador and played cricket again – in Greece! His usual place was No. 11 and he said he was generally mortified to read of his efforts next day in the local newspaper, which gave Joe his full title in the scores. They usually read: His Excellency, the Australian Ambassador, the Hon. J. B. Gullett, bowled—0. One day His Excellency made 17 not out and turned up the newspaper expectantly next day. It read: Gullett, not out, 17.

There is, as I say, a vast difference between a 'bush' game in Australia and a village or club game in England, but the pervading spirit is the same, and so is the language. Some, in England, might show that they have been coached; yet the camaraderie and the humour are similar as the players gather later in the village pub for the *post mortem*.

One who knows and loves his cricket can enjoy a game of any standing, as witness the many spectators who pull into the side of the road during a village game in England, yet the sadness of it now is that never has the game been so threatened. First is the generation gap, the game being thought too slow – possibly too technical – for those many who think that life must always be a bustling and restless business. Some, who possibly haven't the temperament for cricket anyway, decry a peaceful pastime that has no car or 'sex' in it; but the greatest sadness about cricket, international cricket, is that it has been made the butt of politicists and demonstrators. It has become prey to those many who know cricket only as a means to be exploited for their own dubious purposes. Cricket has been caught up in the eddying maelstrom of political and national contention.

I am not, I hope, a racist. This is the initial and pious statement that most make before dilating on racial politics, yet I know that I have good friends in every cricketing country in the world, of every colour of skin and creed, and I have enjoyed playing with and against Englishmen, Indians, South Africans, West Indians and New Zealanders. It is what is in the mind that matters, not the outward appearances. The first importance is that men are cricketers and offer cricketing friendship and understanding. Nor, and this, I think, is important, have I looked at a cricketer and held him responsible for the politics and the actions of his government, nor to represent them.

I have spent twenty-five years in the hurly-burly of newspaper politics in Canberra and possibly am entitled to be a little cynical about politics and politicians. I know, too, how the mass media can be infiltrated and used to whip up mob hysteria over some piffling issue that is barely remembered in a decade's time. Politicians – not to be confused with statesmen, who certainly don't abound in any country – concentrate upon the electoral gain to be won, ignoring the honesty of a basic issue. And, prodding its lenses in and making capital out of most things, is television – the outstanding entertainment medium of the age, yet so often concentrating upon promoting the sensational, the trivial and the snide. It seems a simple medium to infiltrate.

So much do the mass media bombard the populace, so vast and prolific are its outpourings, that the most difficult thing to recognize these days is the truth. One, seemingly, is forced to take sides. There seems neither room nor time for reserved judgments, for a person to sit on the sidelines and reflect before making up his mind. One must be either for or against, and that in a militant manner.

I sometimes wonder whether television will prove to be for the ultimate good of sport, or one of its greatest dangers. I am inclined to think that it sucks the heart and soul out of a sport, making itself and its projectors the main consideration and sport only a secondary one, to be by-passed when some other attraction offers. If one concedes the glittering spectacle that television provides by bringing sport into the living-rooms of millions, one must also reflect upon television's unrivalled capacity to whip up emotions and to formulate opinions by presenting what often are simulated scenes. It nauseated me to see a policeman shoot a prisoner through the head in Saigon; to see beatings and bayonetings in Dacca – almost as if provided for the television camera.

The camera shrieks for action. Peaceful scenes make dull viewing and it is an easy matter to contrive some 'happening' so that there is a 'show' for the camera. The presence of the camera, itself, is often an incentive for action. An interesting facet of a demonstration is that even if all its sincere participants don't want violence, those opposing the demonstration can whip up violence by engaging 'phoneys' to do the job and so denigrate the demonstration.

The hackles of some, anticipating my line of thought, will already have begun to rise! The point I make is this: what is so often portrayed of demonstrations on the television screen, should not be interpreted as the feelings of the majority. Nor should such demonstrations be allowed to enforce a decision upon a majority. That, surely, is basic democracy. A minority cannot arrogate to themselves the right to abuse their fellow citizens and disrupt their sport.

I concede that there are many with honest convictions who find it impossible to watch South Africans engage in sport because to do so might be interpreted as approval of South Africa's apartheid policy. Such an opinion is to be respected. Also to be respected and tolerated is the freedom of conscience of others who, finding apartheid just as abhorrent, don't necessarily blame South African sportsmen for the political system under which they live. And, further, who think that a continuance of sport with South Africa, instead of a boycott, could ultimately bring about a relaxation of apartheid.

I know many white South Africans who abominate apartheid. Through several visits, I have a fair knowledge of South Africa and its problems, and I am glad my country hasn't similar problems. I once had a seventy-five minute private interview with Dr Verwoerd in Pretoria – and, because of some arrant nonsense he was later to express over the D'Oliveira case, I am pleased in retrospect that I kept a glowering Ben Schoeman thirty minutes late for his appointment with the Doctor! In a most pleasant talk, which had been arranged for me through the auspices of Sir Robert Menzies, a good friend of Dr Verwoerd's, I had the temerity to tell Dr Verwoerd that no democratic country could tolerate his detention laws. He claimed that desperate ills needed desperate remedies; that his government was certain that anybody 'put inside' under the detention act was a communist, was a possible saboteur. That didn't wash. South Africa's secrecy about the detentions, its harsh treatment of coloured criminals, its abnormally high rate of capital punishment against the coloureds, are difficult to explain.

I was in England in 1968 and was a close observer of the many nuances of the D'Oliveira case. D'Oliveira, himself, I know to be a gentle person of dignity, charm and impeccable behaviour, the latter often in extreme circumstances of publicity. He could well have asked at times to be saved from the embarrassment of some of his 'friends'. One with a knowledge of politics could detect the undertones and the objectives in some columns and it was amusing that one or two writing minnows should have subjected to virulent criticism anybody who did not see pen to pen with them on all aspects of the D'Oliveira affair. Some commentators, vigorous iconoclasts but often with no substitute for what they seek to destroy, rarely attempt to give a balanced picture. Perhaps they can't.

I once played a full series of five Tests in South Africa against Dudley Nourse, a magnificent batsman, and I considered that I knew him well enough to write to him when he was manager of the South African side in England in 1965 and suggest the infinite amount of good it would do, I thought, if he invited D'Oliveira (then in England) to play in one or two games against the counties for the Springboks. This, I suggested, would have an immense and beneficial effect upon D'Oliveira's own people in South Africa; it would be a just cricket recognition of D'Oliveira himself; and it would be a first move in breaking down prejudices in and against South Africa. It was possible to extend such an invitation at that time in England, if not, for obvious reasons, in South Africa.

Nourse could not have invited D'Oliveira of his own volition. He would have had to contact his Board first and they, things being what they are in South Africa, would have had to contact Dr Verwoerd. In the light of subsequent happenings, Dr Verwoerd might have been more pliable than Mr Vorster. Nothing, however, came of my suggestion. Nourse possibly found it too embarrassing.

Almost everybody played politics in the D'Oliveira case and possibly nobody more so than Mr Vorster. It could have been that his main objection to D'Oliveira coming with the MCC team arose from his fear of a race riot in Cape Town had D'Oliveira been given out, by a white umpire, in a close decision. I saw a riot by the coloureds at Port Elizabeth in 1963 when they objected heatedly to a decision referee Piet Myburgh gave against the Wallabies in awarding the Springboks a try. The coloureds threw bottles; the police, of both colours, entered the field and pelted the bottles back into the coloured's meagre stand. They erupted on to the field, the petrified Wallabies retreated to the far corner side-line and shots were fired and cars overturned in the general upsurge. It wasn't a pleasant experience, disrupting the game for some four minutes or so.

Having refused to accept D'Oliveira, Mr Vorster charged in and accused Mr Harold Wilson of playing politics when Mr Wilson manoeuvred the cancellation of the 1970 tour of England by the Springboks. Mr Wilson, being in office and being a pragmatist, didn't want mob crises on his hands just prior to a general election. Mr Edward Heath, then being in the safe seclusion of opposition, could afford to bang the big drum. Politics, politics, politics!

Nobody received more criticism in the D'Oliveira affair than MCC, yet it was MCC that gave D'Oliveira his just deserts of a niche in Test cricket. MCC must have known where they were heading when they gave D'Oliveira their blessing, but I have yet to read of MCC getting any credit for that.

It is trite to write that South Africa is the most complex country in the world. Whereas there are six coloureds to one white in South Africa, there are ten whites to one coloured in the United States, where racial troubles have been most pronounced. Race is surely the world's number one problem. I have attended two Commonwealth Parliamentary conferences in Canberra, with every colour represented and where criticisms of most things are rife with double standards well in evidence. Several countries that berated South Africa most in 1970 were doing secret trade with Mr Vorster's country. In one hectic session, a delegate from Trinidad, speaking on the population explosion, told his African brothers that two centuries ago they, in Africa, did something to counter this by 'putting them in the pot and eating them very hot'. A Kenya delegate took strong exception to this, as well he might, and angrily asked his black brother to say which country and which tribe did this. The Trinidadian lamely replied 'Pigmies' and then had to withdraw and apologise. 'A silly thing to say,' said the man from Kenya.

After another hot session, a British Conservative M.P. walked out of the chamber and said in a dazed manner: 'Enoch Powell is a Liberal compared to some of these fellows.'

There was a quaint speech by Waruru Kanja, from Kenya. He had been an intelligence officer for the Mau Mau. 'I have forgiven the British people who have tortured me,' he said. 'I see a good face and a good helping hand which came from a British member of Parliament when I was in the condemned cell. I have met him here and I am grateful to meet him. I ask the Leader of the British delegation to convey to her Majesty, the Queen, my *par excellence* sincere good wishes from one of those people whose sentence she commuted and freed from the condemned cell to become a member of Parliament.' He was referring to Arthur Bottomley, British M.P., who, as Commonwealth Minister, signed Kanja's freedom.

Two other delightful black men at this conference were Malawians, the Hon. K. H. Nkwabilo and R. J. Swmbereka. Some 200,000 of their countrymen work in South Africa. On their way to this conference, they stayed at leading Johannesburg and Cape Town hotels as 'honorary whites', an interesting concession by Mr Vorster. As everybody did at this conference, they abominated apartheid but didn't think threats or boycotts were the solution.* I found it interesting at this conference that not one of the coloureds to whom I

---

* This conference had one disappointment for me. I was longing to hear Chief Mukhulumngqandi Mamba, a Senator from Swaziland, speak on the population explosion. He didn't, which was a pity. He has fourteen children! I loved the story of two elderly female tourists talking in King's Hall after listening to one of the sessions in the Chamber. 'I never knew,' said one old dear, 'that we had so many black men in our Parliament.' We have only one and he, Senator Bonner, of Queensland, is a recent addition.

spoke thought that boycott was the answer to apartheid. Just previously, Gary Sobers had made a surprise visit to Rhodesia to play a single-wicket contest with the Springbok, Barlow, and Sobers got a stinging barrage of criticism from the West Indies. One who didn't criticize him was Mr Cameron Tudor, the Deputy Prime Minister of Barbados, Sobers's home island. He thought Sobers's visit might do some good.

Apartheid appals me. I have always resented the rude, inhuman manner in which some whites address coloureds in South Africa. Understandably, because of the population figures, many whites have a constant fear that the coloureds will rise against them. It is remarkable in this country of considerable affluence for the whites (the millions of coloureds, whose cheap labour has contributed to this white affluence, obviously also depend upon the country for their livelihood) that the coloureds always seemed to me to be the much happier race there. Yet it would be churlish to deny the magnificence of South Africa as a country and its varied achievements.

South Africa is not simply divided into whites and coloureds. The whites themselves divide down the centre, the Afrikaners and the British. Here are two teams:

Vorster's Team

B. J. Vorster	H. Muller	B. Coetzee
B. J. Schoeman	M. Viljoen	S. L. Muller
N. Diederrichs	M. C. Botha	S. P. Botha
D. C. H. Uys	P. C. Pelser	C. P. Mulder
P. W. Botha	C. de Wet	J. P. van der Spuy
Frank Waring	M. C. G. J. van Rensburg	J. J. Loots

Backer's Team

Ali Bacher	M. J. Proctor	T. L. Goddard
R. G. Pollock	H. R. Lance	A. J. Traicos
B. A. Richards	D. Lindsay	P. H. Trimborn
E. J. Barlow	D. Gamsey	M. A. Seymour
B. L. Irvine	P. M. Pollock	G. Chevalier

The first is Mr Vorster's cabinet; the second the South Africans who played against the Australians in South Africa in 1970. Oddly, the only English-like name in the cabinet is Frank Waring, a former Springbok footballer, who is Minister for Sport. I met Mr Waring in Pretoria once and found him reluctant to express an opinion on most pertinent subjects, but the interesting thing about the two teams named above is how the Cabinet is so strongly Afrikaans and the cricket team so predominantly of British stock.

It was a criticism of Mr Vorster in South Africa in 1971 that he seemed to bear resentment against Springbok cricketers. He certainly didn't go out of his way to make things easy for them.

I represent in Australia the large Argus Group of South African newspapers, an English-language group, and they haven't hesitated to criticize Mr Vorster over some of his policies. Nor has the Prime Minister hesitated to criticize the Group, even hinting at some form of press censorship. Mr Harry Oppenheimer, the mining millionaire, stood up valiantly to the Minister of Mines over the employment of natives in mines and, I think, won his point. It takes guts to criticize in South Africa and it was a courageous thing the Springbok cricketers did at Newlands, Cape Town, in 1971 when they walked off the field in protest at Mr Vorster's refusal to allow them to consider two coloureds for the tour of Australia.

The world publicity which this gesture got would not have endeared the Springbok cricketers to Mr Vorster. Marais, the Springbok Rugby captain, shrugged it off by saying in Australia that the South African cricketers were professionals, an odd thing to say and which, if true, which it certainly wasn't apart from a few instances, didn't seem to have much to do with the case. Certainly, the Springbok footballers had never done anything to buck their government. The team that came to Australia had not much to show against cricket's Dr Ali Bacher, who works in a coloured hospital.

It was quickly apparent that politics would play a big part in the Springbok Rugby tour of Australia. The new Prime Minister, William McMahon, constantly repeated that politics would not be allowed to enter sport, but he made a pretty notable dive into the arena by promising the Springboks transport from the Royal Australian Air Force if their private arrangements fell through. They didn't, flights often being made in tough circumstances by small planes (the two national internal airlines boycotted the Springboks), but McMahon had made the gesture, and politics were immediately rampant in the tour.

Before this Rugby tour took place, John Pitts, an assistant editor in Johannesburg of my group, arrived in Australia to try and gauge the temper of things. He saw State Premiers and Sir Donald Bradman, Lord Mayors and Bob Hawke, president of the Australian Council of Trade Unions, gave him a long interview. We had no difficulty in seeing, at short notice, Prime Minister McMahon and the former Prime Minister, Gorton, who both gave us over half an hour. But

Labor's leader, Gough Whitlam, whom I have known closely over many years, greeted us as if we had both come from a leper colony. He didn't have the time to see us; he was too busy.

Whitlam, possibly thinking that Hawke had over-projected himself on television on the subject of tours by the South Africans to Australia, seemed to me to be trying to play it safe, not quite certain how much political mileage there was in the subject. McMahon, on the other hand, seemed to be convinced there was a lot to be gained from a general election on law and order. Some time before, Whitlam had urged churchmen not to allow the South African women net-ball players the use of their courts in Australia. He had also urged the government department not to give the South Africans any facilities while they were in Canberra. It seemed odd, to me, to whack girl net-ball players because of their government.

One night in Canberra, in 1970, I watched these South African girls play net-ball. Over the whole period of the game they, and their Canberra opponents, all young girls, were subjected to concerted chants of 'Go home, racist pigs' and a continuous blowing of whistles. If this wasn't infantile larrikinism, I have never seen it. Rubbish was thrown on the court and, at one stage, a party of yahoos jumped on to the court, broke down the goal-net and squatted.

It was a puerile exhibition of bad manners, offered not only to those who played but those who had come to watch, and would alienate rather than gain support for a cause. If anybody dared to remonstrate with the demonstrators, he or she was met with a virulent stream of abuse. It was a pathetic show that will bring blushes to some of the demonstrators when they mature. In Sydney, some of the demonstrators yelled an incessant splurge of indecencies in Afrikaans at the touring girls.

'The age of chivalry has gone,' declaimed Edmund Burke at the news in London of the guillotining of Marie Antoinette. 'That of sophisters, economists and calculators has succeeded. The glory of Europe has gone for ever.' He would, had he lived now and seen the exhibitions in Australia in 1970 and 1971, have added demonstrators to his list.

I saw all three Rugby Tests which the Springboks played in Australian in 1971. In their setting, they were a travesty of sport and good behaviour. Had petitions been set up outside the grounds, addressed to Mr Vorster and expressing opposition to apartheid in sport, I would have signed every time before entering the ground and I think this would have been a fitting and decorous protest to the South African Government. As it was, I deplored the ground invasions and the incessant whistling although these came from a small minority.

The Queensland Premier, Mr Bjelke-Petersen, who is a member of the Country Party, gave the impression the end of the world was nigh when the Springbok Rugby side went to Queensland. He declared a state of emergency, to be expected only in time of earthquake, flood or plague. It was a good example of the over-kill, the final absurdity, and the Premier was probably not surprised when the unions hit back and declared a day of strike against the emergency. One way and another, it was estimated to have cost the Queensland state some eight million dollars. During the Springbok visit, the government won two by-elections, which probably didn't surprise Mr Bjelke-Petersen and was said to have further impressed Mr McMahon on the possibilities of a law and order early general election.

Hundreds of police, with their paddy-wagons on the ground for those arrested, lined the pickets inside and outside the playing areas of the Sydney and Brisbane grounds. It was a costly business, the police expenses being estimated at over a million dollars. It was inevitable, after this, that the cricket tour could not take place yet what put the seal upon its cancellation was Mr Vorster's previous decision that coloureds would not be allowed to tour with a South African side. Had Mr Vorster agreed to this, I am sure it would have appeased and cut the ground from underneath most demonstrators in Australia, leaving only the small hard professional core of these gentlemen who, if they make it, will undoubtedly demonstrate in Heaven.

I flew from Canberra to Sydney to attend the final Board meeting on the tour. For some weeks prior to this, I had sought an interview with Mr McMahon in Canberra, but the Prime Minister fobbed me off. Accidentally, one day, I met him in King's Hall as he was hurrying off for a game of squash.

I reminded him that when he became Prime Minister he had told us members of the Press Gallery that his door would always be open to us for queries. 'Yes,' he said, 'but I have been very busy.' 'But I wanted only a minute or two with you,' I said. 'Yes, I knew that,' he said, 'but I knew the type of questions you wanted to ask me, and you knew I wouldn't answer them.'

Obviously, at this time, Mr McMahon was sitting on the political fence with his ear to the ground. He was watching to see what gain, if any, there was in law and order arising out of a sporting tour. I knew that Sir Donald Bradman had written to him, seeking guidance, a full month before. Not receiving an answer, Sir Donald wrote again. I was told that the answer didn't come, finally, from Mr McMahon but from an official of his department. There wasn't much help or guidance in it. It told Sir Donald that his Board had to make up its own mind on the tour.

In newspapers, I gave Sir Donald high praise for the deft diplomatic manner in which he handled a most difficult situation – without any help from either Mr Vorster or Mr McMahon. To assess the situation, Sir Donald had talks with state Premiers and state police commissioners. He had a long talk with Bob Hawke, the Trade Unions chief (and, in passing, a very capable cricketer who was said to be the most brilliant cover-point known at Oxford University since the war).

I sat near Sir Donald in Sydney when he announced the Board decision at a Press conference. His statement ran, in part: 'While there is substantial evidence that many Australians feel that the tour should go on, the Board has equally been made aware of the widespread disapproval of the South African government's racial policy which restricted selection of the South African team.

'The Board faced the unenviable situation that whatever decision it made would meet with the displeasure of a large percentage of the people, but it could not let that factor interfere with it in coming to a decision. We have gained opinions from all sections of Australian society and we feel that there would be internal bitterness between rival groups, and demonstrations on a large scale would be inevitable. There would be tremendous difficulties for the police if the tour took place and there would be the strain on international cricketers of playing under such circumstances.

'Accordingly, with regret, the Board has decided to advise the South African cricket association that, in the present atmosphere, the invitation to tour is withdrawn.'

Questioned on the statement's reference to apartheid, Sir Donald replied: 'Our Board is not interested in politics. We cannot deny that the South African government has brought its politics into cricket.'

I then asked him what I thought was a pertinent and natural question: 'Do you think the tour would have been cancelled had the South African government agreed to the inclusion of two coloureds?' He answered: 'No.'

I had a cable deadline to meet to South Africa and, soon afterwards, excused myself to Sir Donald and left his conference.

In South Africa Mr Vorster said it was a victory for the riff-raff. Mr Waring saw the decision as a victory for anarchists and a lawless minority. It was Mr Waring who bitterly criticized the Springbok cricketers for their walk-off and twitted them to say they would agree to play racial-cricket. When they did so agree, Mr Waring countered by saying it wasn't legal. He condemned them, then, for doing what he had challenged them to do.

An interesting sequel to the story I sent that night to South Africa was that Mr Vorster later doubted the veracity of it. He claimed that he had a letter from Sir Donald, through the South African Ambassador in Canberra, Mr John Mills, in which Sir Donald denied that he had ever made such a statement on the coloureds and the cancellation.

This was a reflection upon my journalistic reputation. Nobody would write such a story out of his head. I telephoned several Sydney journalists who were at the press conference and they supported completely my version of what I had asked Sir Donald and his reply. I then telephoned Sir Donald in Adelaide and he assured me, immediately, that he accepted my version of what had happened. 'I was under great stress and strain that night,' said Sir Donald. 'I have no recollection that you asked me such a question. If you say you did and I answered 'No', I accept your assurance unreservedly. I will say, now, that had the South African government taken a different view to the coloureds, the tour would have been acceptable to most Australians.'

Sir Donald was not extremely happy that a letter he had sent to Canberra marked 'Private and Confidential' had been made public. I told him that the job of an ambassador is to send home whatever news and views he can get. It was a matter for Mr Vorster whether he made the letter public, which he did at a national congress of his party.

All this is somewhat piffling but it demonstrates, I think, how touchy the South African government was to the reaction towards its attitude on coloured cricketers. There has been some evidence since, I think, that a change in outlook is on the way in South Africa. Sport could be the break-through in ameliorating the general apartheid problem.

Because of my South African work, I have had close dealings with Gary Player for many years and our relations are most friendly. Late in 1971, I covered the Dunlop International golf tournament in Manly, Sydney, and, as is my habit, made contact with Gary. He asked me specially to write an article back saying how he thought Papwa Sewgolum, the Indian South African, making his first tour of Australia, was a credit to South Africa and that the country should be proud of him. Player had been drawn with him the preceding day.

'Gary,' I said, 'this is interesting. You played with Papwa and the skies didn't fall in. What difference is there between a coloured South African golfer playing with you in Australia and a coloured cricketer playing with white South Africans in Australia?'

Player said he didn't think any coloured cricketer was good enough to be chosen. My obvious reply to that was that if they didn't get the chance, they couldn't prove themselves. I instanced to him D'Oliveira, who would never have played Test cricket had he not gone to England. I made the further point to him that it was not so much the ability of the players but the gesture towards them that would have impressed Australians.

Some think – this was not Player's opinion – that D'Oliveira was not good enough to gain a place in recent South African teams, which have certainly been powerful. This, I think, is rather an illogical reflection upon the strength of the English Test team, in which D'Oliveira has certainly been a more than average performer.

I know that Gary Player is close to Mr Vorster. When he is at home, he plays a weekly game of golf with the South African Prime Minister and I am sure Mr Vorster listens closely to Player's opinions. I once gave Gary a written brief on why Evonne Goolagong should be invited to South Africa. She was, subsequently, and she was tremendously popular. She went from Johannesburg to win the Wimbledon and French titles yet, were she a South African, she would not have been given this opportunity.

The present South African cricket team is the best in the country's history. It is, to my mind, undoubtedly the best side in the world today. It is well led, it is sound in technique, in inspiration and interpretation of the game and it is well-disciplined (clean flannels every day of a Test, no long hair!). It plays Test cricket as Australians once played it, tough and hard, asking no quarter. I doubt whether an international team of any era possessed at the one time two such devastating batsmen as Graeme Pollock and Barry Richards. One day in 1970 in Durban, they tore the Australian attack apart, the South Africans declaring with the phenomenal score of 9–622 an hour after lunch on the second day! Australia, in this series, suffered its heaviest defeat in Test history, 4–nil. Not a single Australian made a Test century.

Before that series began, the South Africans who played in it had made these first-class centuries: Goddard 26, Graeme Pollock 25, Barlow 20, Richards 19, Bacher 12, Lance 10, Lindsay 8, Proctor 5 (he was to make five successive first-class centuries in South Africa in 1971), Irvine 5 and Gamsy 2. There surely has never been another Test side in history so flush with first-class centurions.

In late 1971, Gough Whitlam, as his party's leader, went on television to say that no Labor Government in Australia would grant visas to sportsmen from any country which practised apartheid. So South African sportsmen, as far as Labor is concerned, have still to carry their cross! Australian Labor, in recent times, has had the habit of rushing pell-mell into decisions that aren't really necessary or that carry much political weight. They don't allow much latitude in finessing for the future, it seems to me, and I could not imagine either Mr Curtin or Mr Chifley, two very distinguished Labor Prime Ministers, committing themselves to such dogmatic decisions that appeal only to a varied few. A pertinent question that could have been asked of Mr Whitlam was would he, logically, carry his boycott over to South African trade? Those Australian firms, likely contributors to Party election funds and who trade with South Africa, would like to know the answer to the last question. We sold South Africa in 1970–71 some 86 million Australian dollars worth of goods. Australia bought in return only 21 million worth.

On inhibiting policies by some countries against their peoples, Mr Whitlam could well have cast his net wider than apartheid.

So it is all mixed up and involved – trade, politics, race and sport. Sport has the battle ahead. A recent United States ambassador to South Africa said, on his return home, that he thought the coming generation of Afrikaners would adopt a more humane, a more Christian attitude towards the coloureds. No government likes to be preached at from abroad, to be told by others (who might have the odd mote in their own eyes) what they must do, yet one hopes for the sake of magnificent sportsmen, cricket and rugby, and humanitarian reasons, also, that the South African government will concede ground. It cannot always remain colour-blind. The world cannot settle its racial problems by force. Therein is chaos. Sport could lead the way.

Having seen the political machine work from the inside, I can well understand why so many young people should be cynical of governments. I am not against all demonstrations. Indeed, knowing the background from the inside of Canberra, I was long an opponent of the Vietnam war and the manner in which Australia entered it. The young demonstrators, most of them utterly sincere in their convictions, would argue that a show of public disapproval is the only means available to them to change what they think needs changing and, in this, they would point to the steps which the suffragettes took to obtain their rights. All this is valid reasoning, no doubt, yet I detest seeing sacred sporting turf desecrated by politics, banners, smoke-bombs – and parading police, on official duty. I am possibly old-fashioned but I think only those who have won the honour for their country deserve to walk on an international field. A sporting field, a sporting ground, are places for good manners and good behaviour.